Dispatches from the Gilded Age

ALSO BY JULIA REED

Julia Reed's New Orleans

South Toward Home

Julia Reed's South

One Man's Folly

But Mama Always Put Vodka in Her Sangria!

*Ham Biscuits, Hostess Gowns, and Other
Southern Specialties*

The House on First Street

*Queen of the Turtle Derby and Other Southern
Phenomena*

Dispatches from the Gilded Age

A Few More Thoughts on Interesting People, Far-Flung Places, and the Joys of Southern Comforts

JULIA REED

Edited by Everett Bexley

ST. MARTIN'S PRESS
New York

First published in the United States by St. Martin's Press,
an imprint of St. Martin's Publishing Group

DISPATCHES FROM THE GILDED AGE. Copyright © 2022 by The Julia
Evans Reed Charitable Trust. FOREWORD. Copyright © 2022 by
Roy Blount Jr. All rights reserved. Printed in the United States of
America. For information, address St. Martin's Publishing Group,
120 Broadway, New York, NY 10271.

www.stmartins.com

"The 'I Don't' Honeymoon" is republished with permission of News
Corporation; Dow Jones & Co., from *The Wall Street Journal*, by
Julia Reed, October 2011; permission conveyed through Copyright
Clearance Center, Inc.

Designed by Donna Sinisgalli Noetzel

Library of Congress Cataloging-in-Publication Data

Names: Reed, Julia, author. | Bexley, Everett, editor.
Title: Dispatches from the Gilded Age : a few more thoughts on
    interesting people, far-flung places, and the joys of Southern
    comforts / Julia Reed; edited by Everett Bexley.
Description: First edition. | New York : St. Martin's Press, 2022. |
    Includes index. |
Identifiers: LCCN 2022007362 | ISBN 9781250279439 (hardcover) |
    ISBN 9781250279446 (ebook)
Subjects: LCSH: Reed, Julia. | Reed, Julia—Travel. | United
    States—Social life and customs—1971– | United States—
    Civilization—1970– | United States—Humor.
Classification: LCC E169.Z82 R44 2022 | DDC 973.92—dc23/
    eng/20220316
LC record available at https://lccn.loc.gov/2022007362

Our books may be purchased in bulk for promotional, educational,
or business use. Please contact your local bookseller or the Macmillan
Corporate and Premium Sales Department at 1-800-221-7945, extension
5442, or by email at MacmillanSpecialMarkets@macmillan.com.

First Edition: 2022

10 9 8 7 6 5 4 3 2 1

To Clarke and Judy

Contents

Contents

Dispatches from the Gilded Age

Foreword

by Roy Blount Jr.

S uch a downer to think of Julia as departed. Better to remember how she would arrive. For instance at Joan's and my half-of-the-year house in an out-of-the-way New England village. As my wife recollects:

> She came in the door carrying bags and bags of presents and sat herself down as if she'd been here thirty times—so comfortable being in a new place, she made you feel comfortable. Not in some take-charge way, but in a subtle way, an elegant way. And amazing food and bowls and things she'd brought, and she'd determined that we could get the best fried chicken in the world at a place twenty minutes from here. I can't think of any of our other friends arriving like that. She knew how to play it so well. Her confidence could sometimes be irritating, but you didn't have to put her at ease, she made you feel at ease. And bringing the whole world in, not just Mississippi brown water and Nashville la-di-da, but Vermont cheese, tales of Algiers . . .

It feels like that to read Julia. As it did to dine out with her—for instance one Thanksgiving at her house in New Orleans, all of us dressed as either Pilgrims or turkeys, or one long afternoon during Mardi Gras, at Pêche, as she geared up to reign atop a mammoth high-heeled shoe on a float in a parade that she brought to a halt outside a friend's house so she could pop in and powder her nose. She had many friends, including me, who didn't know one shoe from another, but years later, when she parted ways with one cancer specialist, she would pointedly mention that doctor's hopeless taste in shoes.

Very few notable humorists have been virtuoso hands-on organizers of elaborate events. Julia was. Four years ago we were in Julia's Cadillac. Julia was driving—and sipping a Scotch, and running late, and yelling at irresolute drivers up ahead, and working her phone—toward a food-and-drink-rich reception at a cotton gin, as part of her annual Greenville, Mississippi, Hot Tamale Festival. Just recently, I learned that Joan switched on her audio-recording function during this ride. The tumult is hard to reconstruct, except for the laughter. If while reading Julia you can hear her chortle and cackle, then you can fill in that element here.

> **Julia:** Siri, call Hank on mobile. See how she can handle that one. Shit. Oh, nailed it! Hank . . . I'm in my car, that's where. On the road, just hauling it, but I'm not driving back 'cause I'm getting ready to be the drunkest person in the room. Have you got Dave D. and all those . . . AllrightAllrightAllright, I don't want to hear it. Thank you so very much for doing this you're an angel bye.
>
> **Julia to us:** [A food provider] calls this morning and says, "Can you order me two pounds of brussels sprouts?" What am I, a wholesale grocery? You are in Memphis, Tennessee. It's not like you're flying in from Dakar. Get some brussels sprouts, and get somebody to clean and fry 'em . . . Trying to save money? Don't save money if it means expecting me to do all the work!
>
> **Her father, Clarke, calling:** Hey, Sister? Which road do we take after . . .
>
> **Julia:** There's some breaks in the median, but it's the first left you can take that cuts all the way across onto a new road.
>
> **Clarke:** What else can I do for you?

Julia: Hang up the phone that would be excellent bye. [Clarke hangs up.] Mom'n'Daddy were having their usual getting-dressed brawl, and I had to clear out of there 'cause I was laughing so hard. Momma's holding up earrings to me, "Don't you like those better?" "No'm, I really don't." "I thought those were your favorite. I thought these were the ones you didn't like." "I'm liking them tonight!" I'm thinking, "Put the fuckers on!"

A rousing party in the cotton gin that night. And next morning downtown Greenville, Julia's usually life-challenged hometown, was bursting with hot-tamale stalls, distinguished chefs, notable food writers, and voracious folks. And the next day, festival participants picnicked on a sandbar in the Mississippi River, Calvin Trillin recollecting Greenville's relatively unmalign role in the Civil Rights Movement, Julia's friend Bo Weevil taking Jessica Lange out in a boat to dodge huge leaping Asian catfish, and Julia's friends-from-childhood (all of her friends seemed to be lifelong) the Brent sisters picking and singing something lovely.

One political note:

Just about all of my other Southern writer friends, and I, have been confirmed staunch Democrats. Julia, from childhood, was a Republican—of a decidedly secular, anti-Trump, anti-death-penalty, gender-and-race-friendly, Delta-proud variety all her own. So it's not just lip-smacking evocations of food and lipstick she leaves us with, but also spicily incorrect punch lines like the one at the end of her yarn about a train ride with competitively engagé feminists. And time-capsule spritzes like this:

If you are lucky you learn about fashion from watching your mother. . . . She took a suitcase full of minidresses to the Republican Convention in Miami in 1968 and brought back a pile of paper dresses, The Thing that summer. I still have a gold one, with a big ruffled collar, so shiny you can see yourself in it. But I also see NIXON'S THE ONE and Bebe Rebozo and SPIRO IS MY

HERO and my mother at a party on a yacht docked outside the Fontainebleau Hotel. Four years later I can see her in a cool white linen suit covered in paint thrown by antiwar protesters, and Abbie Hoffman wearing a dress that's really a flag, and this time . . . Kay Graham's there, and Kissinger just back from China, and Joe Alsop got drunk and ate spaghetti with his hands.

Let them read the goddamn book, Julia is saying.
Okay you're an angel bye.

PART 1

How It All Started

"Had Jean Harris not murdered Herman Tarnower, her longtime lover and author of the wildly successful *The Complete Scarsdale Medical Diet*, I might not have had a career.

This, in a—sort of—nutshell, is what happened: During my junior year at Madeira, the almost entirely all-male board decided with typical wisdom to replace our brilliant but decidedly masculine headmistress (who went on to become town supervisor of Shelter Island, New York) with Jean Harris, even though her most recent job had been manager of sales at a Manhattan-based company that sold cleaning contracts to office buildings, and when I later interviewed a former board member at a previous school where she'd been head, he blamed her for its ultimate demise. When she was introduced on the hockey field during the spring Fathers' Weekend (in a bow to the number of divorced parents, the traditional Parents' Weekend had been split in two), I took one look at her, turned to my father, and said, 'One day they are going to come get that woman in a truck.'

My father, like most of the rest of the assembled dads, had already pronounced her 'attractive' in her knockoff Chanel suit, and mumbled something about my dislike of authority (which is not exactly true—I just prefer it when the people nominally in charge of my well-being possess some modicum of sanity). At any rate, the following year proved my instincts right. She walked through campus head down, yanking at her hair; once, at a 'relaxed' meeting at her house, she sat with us on the floor and pulled up huge clumps of carpet. We had no way of knowing that she was taking the methamphetamine Desoxyn (along with Valium, Percodan, Nembutal, and other goodies revealed to have been in her medicine cabinet), or that she was in the grips of an increasingly desperate obsession with the famous Dr. Tarnower.

Whereas her predecessor didn't much care what we did as long as we worked our asses off academically, Harris clearly had more literal goals in that department. She put the entire school on what turned out to be the Scarsdale Diet, she hammered incessantly at our general lack of ladylikeness, and twice in her yearbook letter to our graduating class, she underlined the importance of a 'stout heart.' No wonder—in a scenario familiar to country music fans everywhere, it turns out that she was being eclipsed in Tarnower's affections by his younger, blonder office assistant, a woman whom the high-minded Harris derided in a letter to her lover as 'tasteless,' 'ignorant,' 'cutesie,' and, for good measure, 'a slut.' It was the latter's frilly negligee and pink curlers that Harris spotted in Tarnower's bathroom on that night in 1980 when she pumped three bullets into his chest from several feet away, an occurrence she forever termed a 'tragic accident.'

By then I was a sophomore at Georgetown and a part-time library assistant/phone answerer at *Newsweek*'s Washington bureau, a job I'd gotten via Madeira's ingenious cocurriculum program, in which the students are bused off to D.C.-area internships once a week. On the morning after Harris shot Tarnower, the bureau chief woke me up with an order to get out to my old school. When I asked him why on earth, he barked, 'You idiot, your headmistress just shot the diet doctor.'

Looking back, I realize I had none of the usual reactions. Instead, I threw on clothes, jumped in the car, made my way past the guards (with whom I'd made sure to be on extraordinarily good terms during my slightly shady school tenure), and got the scoop on all that had transpired before Harris drove off campus armed with a gun. On the way back, I stopped at a pay phone to make an especially fulfilling 'I told you so' call to my father (even the truck part was right—deliciously, Harris had been transported from the crime scene in an old-fashioned paddy wagon). Then I typed up my notes, filed my story to New York, and got my first-ever byline. I was nineteen and only the tiniest bit sorry that the good doctor had given his life in service to my future as a journalist."

1

The Lady and the Doctor

(1980)

They had been friends and frequent companions for at least fifteen years. He was a prominent cardiologist who last year, at sixty-eight, became famous when he published a best-selling book, *The Complete Scarsdale Medical Diet*. She was a well-bred socialite who was headmistress of the Madeira School near Washington, one of the nation's toniest private schools for girls. One night last week, Jean Struven Harris, fifty-seven, drove to Dr. Herman Tarnower's 6½-acre estate in Purchase, New York, with a strange request: She wanted him to kill her. But before the night was over, it was Tarnower who lay dead—and Harris stood accused of his murder.

Tarnower was shot just before 11 p.m. Police received a report of a burglary in progress at Tarnower's secluded, Japanese-style home. When patrolman Brian McKenna arrived, he met Harris coming out the long driveway in a Plymouth sedan. "There's been a shooting in the house," she told the officer, who raced inside to Tarnower's second-floor bedroom. There, the cop found the doctor lying in his pajamas between two twin beds, bleeding from bullet wounds in his shoulder, arm, and chest. Tarnower was rushed to a nearby hospital, where he died about midnight.

Two other policemen who arrived later at the house found Harris standing by inside. "I shot him. I did it," she told patrolman Daniel

O'Sullivan. "She stated that she had driven with the weapon in the car from Virginia with the intent of having Dr. Tarnower kill her," O'Sullivan testified at a court hearing last week. "She said she had no intention of going back to Virginia alive. She stated they had an argument in Tarnower's bedroom, that he pushed her away and said, 'Get out of here, you're crazy.'" Precisely what happened is unclear, but police say that Harris led them to a .32-caliber revolver in her car. It was the gun that killed Tarnower.

Bruises: Harris was charged with second-degree murder and released on $40,000 bail. Her defense attorney, Joel Aurnou, noted that she had severe bruises on her face and arm and hinted that she might have acted in self-defense. "We have not ruled out the possibility that Jean Harris might be a victim," Aurnou insisted. Countered Assistant District Attorney Joseph Rakacky: "We will contend that the dispute rose out of the personal relationship."

By all accounts, Hi Tarnower was a quiet and private man, a bachelor devoted to his cardiology practice, an outdoorsman who enjoyed fishing, hunting, and golf. Through his work with heart patients, Tarnower developed a high-protein, low-carbohydrate diet that he mailed free to anyone who asked. In 1978, he teamed up with Samm Sinclair Baker and presented the diet in a book that became a bestseller and sold 2½ million copies in a paperback edition. But the fame didn't seem to change him. "The last thing he would have wanted was to be known as the diet man," said longtime friend Sidney Salwen. "The diet was incidental. He was first and foremost a cardiologist."

Romance? The first of several acknowledgments in Tarnower's book thanks Jean Harris "for her splendid assistance in the research and writing of this book . . ." Coauthor Baker balked at the acknowledgment. "Whatever she did for him, I don't know," he says. What was clear was that Tarnower and Harris, a divorced mother of two grown sons, had been close friends for many years, and some suggested that they were romantically involved. She had been a frequent visitor at his home, and though she lived on the Madeira campus in Virginia, she owned a house not far from Tarnower's. A friend of Tarnower's who sometimes teased him about being a bachelor said that he had "lots of dates. But he never indicated that there was anyone special."

Recently, Tarnower was seen socially with Lynne Tryforos, a divorcée in her mid-thirties who worked as his assistant at the Scarsdale Medical Center. Tryforos dined with Tarnower, his sister, and his niece the night he was killed, but they had left by 9 o'clock, before Harris arrived. Tarnower's relationships with Harris and Tryforos led some to speculate that jealousy might have been a motive for the killing: "This was a lovers' triangle," insists one neighbor. "Mrs. Harris was quite a refined lady and he baited her by taking on a young, exotic looking and beautiful assistant."

But if Jean Harris was a refined lady, she also seemed quite troubled and nervous at times. Before coming to Madeira, she was director of the now-defunct Thomas School for girls in Rowayton, Connecticut, where she was said to have shown a violent temper and was given, said one associate, to "unexplainable emotional outbursts." In her early days at Madeira, there were some complaints that she was too demure in her stewardship and ill at ease in her new surroundings. Though parents applauded her emphasis on discipline, the students found her so obsessed with honesty and self-responsibility that they nicknamed her "Integrity Jean." Two weeks ago, she expelled several students for drinking and smoking marijuana. The episode seemed to upset her. Two days before Tarnower's death, a student found her normally immaculate living quarters in disarray.

The full story of Harris's relationship to Tarnower may come out in the trial. For now, there is only speculation. At Madeira last week, students recalled a sentence that Harris once wrote in the Madeira alumna magazine. "If my educational philosophy has a schizophrenic ring to it, perhaps the same could be said of myself as a woman."

PART 2

Fashion and Beauty

2

Clothes Encounters

(1993)

When I was a sophomore in college, the fall fashion magazines pronounced it "the year of dyed furs." And there was a photograph in *Vogue*, I think of Lisa Taylor, and she was wearing a cobalt blue squirrel coat. I wanted that coat so bad, all I thought about for months was how I was going to get my hands on enough money to buy it. I was earning about $45 a week at the time, so it was clearly impossible, and now I am spending a lot of time in Louisiana, where in one parish the opening day of squirrel season is actually a school holiday, and squirrel is something kind of greasy that you eat and do not wear, much less dye blue, so a coat made of squirrel seems decidedly less enticing. But the point is that when I think of that coat, I am back in my rented apartment in Georgetown. I can see myself lying on my bed, on my stomach, looking at that coat instead of studying my logic textbook (a subject I clearly should have paid more attention to). I can tell you exactly what went on that fall, whom I loved, what I prayed for. I remember every year of my life by the clothes that I wore—or at least the ones that I wanted.

The word *fad* implies something ephemeral, silly, even wasteful. This year's fad is next year's Goodwill donation and all that stuff. But still I wait for them. Right this instant they will tell me what's going on in the world of fashion—and in some cases what's going on in the world—and a little later they will tell me what went on with me. Webster's says a fad "suggests caprice," not necessarily a good thing, but it can also suggest so much more. Like the hit song of a particular summer, "this year's look," "the season's rage," can recall the milestones or just the moments of your life and the life of the world around you.

Of course, sometimes you get to remember twice, the nature of a fad being that it gets resurrected. I remember Pucci the first go-round from my mother's Pucci dresses, Pucci nightgowns, Pucci bikini underpants. All I wanted to do was grow up so I could be cool and wear Pucci, and lo and behold I could, although by that time I didn't want to. The night before I sat down to write this I had a dream about a perfect pair of platform shoes—I haven't succumbed yet because I feel as though I did that already, but now I may. Not long ago I pulled out the dress I wore to the party after my high school graduation. It's sheer and floaty with a handkerchief hem and watercolored ferns. That night I wore it with high, high heels and my grandmother's diamond bracelet and snaked my best friend's boyfriend. This summer, like everyone else, I wore it with flats and a cross on a thong around my neck and felt not vampish but waifish and therefore too sweet to snake anybody's anything.

Most of the clothes I've saved in my closet cannot be recycled physically; they hang there as aide-mémoire to a life. I see the labels Donald Brooks and Chester Weinberg and I am again curled up on the floor of the bride's dressing room at Hafter's department store on Washington Avenue in downtown Greenville, Mississippi, and I am as happy as I ever was during my childhood. I am watching my mother try on clothes for the season, or usually, frantically, for some big event for which she is dieting and buying new clothes at the same time, and I am struck by the importance of it all: the lunch, always chef's salad, called in from Jim's Cafe across the street because we could not possibly stop; the enormous piles of clothes tried on and tossed off on top of dozens of strappy sandals from the shoe department downstairs and pieces of lingerie—"the kind you will have when you are married, Julia"; all the people coming in and out, smoking cigarettes and drinking things regular people never drank, like iced coffee, and saying things like FABULOUS and TO DIE.

If you are lucky you learn about fashion from watching your mother. I cannot think of my mother without thinking of her clothes and the exciting places she went in them and the stories she told me about the things that happened to her when she had them on. She took a suitcase full of minidresses to the Republican Convention in Miami in 1968 and brought back a pile of paper dresses, The Thing that summer. I still have a gold one, with a big ruffled collar, so shiny you can see yourself in it. But I also see NIXON'S THE ONE and Bebe Rebozo and SPIRO IS MY HERO and my mother at a party on a yacht docked outside the Fontainebleau Hotel. Four years later I see her again in a cool white linen suit covered in paint thrown by antiwar protesters, and Abbie Hoffman wearing a dress that's really a flag, and this time the party's at an Italian restaurant and Kay Graham's there, and Kissinger just back from China, and Joe Alsop got drunk and ate spaghetti with his hands.

To Nixon's 1969 inauguration my mother wore snakeskin boots and a short, short fur coat made of blond mink paws with a ludicrous lynx collar that is still hanging around in her own closet. So is a black jersey halter dress with huge multicolored stars all over it that was my very favorite. It was from her jersey phase, those sexy seventies years of Scott Barrie and Stephen Burrows and Clovis Ruffin. When I see that dress, I see my mother at yet another party. Her hair is pulled back and she's dragging on a Salem. On her ears are gold hoops by Kenneth Jay Lane that came in a tall, round black box with a dozen interchangeable plastic hoops in every color that hooked on to the gold, and everybody had them, just like they had KJL's knockoff Cartier tank, and bras from John Kloss for all those jersey dresses.

In those days I was a fashion faddist only vicariously. It is tacky for a child to be fashionable, so I was made to wear Florence Eiseman dresses and thin white socks with Mary Janes, unless I was playing, in which case I was allowed to wear corduroy jumpers with white turtlenecks and close-toed sandals. All of these clothes were purchased by my grandmother, who bought my cousin and me identical outfits (we even had matching little girls' purses—wonderful organza-covered cubes held by a drawstring). Then my cousin started wearing long-sleeved dresses without all those

piqué flower appliqués, and she had a Peter Max scarf, and suddenly
wearing all those short-sleeved dresses with round collars and thistles
growing up the side started to make me cranky. Also the Duvall brothers
were giving me a lot of grief on the school bus, so I asserted myself and
made my first fashion choice: a hot pink culotte suit and a Day-Glo
striped turtleneck I found in the Sears catalog, which had by that time
adapted the "mod look" for the middle class.

After that I was unstoppable, a veritable timeline of fashion trends.
My grandmother, having made an abrupt turnabout in her ideas about
what children should wear, sent me brown corduroy gaucho pants, which
I wore with crushed patent-leather boots and a snakeskin-print blouse.
I was in the fifth grade and so proud, until in the drugstore one day I
heard someone say: "*Look* at that little girl." Undaunted, I wore a plaid
maxi with a poet's blouse to school in the sixth grade, along with: a powder blue angora pajama suit with silver metallic thread woven through
it and a burgundy velvet pantsuit with epaulets and brass buttons. My
mother was mortified at my grandmother's and my collaboration, which
also included an extremely sophisticated Franck Olivier pleated chiffon
blouse cut like a man's shirt, but I was on a roll until I finally settled into
an extended hippieish period of Mexican work shirts and Indian cotton
dresses and turquoise jewelry and clogs and huaraches and lace-up espadrilles and natural leather sandals on four-inch platforms—in short,
all the things that were the rage this summer.

I couldn't imagine wearing all that stuff again, not after I had finally graduated to the Donald Brookses of my day—Bill and Oscar and
Calvin and Ralph. But then I found myself working harder in a hotter
climate, and all of a sudden wearing all those loose, sheer clothes and almost no makeup seemed like the only thing to do. It was the first time I
had thought about clothes and their effect on my mood from the inside
out. I was in fact cooler, looser, unadorned. Like my face and my clothes,
my personality was subdued. I had stripped down to bare essentials.

Until then I had been used to thinking about how clothes made me
feel in terms of their effect on other people. If I put on a suit that makes
me look confident and pulled together, then other people have the illu-

sion that I am, and I begin to believe their perception. Everybody knows that clothes are camouflage, a protective coating or a signal to others about how we wish to be perceived. But they don't always hide our personalities so much as contribute to them. I once asked a man not ordinarily given to such extravagance or whim, a man who should have been lying low, why he had agreed on the spur of the moment to meet me in a certain restaurant, a highly visible, theater-like place. And he told me it was because he wanted to see me walk through the door in the black Chanel suit he knew I'd wear to such a place. He knew my walk in that suit—brisk, imposing, with the touch of attitude the clothes afforded me. He also knew that on that particular day I was not in the world's best shape, and the dichotomy between the pulled-together exterior and the discombobulated business going on inside is always interesting.

That was before the pared-down summer, before another man, a musician too Zen-like to take his pleasures from a woman walking through the door of a famous restaurant, asked if I could imagine what it would be like to wear Issey Miyake every day and nothing else. It was sort of thrilling, in a way, to think of being inside those cocoons, free to be whatever you want, wafting around in flat shoes and black tights. I think, in the end, it would make me a bit neurotic. As a friend of mine said, Miyake is for the thinking woman, but the woman who is usually thinking too much.

Anyway, I knew what the musician meant. There are those clothes, like my waif dresses, that don't enhance but make you honest, that make it easier for you to be true to yourself when you play your bass or whatever. But I'm not sure I want to be driven that far inward all the time or forced to re-create myself underneath those gigantic Miyake kite-winged raincoats, which are fabulous but a little scary. I like the clothes I wear to become part of me, like the people I love or the books I read or the places I always go back to. In a new book on the subject, a doctor says that "Prozac seemed to give confidence to the habitually timid, to make the sensitive brash, to lend the introvert the social skills of a salesman." Yeah, but some people say it can make you want to kill people, too. Isn't fashion so much safer?

Which is why I am so glad that this year's fashion fads involve tons of velvet and thigh-high boots, romantic blouses and coats to the floor. There are also skinny black evening gowns sexy as negligees, and, at the couture, the New Short is back according to Karl Lagerfeld, and thank God. They are all the things I wanted in the other years they were in style, and now that they are back, I will have them, the things lurking in my imagination for so long: a red damask evening coat to the floor, a black velvet cape, a white lace poet's blouse, a tiny skirt from Versace, a Manolo boot almost to my waist. This time I will wear them instead of dream about them, and years from now when I find them in my closet I will remember what havoc I will have wreaked and I, like my mother, will be able to tell their stories. For these are precisely the things that make me feel powerful and feminine, the perfect accoutrements to give a woman strength to glide through restaurants on otherwise cloudy days, to survive tragedy and create great, wild, dangerous fun.

3

Lip Service

(1994)

can tell you are in love because your mouth is different."

Oh my God. It was a man talking, and I was quietly thrilled, sure I was about to be both stunned and exposed by some soul-searing example of male clairvoyance.

"What do you mean?"

"Well, it's darker," he said. "Redder, more defined."

OK, so the telltale nuance turned out to be MAC's Chili. But he had a point. If I am in love, I feel sexier and less shy about calling attention to my mouth. My lips were in fact darker, deeper, and certainly as close to red as I've been ready to get in a very long time. "Red," says French makeup artist of the moment Stéphane Marais, "makes the mouth a focal point. And isn't the mouth the part of the face that reveals the most sensuality?"

Yes, and if you are in the mood to play up that sensuality, putting on red lipstick is much simpler, less painful, and infinitely more sophisticated than, say, shooting up your lips with collagen. There is something a bit desperate about trying to make your lips puffy by any other means than a good round of out-of-control kissing and accidental lip biting.

Red lips, on the other hand, are not at all desperate, but, says Marais, "provocative and exuberant, a way of showing the sexiest side of a woman." In his book *Bodywatching*, Desmond Morris goes so far as to say they show sex itself—red lips signifying a secondary, and exposed, genital region. Whatever, there is no question that red lips are about passion and desire. It is impossible to think of them without remembering that famous photograph of Maria Callas, mouth wide open, unleashing a torrent of power. The picture is in black and white, but you know her lips are red.

Maria Callas was a Woman, grand and powerful and volcanic in her eruptions, a diva after all. She would have been hard-pressed to understand the recent flirtation with the grunge look and waifs and clothes that made everybody look like little girls. Little girls don't wear lipstick (with the exception of Paloma Picasso, who said she started wearing her trademark red when she was three); they have tantrums, not eruptions; they are flat-chested and have mouths that no one would notice. A man I know has a theory that women invariably chop off all their hair when a lover leaves them as a sort of desexualizing, just as the waif look was about removing traces of glamour or artifice, except maybe dirt. "All that deconstruction was fighting the tradition of femininity, denying the sex appeal of women," says Marais, who was responsible for much of the new red on this season's runways and who himself has created a line of red lipsticks for Shiseido. "But it was to the point of looking ill and neglected. In the end it could look depressing."

In the first place, there are few among us who should be without at least a touch of artifice, and anyway, women like artifice, probably more than men. It gives us a certain amount of control; it allows us to send signals. The man who literally read my lips knew from a simple change in color what was happening at the deepest level of my life.

Also, lipstick—serious red lipstick—enables you to hide. Makeup artist Kevyn Aucoin said he wanted the red-lipped models he sent down the runway for Todd Oldham to look like Marilyn Monroe on a Saturday afternoon. The girls were almost devoid of any other makeup, and I knew exactly what he meant. Marilyn might be a mess, but she could smear on some lips, pull on some shades, and wrap a scarf around her head and be, or appear to be, OK. It takes a whole lot longer to do full eye makeup, and lips give you equal power.

I asked a colleague who has always worn red lipstick why, and she said it was because she was too lazy to do her eyes. In a pinch we all need something to help us face the music, the day, the prospect of rounding the next corner. "It gives me confidence," said another veteran. "It's so aggressive, you have to follow." During my misspent youth I had a friend who we always made buy the beer because she was never carded—she put on huge Diane von Furstenberg sunglasses and bright red lipstick before going into the store. It worked every time—instant thirty-five, or at least, for our purposes, eighteen.

Cleopatra used henna and cochineal (a red insect) ground to a powder to make her lips red. Elizabeth Taylor, playing her, probably wore Revlon's famous Fire and Ice, the "foolproof formula for melting a male!"—not that Liz needed it. The ad featured a quiz to see if you were up to the shade: "Have you ever danced with your shoes off? Do you sometimes feel that other women resent you?"

This was pretty racy stuff for 1952, but poets have felt the power of red all along. John Masefield wrote of the "dear red curve of her lips," while Robert Herrick extolled his beloved's lips as a "cherry, ripe, ripe, ripe." Juliet's lips were invariably "crimson" to Romeo, and Ella Wheeler Wilcox cut right to the chase with "I love your lips when they're wet with wine and red with a wild desire." OK, she was a woman, but she touched on a key point, which is that red equals wicked or sex crazed or both. "Her lips were red, her looks were free," Coleridge wrote, and we all know what free is a metaphor for. I asked another colleague why she wore red lipstick, and she didn't miss a beat: "'Cause I'm a ho."

The man with the hair theory uses rather tortured logic to explain why women who wear red lipstick may be free but not truly wicked. "The great virtue of red lips for women is that they can leave the mark of Cain, thereby cutting down on blatant bites." In other words, wreaking havoc with lipstick on the collar is sweeter than drawing blood on the neck. This is obviously a big thing with men. I asked another man if he thought "sexy" when he saw a woman with red lipstick. "No," he replied, looking rather pained. "I think messy, telltale, shirt collars, that kind of thing." Keep in mind that the Duchess of Windsor wore red lipstick, though she was not a woman you would necessarily call sexy, either. Whatever it was she undoubtedly had, you couldn't tell it from that uptight red slash that was her mouth.

My grandmother wore red lipstick. She left its imprint on countless butts of Pall Malls in ashtrays throughout her house. I still have one, pressed inside a book like a flower, but that lipstick-stained butt is somehow a more fitting remembrance. Red lips demand something—an attitude, a beauty mark, a temper. My grandmother had all but the beauty mark (she preferred jewelry), and there was no question she was up to the color. My mother didn't have to be, since she spent her glamour years in the silver sixties. She still wears frosted pinks and corals. But she has always been after me to wear red. When she sees me in my normal brown or nude she goes nuts. She is convinced it's a sign of some deep-seated trauma, like when I was a child and hid my thumbs in my fists. If I wear red she knows I'm happy, or at least I look it.

Indeed, says Marais. "Red lips bring freshness to the face. They are gay and amusing, especially when you are not used to seeing women in them." I had a fiancé once who wanted me to have blond hair and red lips, so I did. But I did not feel gay or amusing; I felt ridiculous, false. And for years afterward I wore nothing but black clothes and brown lipstick, as penance, I guess, for having led everybody, including myself, on. Red lips are not something you should acquire because somebody asks you to. You have to mean it.

Makeup artists would have us believe the new red is more real and fresh and natural-looking than the glittering hard seventies red or the over-the-top, wet-lipped movie-queen red of the thirties and forties, and it is. Still, the girl at the Chanel counter told me that most people feel safer with corals and browns. Marais insists that any skin tone can handle red and that it "illuminates" the face. And I read the other day in an Irish newspaper that the darker the red the greater the protection against the sun. But I don't think that's why the wary may switch. I suspect it will be for the thrill of wearing colors called Glam and Outrageous and Drop Dead Red, of forcing men to think about their collars, fearfully or not, of seeming confident and sexy and maybe just a little in love.

4

Portrait of a Lady

(1995)

When my uncle imitates my grandmother, he puts a large crystal ashtray on his ring finger. She wore an enormous pear-shaped diamond on that finger, so big we called it the headlight, and whenever she was nervous or about to say something she shouldn't, she would stroke it. My uncle would lean over to me and say, "Watch out, she's stroking the headlight," and then blam, the room would be leveled, jaws would drop open, and she'd go on about her business. She had a lot of jewelry—big, serious jewelry (or jewels; as Oscar Heyman, the man who sold her some of them, once explained to my extremely amused father, "There is jewelry and then there are jewels")—and she wore it all the time, every day, even when she took my cousin and me fishing or to the woods to build fairy houses out of twigs. She could not have fathomed being without it, any more than she would have ever considered descending the stairs of her own house without perfect hair and full makeup or without being dressed completely, in little shifts with matching cashmere cardigans in the summer and wool chemises in the winter with matching shoes and bag and a girdle and stockings even when she had no plans to leave the house, even when she was going no farther than the sunroom to do a crossword puzzle. At night she wore chiffon evening gowns with beaded tops and a silver fox stole and Delman evening shoes and little *peau de soie* bags containing her Pall Malls and some face powder. I never saw her actual fingernails or toenails, just enamel—two perfect coats of Revlon's Windsor.

I don't think she ever thought about why she looked like she looked or wore what she wore. I know her hair and her clothes and her jewelry gave a very shy woman confidence, courage, and sometimes even balls, but I don't think she was ever that introspective about it: You dressed, you looked nice *always*; if you had diamonds you wore them; if you didn't you made damn sure every hair was in place, your clothes were pressed, and your shoes were polished. It was that simple. You owed it to yourself and the people around you.

My grandmother would have approved of fashion's current direction.

Suddenly clothes are beautiful again, rich-looking, well cut, sexy and demure at the same time in that Grace Kelly kind of way. Marc Jacobs, who once led the pack in elevating grunge to high fashion, is designing furs and real diamond jewelry—his latest "bride" wore a scattering of diamonds (the most divinely feminine and extravagant way to wear them) on her white lapel. At the intimate showing of his spring collection, John Galliano pinned huge—and real—flower brooches to cloche hats and kimonos and fastened a silk moiré jacket with a $250,000 dragonfly pin from Fred Leighton. He also showed veils and forties fluid pantsuits and perfect fitted jackets and strapless tulle ball gowns that looked as though they should come with their own orchids and dance cards. Stores are selling pocketbooks (remember that word?) again and not backpacks; gloves; suits in pastel colors (Bill Blass made some of the best ones in pink and yellow, solids and checks). One of today's hottest designers is Philip Treacy, and all he makes is hats. "There is a generation of women," said one retailer at the shows, "who want the illusion of couture."

Whatever, diamond sales hit an all-time high last year, topping $12 billion. Despite the best efforts of PETA and Ricki Lake, fur sales also rose, for the second year in a row. Women are going to the hairdresser to get their hair done, not just cut and blown, and they are no longer embarrassed to admit it. People are sick of feeling guilty and looking ugly. If there is no order in the world, no universal and mutually understood standards left by which to measure ourselves, at least you can impose some order on yourself. In *Steel Magnolias*, when Dolly Parton announced that since she was fourteen her thighs had not left the house unless they were encased in Lycra, Olympia Dukakis told her she was raised right. Damn straight. Nobody wants to see your flabby thighs any more than they want to see your politics worn literally on your sleeve. But we go through these very unfortunate and often actually dangerous periods of puritanism in this country when looking nice is equaled with possession by the devil or being Nancy Reagan. Everybody is supposed to lock up their jewelry and sit around looking depressed about the environment in clothes with the seams on the outside.

In the sixties this manifested itself in patched blue jeans and tie-dyed T-shirts and the bombing of draft offices. During this most recent bout of puritanical tyranny—an early-nineties backlash motivated in part by the fear of looking like a leveraged-buyout-artist's second wife—everybody wore the same thing I wore in boarding school. When I look at my yearbook now, we all look like depressed truck drivers. It wasn't good for our self-esteem then; think what it does for that of an entire nation. "On a fashion level," said one L.A. retailer, "[the spring shows] marked the death of deconstruction." On a psychological level they marked a collective coming-out party. People can take only so much and then they want it to be Morning in America again. So they vote Republican and dress up.

Even deep-dyed liberals like Hillary Clinton get a little obsessed with their hairdos and secretly try to make a lot of money. *Most* people want to make a lot of money, and then they want to hang on to it and wear things that make them look like they have even more than they do. You do not have to be a rocket scientist to figure out that if you look more like Grace Kelly than, say, Courtney Love, you are more likely to get a good table—or any table—in a restaurant; people will accept your checks; salesladies are more apt to ask if madam would like to open a Bergdorf's charge because it is absolutely *no* trouble, really. If you look rich you are treated like a rich person. If you look like Courtney Love you are asked to leave the lobby of the Ritz. Period. This is the kind of thing someone like Estée Lauder was born knowing. "I've always told Evie," she told a reporter, referring to her daughter-in-law Evelyn, "'If you don't look successful, you won't be successful.' You have to dress expensively even if it means selling your soul to get that one fabulous suit which, if you have no other, you wear all the time."

This, of course, is the stuff of fiction: the mother who scrimps and saves and sews till her fingers bleed so that her daughter can go out into the world, her one shot with her nice frock and matching hat and gloves, to get a man, to gain a fortune. Clothes can be the ticket to the life to which you aspire. Remember *Stella Dallas*? Reba McEntire sings a song called "Fancy," in which Fancy's mother spends her last penny on a red satin dress for Fancy and sends her on her way. Fancy ends up with a mansion in Georgia and a town house in New York. This song was a big hit, which is no surprise, since a large number of the people who listen to country music are people for whom the grunge look is a part of their daily working life and not a fashion statement. When these people don't have to dress like that anymore, they don't. Tammy Wynette spent her childhood picking cotton. Now she doesn't go out of the house without forty pounds of bugle beads on her back. She knows. This is America, after all; that's what it's for, for God's sake. If people in America did not want to get rich, they wouldn't have come here in the very first place. And if they did not want to look rich, there would be no rhinestones, cubic zirconium, designer knockoffs, $999 mink coats bought on time. Women would not put aside a month's grocery money to buy a single Chanel camellia.

Those people who do not have to save money to buy Chanel have a responsibility to live up to their good fortune. I object to those old-money Yankee women who wear no makeup, fake pearls, and castoffs from the Junior League thrift shop. This is disappointing and pretentious. I much prefer those unabashedly ostentatious Texans who flash ten-carat diamond rings—"It's my tenth anniversary, honey"—or the Revillon man at Houston's Saks Fifth Avenue, who told me that fake fur was just "so unwonderful." There is nothing worse than rich people with guilt. They do ridiculous things like give George McGovern's presidential campaign $1 million or hobnob with the Dalai Lama and hang out in $10,000-a-week ashrams. Rich people should act—and look—like rich people, just like royalty should act like royalty and not white trash or guests on *Oprah*. The photographer Edward Quinn, who took brilliant pictures on the Riviera in the 1950s, recently lamented that "now the stars have to be seen in jeans and sweaters. It disappoints me because it's become a sameness, a uniform." The other night I saw a very fabulous movie called *The Rains Came*, in which George Brent tells Myrna Loy that he admires their hostess, the maharani of Ranchipur, a "tough egg," because "while queens do everything in their power to look like housewives, she still dresses the queen." Quite right.

Vogue itself was founded by very rich people (including Cornelius Vanderbilt) and billed as "the dignified authentic journal of society, fashion, and the ceremonial side of life." It has been a long time since fashion was entirely dictated by society, and there are far too few ceremonial sides to life, but there is still that lingering connection. Otherwise there would be no Jackie O. sunglasses, Kelly bags, the idea that possessing a simple accessory is to have a piece of a whole other world. Five hours after Princess Diana got married, the British department store Debenhams put a copy of that wedding-cake wedding dress of hers in the window, and it was still selling five years later.

Fashion has always been about yearning. The clothes now are not only about a yearning to look or to be rich, to be like those people; they seem to want to re-create another time, a more civilized, dignified but also glamorous era. Perhaps if we look like Jackie or Grace or Audrey they won't be lost to us, and neither will the mores of their age. An age in which we were better-mannered, polished, when brides got trousseaus and left their weddings in pastel douppioni leaving suits adorned with circle pins and oversize charm bracelets and asked their mothers what to put in their pocketbooks. When boys in white dinner jackets came to pick you up and your dress was so big you had to sit by yourself in the backseat. When I look at Galliano's ball gowns, I see my mother's scrapbooks crammed with Fortnightly Club dance cards and the boys' penciled scrawls, countless clippings from the social pages, satin ribbons from corsages turned to dust between the pages. My own scrapbooks do not contain the same remnants of innocence or glamour or romance; they contain pictures of people in cutoffs. I never got to feel like my mother did in those dresses.

These clothes also signal a return to what my grandmother always did, dressing for an occasion. They are about getting dressed to go to work or lunch or shopping or an interview in something besides leggings and a jacket, even if the leggings are from Prada and the jacket is Chanel. It is a chic look, that, but it somehow doesn't seem as respectful to an occasion, any occasion, as a nipped-in-at-the-waist black-and-white houndstooth suit with a little belt and seamed stockings with fabulous heels. Rich people are brought up to rise to the occasion and to dress for it, and there is a dignity in that: Jackie Kennedy standing firm in her blood-spattered pink suit, Myrna Loy in that same swell movie unruffled in an evening gown and jeweled cuffs even after an earthquake and a flood. When she finally changed clothes, she curled her hair before ministering to the cholera-stricken. This is not a bad thing for the rest of us to emulate.

As I write this I am looking at a photograph of my mother's best friend, Bossy. It was taken when I was about five or six, and she is quite beautiful and young and she is sitting in our living room holding a glass of Scotch. She is wearing a handmade lace-and-batiste blouse underneath a black crepe jumper with a little pin at the neck and white gloves. She looks like she is going to a wedding or a cocktail party or possibly an audience with the pope, but she was just going out to dinner with her husband and my parents, which I find astonishing since there were only two restaurants in my hometown then, Doe's Eat Place and Lillo's Dine and Dance, both of which were white clapboard roadhouse-looking places serving steak and spaghetti and featuring at their respective entrances a hot-tamale machine and a jukebox. The place was clearly not the point. The point was she was going out, so she dressed. And her face is so hopeful. Fashion, after all, is also about possibility.

Now, at the time she was not a particularly wealthy woman; she just looked it. It's the white gloves that did it. Audrey Hepburn wore white gloves in *Charade*, with a white pillbox hat and a red suit. She wore almost no jewelry, but she looked rich. Audrey was, as they used to say, well groomed. So were Carole Lombard and her entire family in *My Man Godfrey*, and Myrna Loy in everything. They all had sleek, shiny hair, which is also making a comeback. My own hairdresser, the particularly well-groomed and gorgeous Tim at Manhattan's Stephen Knoll salon, has taken to putting just a smidgen of oil on mine, and he refuses to make it big anymore. It's a good thing, actually, because if you don't have slick hair when you put on Galliano's ball gowns you will look like a prom queen from West Texas. Elizabeth Taylor hasn't looked rich since her hair was all one color and a lot closer to her head, and all the rocks in the world won't change that.

Grooming in the end is more important than the rocks, and, like the white gloves, it's a whole lot cheaper. Jackie would not have looked half as chic in her white pants and striped tee if the rest of her hadn't been so well taken care of. After my grandmother died I asked one of her friends what she remembered most about her, and she didn't mention the eye-popping jewels or the furs or even her post-headlight-stroking pronouncements. She said, "She could get a spot out of anything and pack a suitcase like nobody's business." It's true. My greatest pleasure as a child (with the exception of pinning her brooches in my hair and pretending my nightgown was an evening dress) was watching her unpack. Everything was carefully folded in layers of tissue paper or stretched out in dry cleaner's plastic so it would never wrinkle. There were lingerie bags, shoe bags, mending kits, a gold-plated manicure set in a green leather case, Carbona for the dreaded spots, Elizabeth Arden Eight Hour Cream. No one, she taught me by example, looks rich or even presentable with callused elbows, a missing button, a chipped nail. We learn important stuff from our more elegant elders: to use the word *peignoir* instead of, say, *housecoat*, and that gray and brown somehow looks richer than gray and black.

What else looks rich? Linen, wool crepe, silk—especially four-ply.

Linings as beautiful as the things they line. I have an orange four-ply silk skirt lined in lipstick-red charmeuse, and every time I step into it I feel incredibly extravagant. I used to wear it with a four-ply white silk dinner jacket cut like a man's until I finally had to throw it away. White silk is beyond decadent because you know it can't last too long without getting yellowed or spotted or spilled on. It is the ultimate in throwaway chic. White tennis dresses with pleated skirts look rich, and so do jodhpurs. Only rich people can afford the ludicrous upkeep of horses, which is why Ralph Lauren is such a genius. He gave us jodhpurs without the horse, just the association. Things that match always look rich and are a big hit this season: dresses and jackets or coats, hats and gloves, shoes and purses, nail polish and lipstick, twinsets, luggage.

When you have on any one (or two) of these things, when your nails aren't chipped and your hair is shiny, you feel different, better, more pulled together and in control. I was talking about the effect of all this with a male friend who has recently taken to wearing a homburg, and he asked me if I'd ever carried a loaded gun. When I told him no, he explained that it "shifts your posture, kind of like the first time you ever carry $1,000 in cash." That I could understand. When I put on my new black Bill Blass evening suit and my black satin Manolo Blahnik T-straps with five-inch heels there is not a room in the world I can't walk through. But if I'm on the street without makeup and in my black sweater with holes in the elbows, I hide from most people I know. Everybody called grandmother the Duchess, for obvious reasons, but she was actually the sweetest and shyest soul on the planet. It was all that jewelry and outer perfection that made her stature so regal, that enabled her to face my grandfather and the world and, occasionally, to lambaste them both. We all become, at least for a while, the faces we present to others.

There is an old home movie taken by my father of my mother and Bossy, her white-glove-wearing friend. They are at a resort in Nassau, and they have on movie-star dark glasses and strapless bathing suits with push-up bras sewn inside and they are smoking with cigarette holders in a very provocative way. They could have easily been movie stars, they exuded such beauty and glamour—a power, really, that I did not often see at home, where they smoked without the benefit of holders and wore decidedly different dark glasses. They were taken up and followed around by all the swells on the island—they looked the part, and so it had become real. (Until one of the grander ladies they'd met called later, when they were all safely back home, and announced she was coming to visit, expecting no doubt a lifestyle as glamorous as the fabulous young couples she had met in Nassau. Instead she found women in wraparound skirts driving station-wagon loads of children and a dry cleaner who was too frightened to clean her Balenciagas.)

My father, who has never had an insecure moment in his life, doesn't understand about clothes or dark glasses or especially beautiful jewelry (Oscar Heyman's advice being totally lost on him, a man who has bought my mother only an engagement ring and an amethyst pin in almost forty years), about dressing to improve your posture and your state of mind. He always acts like he's carrying a loaded gun. Until out of desperation my mother and I started buying him nice shirts from England, he wore discounted Ralph Lauren Polo shirts he got for $12.95 at the local Stein Mart because the polo pony insignia was missing some threads. He therefore did not understand our mortification over the fact that the first year we went skiing (this was prior to his announcement that he would stay home and take a cold shower and burn up $1,000 bills for the same effect), he made us all wear the quilted linings of his hunting jackets instead of the swanky new ski ensembles we all wanted.

Once he flew us in his small plane down to a resort in Florida, and because of the weight we were each given a single paper bag to pack in. We arrived at the hotel early and the bellman asked us if we would like to check our luggage before he had actually seen it. Never has a group of five paper bags been put away so quickly. The bellman was embarrassed, we were embarrassed, and my father thought it was the funniest thing he had ever seen. He is not a guy who will ever feel the need to invest in a Vuitton trunk to boost his self-esteem. The rest of us, of course, could use some help, and thank heaven it has arrived. Thank heaven it is OK to look rich and glamorous and polished and secure again instead of messy and sullen. Not tacky, over-the-top, second-wife, eighties trying-too-hard-to-get-in-the-columns kind of rich, with one too many Cartier panthers prowling all over your chest. But the way rich people used to look in their ladylike, well-cut suits and glamorous evening gowns with dyed-to-match *peau de soie* shoes. The way people looked back when they cared enough to "do" their hair and wore something besides sweat suits on airplanes. The way people looked when they dressed just to go out of the house. Well groomed, nice, hopeful.

5

A Case Study

(1997)

Last July I went to five countries in eight days. I was traveling with the secretary of state; my wardrobe was not the issue (the issue was NATO expansion); packing should've been easy. It wasn't. It never is.

The trip demanded: a suit with a skirt for official stuff, a black pant-suit for everything else, an extra pair of black pants and some T-shirts, a black satin shirt, a white cotton shirt, a pair of Manolo Blahnik loafers, a pair of Manolo pumps. Period. I took all that, but since I pack by the motto "you never know," I also took five separate pieces of chiffon evening wear, some Armani tuxedo pants, an organza skirt, some spike-heeled satin pumps, one pair of low-heeled satin mules, one pair of high-heeled satin mules, and two black satin evening bags. I had an agonizing moment over a brown suit, which would have required an entirely different set of accessories, so, in a rare act of restraint, I nixed it. But I still managed to squeeze in an Armani blazer I bought on sale an hour and a half before my plane left, *just in case*. It still has the price tag on it.

You would think I would know better. I live in two places; I pack a suitcase for somewhere almost once a week. And almost once a week I ask myself if I really need to pack that Bendel's brown-striped mini-suitcase of a cosmetics kit with four kinds of face masks, three eye gels, and two deep conditioners. And the answer is always yes. In the days before Velcro rollers I navigated the globe carrying a very heavy set of twenty hot rollers, and converters and adapters for every country. You never know whom you might run into. You also never know when something might go wrong—I once missed a plane because I was trying to find my suede brush.

I always pack too much and I always curse myself, but I'm not convinced overpacking is a bad thing. Packing, for some people, is an act of efficiency and order. I know a woman who had to promise her husband, as a condition of their marriage, that she would never use a piece of luggage she couldn't carry on an airplane. She packs thin jerseys and silks and cashmeres in a streamlined black leather hang-up bag that has pockets for two pairs of shoes, some lingerie, and a few other bare essentials. Now, this woman has been my mentor in a lot of departments, and she showed me where to get this bag and I bought one, but I could never be that disciplined. I think packing should be an act of the imagination.

Traveling, even on business, even in the worst of circumstances, is about possibility. Including not one but five pieces of black chiffon in a suitcase packed for a tightly scheduled trip in which your only mission is to listen to a cabinet member spout administration policy is, therefore, an act of optimism. When my friend McGee and I went to Africa on safari we were given a list of items to take and a suitcase apiece, a hideous green nylon duffel, which we absolutely were not allowed to augment with an extra one or two of our own. I filled mine with my khakis and my T-shirts and my hiking boots and books, while McGee managed to find room for some strappy silver evening sandals and a white lace-up bustier. She ended up trading the sandals for two Maasai bowls, and she tried to wear the bustier to a Maasai village until it was recommended by the guide that she didn't, but I knew why she'd brought them. Remember the scene in *Out of Africa* when Meryl Streep's undoing her blouse in her tent and Robert Redford comes in and says, "I'd like to do that"? You never know.

Meryl Streep had some good-looking luggage in that movie. My grandparents had luggage like that: parchment-colored canvas cases with brown leather trim and gold initials; caramel leather satchels that looked like doctors' bags; trunks that had been to Paris and Venice and

Rome and on the last voyage of the *Andrea Doria* before it sank. There were mounds of it stored in a room off the bar, and I would go in there with a jar of olives and breathe in that good canvas-y, leathery, slightly musty luggage smell and plot the places I knew I would eventually visit.

When I finally did go to Rome I did not put my clothes, as my grandmother did, in dry cleaners' plastic between layers of tissue paper in a hard canvas case. For reasons I cannot now fathom, I put them in a long cloth garment bag that was far too fat to stuff into one of those airline boxes. I was going to meet the man I almost married. It was a turning point in our relationship and I knew it would be, so I came prepared with enough brand-new clothes to last me a month, including a very sixties silver and white sequined shift. The man who made it for me said, "That's it, that's the dress. He's going to ask you to marry him." And eventually he did, but I don't know where the hell I thought I was going to wear that dress on a four-day trip to Rome.

Anyway, I got back to Dulles airport and watched my bag full of all my new clothes come around the baggage carousel with its entire bottom half in shreds. It was the mid-eighties, skirts had to be at the least mid-calf, and from the knee down everything I owned looked like a fistful of party streamers. The airline reimbursed me a grand total of $600, but in a major stroke of fashion luck, the mini made the first of its many comebacks within weeks, so I chopped everything off and became easily the first girl in Washington, D.C., to have an entirely up-to-the-minute wardrobe. I also immediately went out and bought myself a hard canvas suitcase.

Since then I have become a luggage fanatic. I have an enormous wardrobe trunk with hangers, the kind that was outside Gary Cooper's room at the Ritz in *Love in the Afternoon*, which I have used exactly never. (You never know.) I have cases, soft duffels, leather totes, snakeskin totes, L.L.Bean canvas totes. When someone is dying, one of those things you're supposed to do is keep "a little bag" packed and ready to go when the dread call comes in the middle of the night. My grandmother took so long to die, my mother and I had long ceased to keep ours packed, so when the call came, my mother left without any bag at all, and I left from somewhere besides home. The shopkeepers of Nashville were thrilled to see us—our first act upon arrival was to buy two days' worth of suitable mourning clothes.

Then there is packing for a different kind of phone call in the night. A big soft Hermès Kelly bag has just the right mix of recklessness and extravagance for the impromptu tryst. The first things you throw in— frantically, breathlessly—are not shoes or shirts or even chiffon, but your best underwear, charmeuse nightgowns you never wear at home, perfume, razor, toothbrush, a simple little shift almost as an afterthought, in case once you check into your room you actually decide to leave it. On trips like that everything needs to be effortless—dresses you step into (and out of), sandals you can slide on, a scarf to wrap around your shoulders, sunglasses big enough to hide your face. The things you must be prepared for are different.

On those trips, and only on those, you do in fact know. It is not necessary to be dressed for possibility. Face masks and suede brushes, multiple evening bags and extra T-shirts, would all be superfluous. However, until the lucky moment when that call comes, I strongly urge overpacking.

6

On the Scent

(1999)

Lately my identity has been seriously messed with. First, my hairdresser of more than a decade took off for an ashram in India. Second, within the space of a week, George, who had been serving me overpriced cocktails at the Carlyle hotel's Bemelmans Bar since I'd been too young to order them, retired, and my favorite waiter at my favorite restaurant in New Orleans moved home to Tampa to take care of his aging father. I maybe could have handled all that—although it is not the same to walk into the Carlyle with hair you're a little shaky about and no George to kiss you and tell you you're beautiful even if you're not. But then I walked into Boyd's Pharmacy, where I'd been buying my favorite—my only— perfume for seventeen years, Paco Rabanne's Metal, and was told that it had been discontinued.

This was too much. Scent is one of those ostensibly superficial things—like a hairstyle, a "look," or the jovial assessment of another person—that define us. Also, the only man I've ever really loved told me a long time ago that Metal is the only perfume he's ever even liked. I found it in St. Thomas while on a cruise with my cousin. We had had the misguided idea of taking our old and very cranky grandfather to the Caribbean. Discovering what I knew would be my signature scent for life had been the trip's only bright spot.

In junior high school, like everyone else, I wore Charlie. And patchouli oil, briefly, for the same amount of time I decided to set myself apart by wearing Indian jewelry and Earth shoes. When I wanted to feel grown-up and glamorous I would wear Norell, and then I progressed to Halston and Chanel No. 19 and Lauren, when it was new and therefore cool.

But none of those scents were mine. They were better defined by someone else's personality. Shelley Hack was the face of Charlie; people at Studio 54, a place I could only read about, wore Halston. Patti Hansen and Rene Russo appeared in the ads for Chanel No. 19; a preppy Clothilde modeled for Lauren. I hadn't even seen an ad for Metal. I had simply found it. On my own. On an island. It was chemistry. Like love, like that look across the crowded room, there is no explaining the attraction.

Now, when it is too late, the people at Paco Rabanne have decided to explain it to me anyway. "The style of Metal was consistent with the style of the designs of Paco Rabanne ... edgy—ahead of their time," says the letter from the PR firm. "Those who enjoy wearing Metal do not mind appearing quirky or different. These women are strong and assertive. They like being distinct. They enjoy the limelight." "Right," said a friend of mine when he read the same letter, "you're a weirdo."

Apparently. I am further informed that the scent's "unusual metal note" meant that its "audience was limited in relation to the expensive cost of producing the fragrance." At the same time, the catalog of the designer's spring/summer 1999 collection says that the clothes hark back "to a past which remains enduringly modern as the couturier returns to his origins, with metal plates connected by rings, rivets, and eyelets." It seems to me that a fragrance named for all that chic hardware would be the perfect accompaniment to it. However, not only does Rabanne not ever plan to bring Metal back, they could find me but one bottle—in Tokyo.

They did manage to tell me what was in it: "blend of woods and greens—with tones of rose and a 'hint' of the problematic 'metallic.'" I vow to find something similar and immediately head off to Bergdorf's perfume room. A very nice man named Richard brings out Zaharoff, composed of jasmine, sandalwood, and Bulgarian rose (that would be the "blend of woods and greens with tones of rose"), but instead of the hint of metallic there was a whiff of pink osmanthus—a cousin, I am told, of the vanilla plant—which grows only in the foothills of the Himalayas. The vanilla is troublesome, overwhelming, the opposite of the clean and flinty edge of Metal. But also most every fragrance Richard spritzes on his endless paper strips has an element of it. I feel like I'm in Betty Crocker's test kitchen.

Richard doesn't even work for Bergdorf's; he's just being helpful. He is officially in the store to rep Fable, a new scent by the great-grandson of Evalyn Walsh McLean, the doomed owner of the Hope Diamond. He has not bothered to try to sell it to me, because it smells almost entirely of vanilla—the favorite dessert of Mrs. McLean having been crème brûlée. In an effort to be polite, I venture that I am crazy about crème brûlée. But another salesman finishes my sentence: "Yeah, but who wants to wear it?"

Giving up on finding a relation of Metal, I dropped a note to Anitra Earle, the Chicago-based Perfume Detective. I had dealt with Anitra before, when she managed to find a bottle of my mother's long-discontinued scent, Sortilège, so I was hopeful. Victory was in fact quickly at hand (if she knows she can get it, she'll let you know within 48 hours). Anitra found me a 6.7-ounce bottle of eau de toilette for $78 plus $5 shipping. I implore her to keep looking, and I know she will because she takes her work extremely seriously. "People call me and say, 'It will save my marriage if you can find this scent for me,'" she tells me. "People laugh at the soap-opera aspect of it, but the sense of smell goes more directly to the part of the brain that deals with emotions than any of the other senses. When you look at it that way, what a person's mate smells like is important."

Anitra says her "all-time most-requested fragrance" is Intoxication by D'Orsay, which was very big in the fifties. Recently the company announced it was back in business with Intoxication d'Amour, but it was, says Anitra, a "totally different fragrance." Perfume makers seem to have a bad habit of doing things like that. In the course of trying to solve my own dilemma I ran into my friend Grace, who told me she didn't wear perfume for seven years after her favorite, Bob Mackie, was taken off the market. It was replaced with the similarly named Mackie, but it wasn't at all the same. She finally found something she could wear, Hermès 24, Faubourg, but it clearly doesn't own her heart. She confides that about once a year, and only on some supremely special occasion, she allows herself a single dab of her precious last bottle of Bob.

I tell her I'm about to make a call to another perfume finder and I'll inquire about her lost scent. She is practically in tears, she is so grateful. Within the hour I am talking to Brenda Isley, owner of the Fragrance Factory in the unlikely farming community of Walla Walla, Washington. The first long-distance phone call that Brenda ever made in her life was when she was nineteen years old and newly married. She called New York ("It might as well have been another planet") to Germaine Monteil to try to find her own discontinued scent, Bakir. "I just had to have it." Fifteen years later she quit her job in banking to devote herself to what is clearly her natural calling. "I'm so glad I took this risk. I really feel like I'm helping people." She certainly helped me. She had four 3.4-ounce bottles of Metal at $85 each, and five 1.7 ounces at $65 each, some smaller-size bottles, and even a purse size—twelve altogether. I took them all. Also, she said she thought she could lay her hands on at least one bottle of Bob Mackie. When I gave Grace the news at dinner that night, she literally bowed down to me.

As nuts as Grace and I might be, we are not nearly as obsessed as some people. Brenda has granted dying wishes, she has had people sob into her telephone, she had a male doctor in Boston pay her $350 for a quarter ounce of a scent he used to buy at the Ritz-Carlton. In the latter case it took her a year. "I'm 99 percent successful," she says. "I don't take no for an answer." It's a good thing. "Sometimes people are so desperate I fear for them, and I paste their names on my computer."

With Anitra's bottle in hand and twelve more on the way from Brenda, I am less and less desperate. Plus, someone gives me yet another source, Parfumelle, a store in Fort Worth, Texas, which has three more bottles. At this point, I feel like I'm about to lay down some really fine wine. Except instead of the cellar, I plan to put my bottles in my sweater drawer. Heat doesn't affect the fragrance as much as light. My Metal will be deservingly swathed in black cashmere. And my identity, for the next several years at least, will remain intact. Now if only George would come back and pour me a Johnnie Walker.

7

Knee High

(2003)

Years ago, I was sitting at the bar in Café Loup—the old location, the good one—in Greenwich Village. My legs were crossed and sort of propped against the edge of the bar when a man leaned toward me from about four stools over and told me I had great knees. I don't think I've ever been so flattered. It wasn't a come-on—who would try to pick up a girl by complimenting her knees? The man turned out to be a regular, and I became one, and every time I saw him I gave him a big smile and flashed a little knee. Since then, I have broken my right knee and generally battered my left, but, thanks to the gallant barfly, both knees have remained points of pride on an otherwise flawed body.

It turns out that most people are not proud of their knees. "I think the human body is perfect with the exception of the knee," says my friend M.T. "It's vulnerable, and it's ugly. I hate my knees so much, but when I start working out, they go out."

Knees get a bad rap in general. If you are knee-deep in something, it is usually trouble; if you're knee-walking, it means you're drunk. To be brought to your knees is to be in a position of submission or desperation, says *The Oxford Companion to the Body*; to be cut off at the knees is to be humiliated, disabled, or both.

And then there is kneecapping, a practice favored by the Mob and various terrorist organizations, which involves destroying the kneecaps by shooting them or shattering them with a baseball bat.

Comparatively, then, the news that hemlines are again on the rise does not sound so bad. After all, your knees are simply exposed—they haven't been crushed by Big Pussy or Paulie Walnuts. But M.T. is not happy. She knows she has little recourse. "The knee is just bone and cartilage for the most part," says Marc Felberg, a personal trainer in Manhattan who lately has been helping me with my many body parts I don't happen to be proud of. "There are not a lot of muscle or fat cells. So there's not much you can do to change the actual knee." When people have "fat knees," what they really have, Felberg says, is "a tendency to hold fat in the 'teardrop' of the muscle, where the thigh muscle joins the knee. The fat is really in the thigh and just kind of hangs down there." Your best bet, he says, is to create an "illusion—if you have a well-toned thigh and well-toned calves, the knee itself will look better."

The first thing to do is to strengthen the knees so that they will not, in fact, go out. Felberg recommends biking, climbing stairs, doing squats or partial squats, all of which strengthen the ligaments around the knee, the tendons of the muscles that attach to the bone, and the bone itself, which is most important in fighting osteoporosis. (When I was a child, our maid, Tee, sprayed WD-40 on her knees to improve their mobility. She swore the stuff worked as well on her knees as on the door, and it's true that the knee is a hinge joint. Still, I think Felberg's course is a wiser one to follow.) Then, after strengthening, if you're skinny and have knobby knees that stick out, you can get to work thickening the thigh muscle a bit (with weighted squats, leg extensions, and curls) and working on your calves. "The eye will go to the shapely calf muscles and well-toned quads," says Felberg. Likewise, if your legs are heavy and your knee looks like a dimple in a tube of cookie dough, get on the treadmill. "Don't do bulk work," says Felberg. "Do aerobics to burn down fat so that the leg returns to its natural lean mass."

Also, some people tend to store fat in that "teardrop" even when their legs are otherwise toned. For that, there is, naturally, a surgical option. Thomas Loeb, MD, has created a "microliposuction" technique that sucks fat out of the inner knee and outer thigh. It is called microliposuction because he uses a more delicate instrument than is usually used in liposuction, so the incisions are much smaller. What that means, according to Loeb, is that there is less bruising and "dimpling skin," and "patients can return to work the next day. Even better, they can show off their more shapely legs on the beach in just three weeks."

Loeb is the man responsible for Paula Jones's new nose, definitely an achievement of sorts, but I would opt for Felberg's illusion technique. In that regard, Donna Karan's Essential Toners are useful. Knee socks are not. No one over the age of ten should be caught dead in knee socks, which showcase the knee, acting as a pedestal of sorts. And no one of any age should ever put on that grotesque invention, sheer "knee-highs" designed to look like pantyhose beneath pants or long skirts. My friend Iris learned this lesson the hard way one New Year's Eve at a black-tie dinner. Iris had on a great-looking black gown and some sexy evening sandals. No one knew that her "pantyhose" were actually the dastardly knee-highs until a guest began regaling Iris with the details of her tummy tuck, causing Iris to faint dead away. The first thing people do, apparently, to fainting victims is to put their legs up. I walked in to find Iris flat on her back with her gown bunched up over her thighs and her bare white knees up in the air for all the world to see.

Knees, especially in that position, are inherently funny, but I think we should appreciate knees more. My high school social life would have suffered greatly without the helpful knee-up my best friend gave me, enabling me to slip in and out of my bedroom window undetected on many a late weekend night. So far I have never had to knee anyone in the groin, but I know how to do it if the need for self-defense ever arises. Also, if it weren't for knees, some of the world's great songs never would have been written. Eric Clapton's "Layla," for example ("Layla, you've got me on my knees/Layla, I'm begging, darling, please"), or the

Righteous Brothers' "You've Lost That Lovin' Feeling" ("Baby, baby, I'd get down on my knees for you"). I managed to find a website devoted to songs whose lyrics contain the word knee, a remarkable number as it happens—87 on this site alone. I think the amount mostly has to do with the convenient rhyme of the words *knees* and *please* and the fact that knees—and love and sex—are so closely associated with begging. Witness Alicia Keys's sexy/plaintive "How Come You Don't Call Me?" (To paraphrase: "I'll get down on my knees/Hoping you'll please, please, please/Oooh, why don't you call me sometime. Papa?")

In John Cougar Mellencamp's "Jack and Diane," knees rhyme, for a refreshing change, with "Tastee Freez," the location where Jack asks Diane to "Dribble off those Bobbie Brooks/Let me do what I please." And then there is a much earlier classic: "Picture you upon my knee/Just tea for two and two for tea." Those lyrics did not make the website, but that seemingly innocuous song, with that "you upon my knee" business, has always conjured up a Lolita-like image for me. Perhaps young knees are inherently more appealing—they haven't had much time to collect any fat from the thigh. In the movie *Claire's Knee*, director Eric Rohmer tells the story of a man who becomes obsessed with a younger woman. Before he sees her face, he encounters her knee on a ladder in an orchard and immediately falls in love.

Inappropriate older men are not the only people who find knees erotic. They play an obvious role in a great many sex acts, a fact that has earned them a lot more websites than their existence in song lyrics. Playing "kneesies" under a table is a well-known turn-on, particularly when it is forbidden, and the back of the knee is a particularly sensitive area. If you grab someone's leg hard just above the knee you will give him a painful charley horse; lightly brushing against the crook of the knee will make the same person blush—or more.

I think we should take advantage of the season's new hemlines and give thanks that we have the option to show our knees in the first place. We could live in Iraq, for heaven's sake, or pre-twenties America, or any other place where women cannot walk around blithely showing their knees—or, indeed, prop them up on the edge of a bar. So if you don't like your knees, call the trainer or the doctor or invest in some good tights. And then flash a bit of knee. It's our patriotic duty.

PART 3

People

8

Witness at the Execution

(1993)

t is midnight, March 5, 1993, and I am outside the Louisiana State
Penitentiary waiting for the execution of Robert Wayne Sawyer, a
forty-two-year-old mentally disabled white man with one eye whom
I have seen only in newspaper photographs. The penitentiary, known
as Angola because the slaves who originally farmed these 18,000 acres
came from there, is miles from nowhere on the Mississippi River and
is without question the last place in America I thought I'd be on this
night, especially in the company of a fifty-four-year-old nun from Baton
Rouge named Helen Prejean. But I am, because I've read Prejean's new
book, *Dead Man Walking: An Eyewitness Account of the Death Penalty in
the United States* (Random House), and I wanted to get closer to a process and a punishment about which I thought I had made up my mind.

All my red flags went up when I was told about Helen Prejean: nun,
bleeding heart, lived in a housing project, now works to stop the death
penalty. I expected someone skinny and pale and hopelessly earnest, and
then I met this hilarious powerhouse of a woman with a heavy Louisiana
accent and no habit who laughs all the time unless she is talking serious
business, in which case she is not earnest but honest and compassionate
and unstintingly direct. (I quit trying so hard not to take the Lord's
name in vain when she told me an old Mickey Mouse joke with the
f-word in it.) I thought I believed in the death penalty, but I read the

manuscript of her book anyway—trailing pages through airports across the country as I flew on a series of planes—and by the time I'd reached my destination, the convictions of a lifetime had been overturned.

The book is Prejean's own story: middle-class nun teaching poor children in the New Orleans projects agrees to be pen pal to a death-row inmate ten years ago and winds up friend to both death-row inmates and the families of their victims, witness to executions, testifier at trials challenging the constitutionality of capital punishment, and ultimately an articulate leader and cofounder of a coalition to abolish the death penalty. Along the way she battles a hypocritical church hierarchy (despite the church's rather obvious position that it is wrong to kill, the US Bishops' 1980 statement upholds the states' right to take a life), chauvinistic church authorities (who tried to bar Prejean and other female spiritual advisers from becoming involved with death-row inmates on the grounds that women are too emotional to deal with executions), and a skeptical public who assumed that she was a communist or had fallen in love with the inmates, or both.

She is hardly in love—she cannot even begin to apologize for the men she writes about, but she manages to restore to them a basic humanity. We read their letters with her; we are in their cells as they prepare to die. "When you're meeting with a man an hour before he dies . . . and he's packing up his clothes and putting them in a paper bag and asking for a Sprite, here's another dimension of a human being that you're seeing." She contends that "the redeemable feature in us is that human beings are transcendent of an action," however terrible. But she has also learned that the lives of the victims' families are forever defined by another man's action, and she takes us on a separate journey that ultimately leads her to set up an assistance program for those families, whom we come to know equally well.

By its nature, the book is a moral argument against legally mandated murder, but it is also a practical argument that exposes the extraordinary expense, arbitrary nature, and ultimate ineffectiveness of the process, as well as the political forces behind it. Finally, it is a gripping narrative, driven above all by her conviction that if the public could be as close to this as she has been, we would no longer condone capital punishment in any form. So she takes us there. "How," she asked Paul Phelps, the recently deceased Louisiana corrections department chief, "can we end the death penalty?" "Simple," he said. "Do it in the Superdome."

So far executions are still carried out in the penitentiary's official "death chamber," a tiny room with a window through which the twelve witnesses required by the state watch the condemned man die. Because I am not a resident of the state of Louisiana, I am not Robert Sawyer's spiritual adviser, I am not related to the victim, I do not work for United Press International or the Associated Press, and I did not qualify for the press pool of one, I am as close as I can get to witnessing the death of Robert Sawyer. He will be the twenty-first person executed by Louisiana since the Supreme Court allowed states to resume capital punishment in 1976 and the first by lethal injection.

Inside, Sawyer has eaten his last meal of two bacon, lettuce, and tomato sandwiches, french fries, a strawberry milkshake, and chocolate pie. He has issued what will be the last statement of his life, expressing relief that after thirteen years and eight stays of execution he will be "going home to be with my family" (although God knows why, since his mother tried to kill him before taking her own life with a shotgun, and his father beat him repeatedly) and containing the warning to "young kids" that "drinking and hanging with the wrong people will get you where I am sitting right here."

Outside, about two dozen people have gathered beneath the light of an unusually bright moon, and one that is closer to the earth than it will be for another month. The moon is two days shy of full, or not quite all there, which Helen takes as a metaphor for Sawyer himself, a man with an IQ of 68 who suffers from frontal-lobe brain damage possibly sustained on those two occasions when his mother tried to kill him or in the car accident in which he lost his eye. (This is not information that Sawyer's court-appointed lawyer shared with the jury in his case, but the Supreme Court upheld his conviction and said that judges could consider only appeals based on constitutional error, a ruling that has severely curtailed repeated federal court challenges to state convictions.)

Helen is here for Sawyer—earlier in the week she had been with him at the last-chance state pardon-board hearing—and for Allyson Lamy, a friend whom Helen had asked to become Sawyer's spiritual adviser during a period in which she had been overloaded. Nine years later Lamy, now thirty-one, has grown extraordinarily close to Sawyer, who will be the first man she will watch die. Usually during these events Helen is inside rather than out, but the rest of the crowd seems familiar with their positions at the gate. There is the small corps of rather intense, mostly female, young lawyers from the Loyola Death Penalty Resource Center, a federally funded community defender program that has handled Sawyer's appeals; there are members of the Louisiana Coalition to Abolish the Death Penalty, the group Helen helped found; and then there are the Harveys, parents of a daughter, Faith, who had been brutally murdered, raped, and stabbed seventeen times—by a man Helen "advised" and whose death in the electric chair she and the Harveys witnessed together in 1986. Seven years later the Harveys rarely miss an execution, although Angola is a treacherous three-hour drive from where they live.

I have met the Harveys at their house in Covington, Louisiana, earlier in the week, and my heart has already broken for them. Vernon has shown me a photograph of Faith beneath the folded American flag and posthumous commendations from the US Army and from then-president Jimmy Carter on the wall, and he burst into tears. Faith was to have reported for duty on the morning after she was killed, and it was her recruitment officer who had let the Harveys know their daughter was missing. Elizabeth, a staunch activist on behalf of victims' rights and the reason Helen became involved in their cause, shows me a letter from an inmate who resents their presence at the gates and who promises to "get out of the joint" and "show you fuckers how it feels to face death," starting with "your whore daughter Lizabeth," the Harveys' remaining child. Now they sit in their white Buick, whose windshield is adorned with homemade signs—THE VICTIM'S RIGHTS ARE SILENT FOREVER—covered in Saran Wrap to protect them from wear and tear.

Vernon walks their Pekingese, Charlie Chan, and drinks coffee with the guards—old buddies by now—while Elizabeth sits in the car reading a paperback until the cameras come, and Elizabeth tells the newsman from Baton Rouge that "we are here because Frances Arwood [Sawyer's victim] could not be here." He asks her if she thinks Sawyer should be executed. She says, "He made that decision when he took that girl's life." A man who identifies himself as G.T. wishes to give his statement, but the Baton Rouge newsman has turned off his mike, so he gives it to me instead. "I come out here because I believe in what's being done tonight," he says, explaining that Sawyer could not be mentally disabled, because "if a human being can eat three meals a day, he's not insane. An insane person cannot eat by himself"—a more interesting interpretation than that of the American Association on Intellectual and Developmental Disabilities, which sets an IQ threshold of 70 to 75.

At 12:01 a.m., official injection time, everybody checks their watches. At 12:09 a.m., a guard receives word that the sodium pentothal has made Robert Sawyer's one real eye roll shut, the pancuronium bromide has stopped his lungs from working, and the potassium chloride has caused his heart to cease beating. "He's dead," says the guard. "Hello!" Vernon whoops. A neighbor of Frances Arwood's mother hugs her husband and pronounces justice done. "It's like a blessing. We never have to worry about that lunatic again."

The AP man, who has seen more of this than he'd probably like, comes out and says, "This may not sound so good, but the lethal injection was easier on the witness." I am reminded of a passage in Helen's book quoting Ronald Reagan as governor of California advocating lethal injection over the gas chamber because as "a farmer and horse raiser," he found it a whole lot easier "to eliminate an injured horse" by calling the vet than by shooting him. Allyson Lamy appears and cries and cries and tells us that Sawyer's last words to her were "I love you," mouthed through the glass, and that they had then mouthed together the words of the Twenty-third Psalm as he lay strapped down on the gurney preparing for the injections. Elizabeth Harvey is packing her signs in her trunk, and I read one of them and realize why I have the increasingly overpowering

feeling that I am no longer safe, despite the fact that "the lunatic" is out
of commission. VIOLENT CRIME DOESN'T JUST HAPPEN IN
THE STREETS, the sign says. No. It has just happened—witnessed
by a member of the governor's staff who had arrived with the Bible in
hand and the prosecutor who has requested to attend in the name of
"completion"—at the hands of the state, which cannot get it together to
even maintain the road on the godforsaken spot where we're standing,
much less to solve its current severe fiscal crisis.

I already knew that bad guys, guys like Robert Sawyer, can kill you,
that they can rape you, pour boiling water over you, and set you on fire
with lighter fluid, which is what Sawyer and his accomplice did when
they decided to make Frances Arwood into what amounted to a human
percolator. But, Helen asks, "how are you going to have a society where
it's OK for government to kill somebody? What kind of signal are you
giving to children? You're saying, 'Look, you got a really bad problem
with somebody, and you don't know what else to do; what you do is you
kill 'em. Legalize it if you can, but kill 'em.' I mean, how can you have a
society like that?"

The fact is that 76 percent of the people in this country say they
are in favor of a "society like that." Support for capital punishment has
increased by more than 30 percent since 1966. But Helen, like the late
Thurgood Marshall, contends that the numbers are high only because
the public is uninformed. "The American people are largely unaware
of the information critical to a judgement on the morality of the death
penalty," wrote Marshall in *Furman v. Georgia,* the decision that found
capital punishment unconstitutional in 1972. "If they were better informed they would consider it shocking, unjust, and unacceptable."

It is difficult to be informed when the ritual itself is cloaked in such
secrecy. The executors are always anonymous. During lethal injections
witnesses are not allowed to see the condemned man (only one woman
has been executed in the United States since 1976) actually strapped
onto the gurney, lest they lay eyes on the people performing the task.
Executions themselves are almost always carried out in the middle of
the night. In Louisiana the governor has transferred the task of signing

the death warrant from his office to that of the sentencing judge. If the people closest to the process try to get as far away from it as possible, the public cannot help but be unaware of what death by execution entails. It becomes a joke. Indeed, on the day Ted Bundy was executed, the morning deejays repeatedly and gleefully announced that today was "Fry-day in Florida." I suggest that it's difficult to have sympathy for Ted Bundy. Helen replies that sympathy is not the issue, it's the language, the laughter, that dehumanizes us as a society. And the laughter is made possible through the ignorance.

"If people were shown the machine, made to touch the wood and steel and to hear the sound of the head falling, then public imagination, suddenly awakened, will repudiate both the vocabulary and the penalty," Camus writes in *Reflections on the Guillotine*. "One must kill publicly or confess that one does not feel authorized to kill."

"One reason for the book," Helen tells me, "is to bring people into this country, the country of being incarcerated on death row. We live in these separate worlds. I believe prison embodies some of the deepest struggles we have in a society. It's as though walls are built around certain places, and that's one of my key concerns. How can we build bridges across to each other so people can actually meet each other? More and more, we live out of virtual knowledge instead of real knowledge, because so much is presented out of an electronic medium. And so much is lost."

Helen Prejean did not start out life with such a hard dose of real knowledge. She and her sister, Mary Ann, and her brother, Louis, grew up in a big old two-story house in Baton Rouge with a black maid and yardman and loving parents, Louis and Gusta Mae, to whom Helen dedicates her book, for "loving me into life." The family was close-knit and devout. In 1957 Helen joined the Sisters of St. Joseph of Medaille, but her own bridge to different worlds was not built until 1980, when, as a result of a reform movement in the Catholic Church that emphasized social justice, her religious community made a commitment to "stand on the side of the poor." It was a recasting of the faith of her childhood that Helen at first resisted—she had been taught that "what counted was a personal relationship with God, inner peace, kindness to others, and heaven when this life was done," she writes in her book. "I didn't want to struggle with politics and economics. We were nuns, after all, not social workers . . ."

It seems incomprehensible to me now that she could ever have felt that way, this woman who for three years lived in the bleakest and most dangerous housing project in New Orleans, who leads marches and gives speeches, who tells me now that "you can either be steamrolled by everything in society and just say, 'What can I do?' or you can say, 'I'm gonna go and pick up that little piece right over there. One person—a universe—is important. I'm gonna do something about this.'"

Her change of heart came at a conference where she heard a nun, a sociologist, explain, "The Gospels record that Jesus preached good news to the poor and that an essential part of that good news was that they were to be poor no longer . . . that they were not to meekly accept their poverty and suffering as God's will but struggle to obtain the necessities of life, which were rightfully theirs." To aid in that pursuit, she and three other sisters from her community moved into the St. Thomas projects. They were practically the only white people in a six-square-block community of 1,500 residents. The first night she concentrated on not getting shot, and then she began to construct the first of many bridges.

The women set up shop in a building they called Hope House. They instituted adult-education programs, recreation programs; they were simply *there*, which was extraordinary. They created the Bridge Program in which students from all over the country came to stay for a week. "It was magic, it was wonderful. These kids would say, 'Wow, I didn't know police beat people up. I didn't know you had to wait with a sick child eight hours at Charity Hospital. I didn't know this part of America existed.'" It was her first experience watching what happens when the barriers between two cultures are removed. "That's what fires people with passion."

Her own passion was fired again a year after arriving at St. Thomas when a friend from the Louisiana Coalition on Jails and Prisons, whose office was near Hope House, asked her if she would write to Elmo Patrick Sonnier, an inmate on death row at Angola. Sonnier and his brother, Eddie, had kidnapped a high school couple on a date, raped the girl, forced them to lie side by side facedown in a ditch, and shot them execution style, with three bullets each in the backs of their heads. Helen and Sonnier exchanged weekly letters, and though she says she cannot for a moment forget his crime, "after a while I began to think of him as a fellow human being." He wrote her letters thanking her for the most basic kindnesses, for simply acknowledging him, for giving his name to other people who wrote to him. "I've never had so many friends in all my life," he wrote. "I have you and the Good Lord to thank for that, Sister Helen."

She asked him if anyone ever came to see him, and he said no, so she went. "It was very casual the way it happened. The categories of women visitors were very spelled out—you were wife, ex-wife, girlfriend, relative, or spiritual adviser. So he said I'll put you down as spiritual adviser. I said fine. Then as his execution date got closer, I realized, God, this is an execution, I'm going to have to be with him there."

The execution is described in graphic detail in her book, and it resulted in her decision to become more actively involved in the defense of the inmates she advises, something she says she did for Pat Sonnier too late, and to fight against the death penalty full-time. At a meeting at Hope House, she looked around the room at all the people engaged in the project and thought of all they had accomplished. "Then I thought, no one in the entire state of Louisiana is working full-time to talk to the public about the death penalty. I will do this," she writes. "The decision unfolded like a rose."

She joined forces with Bill Quigley, a lawyer and staunch opponent of capital punishment, and together they formed what has become the Louisiana Coalition to Abolish the Death Penalty to wage a grassroots campaign to educate the public. Among their first tasks was gathering numbers, the kind of numbers that prompted the Supreme Court to declare the death penalty unconstitutional in *Furman*. That decision had not been based on the death penalty's being cruel and unusual but on the "capricious and arbitrary" way it was carried out.

More than twenty years later this is still the case. Ninety-nine percent of all death-row inmates are poor. When black inmates are on trial, the prosecutor attempts to eliminate blacks from juries because they are less likely than whites to impose the death penalty, and without a strong defense attorney (which is rarely the case), the prosecutor will succeed. Blacks who kill whites are far more likely to get the death penalty than whites who kill blacks. In short, for obvious reasons primarily having to do with resources, most people who are on death row are poor, black, or mentally impaired. Robert Sawyer's accomplice got life imprisonment because he accepted the plea bargain that was explained to him by his attorney. Sawyer did not understand the option—presented to him by his own court-appointed attorney as he was escorted into the courtroom—so he declined to take it.

Moreover, executions do not deter crimes. The murder rate in the United States is not higher in the states that do not have capital punishment than in those that do. In the fall of 1987, immediately after the state of Louisiana executed eight people in a particularly busy eight and a half weeks, the murder rate in New Orleans rose 16.39 percent. And finally, because of the drawn-out legal process, executions cost a lot of money. There are automatically two trials for capital crimes, a trial by jury and a separate sentencing trial. When the death penalty is sought, there are always appeals. However, when the DA does not go for the death penalty, there is often no trial at all. In Florida each execution costs approximately $3.18 million. To keep someone in prison for forty years costs $516,000.

These are the numbers Prejean has repeated in weekly speeches and articles since the coalition was formed in 1987. But it was not until she undertook to bridge the gap between the truth about the death penalty and the public's perception of it that she realized there was one gap she herself had not sought to close.

At the pardon-board hearing of her first fateful pen pal, Pat Sonnier, she was approached by Lloyd LeBlanc, the father of one of his victims. "Sister," he asked, "how can you present Sonnier's side like this without ever having come to visit with me and my wife. . . . How can you spend all your time worrying about Sonnier and not think that maybe we needed you too?" The rectifying of that initial mistake is one of the great strengths of the book and the foundation of two sets of remarkable friendships.

Lloyd LeBlanc's words were part of Prejean's continuing education. She had, she says, been naive, simplistic, possibly even afraid to consider how painfully complex the issue of capital punishment actually is. Just as she had earlier sensed a deep loneliness in Pat Sonnier, she now sensed it in Lloyd LeBlanc. Both the killers and the families of those killed are cast into worlds that no one else in society can ever completely comprehend. And to many, the victim's family is almost as horrifying as the killer. "People who it hasn't happened to, they shit you," Vernon Harvey told me. "They walk a long way around you. They don't want to believe it can happen, but it can—when you least expect it."

Into this void stepped Helen Prejean. Her friendship with Lloyd LeBlanc, a construction worker from St. Martinville, Louisiana, and a devout Roman Catholic, began the day they met. Despite her failure to contact him, they talked for an hour. "There is nothing finer than showing love and being friends with people," LeBlanc tells me. And so he allowed Helen Prejean to become his friend. He had already—remarkably—forgiven his son's killer. "When I saw my boy laid out on that slab, I said I forgive whoever did this, because they have no idea what they've done. That was my only son."

David LeBlanc was an altar boy, a senior in high school when he was killed with his girlfriend, Loretta Bourque, on their way home from a football game. Lloyd LeBlanc sits at his kitchen table while he tells me about it. His wife, Eula—who read nothing but cookbooks after David was killed because anything else was too hard to concentrate on—has made an amazing supper of fried catfish and crawfish, rolls, salad, and a baked bayou fish called gaspergou with a creole sauce. But now she has gone to the grocery store with her daughter, Vickie, who lives down the road with her husband, Curry, a sugarcane farmer, and their four children. She still cannot talk about the details of David's death. Lloyd tells me funny stories about David's dog, who ate the next-door neighbors'

Easter eggs every year. He shows me the class ring on his finger, the one David was wearing when he was killed and by which he was identified. He tells me how he finally managed last November, fifteen years after David's death, to get his son's Volkswagen out of storage and go through the belongings inside. He shows me a photograph of David and Loretta facedown in that ditch. It is something he has never, would never, show his wife.

Earlier Lloyd and Eula had shown me different pictures, pictures of David and Loretta smiling for the camera before going out to a dance, pictures of them arm in arm at Lloyd's brother's twenty-fifth wedding anniversary celebration. They showed me a picture of the Bourque family, an enormous group photo that has superimposed at the top a photograph of David and Loretta and a photograph of the child they called God's little angel, a child born with such severe brain damage that he was in a crib until he died at age twenty-one. "The good Lord must have known that if it had to happen," says Lloyd, "the Bourques had a large enough family that it would hurt them but they could stand to lose one, and that the LeBlancs could understand."

Lloyd hones his understanding every Friday from 4:00 to 5:00 a.m., his allotted hour of prayer in the "perpetual adoration" chapel down the road from his house. Sometimes Helen and her brother, Louis, make the two-hour drive to pray with him. At night he makes grandfather clocks in the shop beside his house. He may be the kindest man I've ever met. "That he could kneel by the body of his son and say what he said shows his deepest instincts," says Helen. "He has to keep reaching it, but it shows that here's a man who does not want to be obsessed by hate. And you can become possessed. Not only does your loved one get killed, but you get killed."

Vernon Harvey's anger has literally burst his blood vessels. Since Faith was murdered, he has had open-heart surgery and a stroke. During the trials of Faith's killer, he built Elizabeth a dog-grooming shop behind their house so she would have something to take her mind off what was happening. Vernon is a man who has given CPR to a poodle, but he came within an inch of running a car carrying Faith's killer off the road and into Lake Pontchartrain. He says the only thing that stopped him was the fact that he would have also killed the innocent federal marshals inside. He will never forgive Robert Lee Willie, Faith's killer—he says he wished Willie had fried longer, and when someone asked him how he felt after the execution, he said, "Do you want to dance?"

Elizabeth, a strong, intelligent woman, has turned her anger toward helping other people who have suffered the same loss. She goes with them to court, tells them what to expect through the endless ordeal. Most important, she educates them about their rights. Five days after Faith was murdered, she and Vernon were told by a neighbor, not by the police, that Faith's body had finally been found. They were not told until it was too late that they had the right to see the body and the autopsy report. "In dealing with the DA and the police," Elizabeth says, "you could probably get more information when you get your car stolen than if your child was killed, because then you're the victim. But when someone's killed, they figure the one killed is the victim, not you, and you're pushed to the sidelines. You and your needs don't count, and you can call them until you're blue in the face, and they won't call you back."

Elizabeth works hard to change that. She has met with the governor to encourage programs to educate law-enforcement officials about the rights of victims' families. She lobbies Congress to protest budget cuts for victims' assistance. She also encouraged Helen to get involved.

Helen had contacted the Harveys as soon as she contacted Robert Willie. Their friendship includes a lot of sparring with Vernon, but it is a real one. When Vernon tells me he knows they've "changed Sister Helen a lot," she agrees. "I tell him all the time how much they educated me on victims' rights." Her education began when Vernon told her it was time for her to come with them to a Parents of Murdered Children meeting, with the words "You've been helping all these scum balls. You ought to come find out what the victims go through." She went and heard their stories and recalled the words of St. Augustine. "Late have I loved thee." But not too late. At the next coalition board meeting, she proposed they inaugurate an assistance program for victims' families in New Orleans. They did, enabling Helen to come full circle, reaching out to the two sets of people most often ignored in the actual process of capital punishment.

The killer and his victims' families are ignored, Helen contends, because the death penalty has ceased to be about the criminal and the victim, crime and punishment. It is about politics. "People are good," says Helen. "I've encountered very few really bad people. People don't want to kill people. They are manipulated by politicians who tell them it is the only answer. Politicians do not want to deal with the real crime problem, which is complex, costly—you gotta do some thinking and planning and go in-depth. It's so much easier just to whip out that death penalty." She points out that victims' families did not fuel the call for the death penalty after the court's 1972 decision; that came in large part from the southern states, which have a historical hang-up about the "feds" telling them what to do. As in most things, they wanted to be able to decide their own fate, and now 85 percent of all executions happen in four southern states.

While Helen has faith in people, she has no faith in politicians, hence her belief that only by bypassing them, taking her case directly to the public, can the death penalty ever be eliminated. "Politicians want more than anything to be governor or president, and they will be willing to do anything to attain that." As an example, she offers Bill Clinton's dramatic return to Arkansas in the midst of a tough New Hampshire primary to personally oversee the execution of Rickey Ray Rector. "He did not have to do that," she says. But it worked. He managed to grab some headlines other than those about Gennifer Flowers and his problem with the draft and look like a tough guy in the bargain. No matter that Rickey Ray Rector was a man missing almost a third of his brain (he shot himself in the head immediately after he shot a police officer), he barked like a dog, and he had so little understanding of what was happening to him that he saved his pecan pie at his last meal because he always saved his dessert for later.

Prejean is convinced that with states enacting tougher laws to keep murderers behind bars (thirty states including Louisiana now have laws guaranteeing that a person convicted of first-degree murder must serve a life sentence without possibility of parole), more people will change their minds about capital punishment. Already polls show that support for the death penalty drops to about 50 percent when people are offered the alternative of mandatory twenty-five years' imprisonment without possibility of parole coupled with restitution to the victim's family from the labor of offenders.

Helen knows that no amount of restitution can ever bring a child back, but she prays that other parents can find the peace that Lloyd LeBlanc has found. LeBlanc still believes in the death penalty because "it's the proper punishment for the crime. . . . The law's the law. I got to live by the law, but some people don't have any respect for it." However, he also tells me that when he saw Pat Sonnier electrocuted, "I said that night, 'That is not a way to treat a human being.'"

Above all, he says, peace has to come from someplace else. "Capital punishment doesn't help the victim's family at all. It doesn't have anything to do with that. Mr. Phelps said to me before the execution, 'After this is over, you'll feel a lot better.' Like they were giving me a shot, you know?" He shakes his head. "Can you imagine?"

9

Woman of the World

(1997)

It was a gorgeous July Sunday morning outside St. Petersburg, and Madeleine Albright, the United States Secretary of State, had just completed a tour of the Catherine Palace, a baroque pile built by Elizabeth I for her mother, complete with a room paneled entirely in amber. She had been given a porcelain egg by the palace's curator ("Be sure and tell him I collect eggs," she said to the translator), and been blessed in the palace chapel by a Russian Orthodox priest, who told her in Russian, "This is where we blessed members of the imperial family. We wished them peace [before they went off to battle], and you are on a mission of peace, so I wish to bless you too."

The night before, she had done a little battle herself during a grueling dinner with the Russian foreign minister, Yevgeny Primakov, who was less than thrilled about the NATO decision two days earlier to welcome former Soviet satellites Poland, Hungary, and Albright's native Czech Republic as members, and who was also extremely irritated by the recent violent routing of Serb war criminals. ("Do you think the war criminals should be brought to justice?" she asked him. When he said yes, she challenged him to come up with a better way. He could not, effectively ending that particular part of the conversation.) In the early morning hours afterward she had written in longhand the short but emotional statement she would make later in the day in Prague. It would be her

first visit in her new position, and her first since learning from a reporter
that her grandparents had been killed in the Holocaust, that her heritage
was in fact Jewish.

But now she was going to take a break from all that and indulge in
what she tries to make time for on every foreign trip: shopping. In the
stalls not far from the palace she bought two sets of watercolors and,
after much deliberation but not enough bargaining, a traditional Russian
sable hat for $100 (which she had to borrow from an aide). She also got
to revel a bit in her new celebrity status. "Is that Madeleine Albright?"
asked a man from Minneapolis, who also informed me she had paid too
much for her hat ("I got one for $65 last year"). Earlier that morning, a
crowd of American tourists jammed the entrance to her hotel to catch
a glimpse of her leaving. The day before, in Slovenia, the locals had
stopped and clapped as she passed. Now in the market, a local artist who
had been madly sketching her portrait timidly asked for a five-minute
"sitting" so he could finish. As she stood patiently a crowd gathered,
and the artist looked up, embarrassed: "My hands are shaking standing
before such a big person."

Despite her diminutive stature, Madeleine Albright is certainly the biggest and brightest personage in this administration. No secretary of state
since Henry Kissinger has so captured the public's imagination or gen-
erated as many headlines. It helps, of course, that she is the first woman
to serve in the post, and that her predecessor was compared—in print
and often—to a corpse. And it helps that she is serving in a cabinet so
far distinguished by reticence, mediocrity, or scandal. She is an assertive
advocate of American dominance in world affairs in an administration
in which the boldest rallying cry so far has been to balance the budget
by the year 2000 and whose biggest first-term foreign-policy accom-
plishment was a trade treaty, NAFTA. She speaks for a president who is
congenitally afraid of offending anybody, but she is not so afflicted. She
says what she thinks in perfect sound bites. When the Chinese deployed
4,000 troops to Hong Kong on the very day of the handover, she went

on every Sunday-morning news show and said, "Speaking personally, it's not a good beginning." A lot of what she says is personal. There is no waiting for responses to be cleared and vetted by battalions of State Department analysts and White House spinmeisters. When she was still a UN ambassador, she gave Haiti's military dictator two options for clearing out: "You can depart voluntarily and soon or involuntarily and soon." (A cartoon depicting her uttering the ultimatum in Western garb and holding six-guns hangs on her office wall, and it's true that she is very fond of her cowboy hat and has no problem using firepower.) When the Cubans shot down two American civilian planes over disputed airspace, she famously said, "This is not cojones, this is cowardice." The hyperpolite and reserved diplomatic community was appalled—the Venezuelan representative said he wouldn't have used the word, "not even on my farm"—but the president, delighted to have a spokesman who talks tougher than he, called it "probably the most effective one-liner in the whole administration's foreign policy." Let's hope not, but it was certainly effective domestically. Cuban Americans, a voting bloc the president has assiduously courted, printed Albright's statement on bumper stickers. When she made a speech in Miami, 60,000 people came to hear her in the Orange Bowl. More important, Jesse Helms, the powerful Republican chairman of the Senate Foreign Relations Committee, was smitten.

When she asked Colin Powell, "What's the point of having this superb military you're always talking about if we can't use it?" he wrote that she almost gave him an aneurysm. "American GI's were not toy soldiers to be moved around on some sort of global game board," he huffed in his book. After the first NATO air strikes she had advocated drove the Serbs to the bargaining table, she told Elaine Sciolino of *The New York Times* that she "felt some vindication. It wasn't easy being a civilian woman having a disagreement with the hero of the Western world." She paused. "But maybe he'd want to rewrite that page now."

A memo she wrote after her exchange with Powell, criticizing American policy and calling for military force, helped lay the groundwork for the Dayton accords. She didn't get credit at the time, but she took it wistfully in stride, telling a reporter that it didn't matter, that one day "the meek shall inherit the earth." She's not meek, but she did inherit the earth, or at least the patch of it in Washington's Foggy Bottom that she desperately wanted. She has already won the first major internal policy battle with Secretary of Defense William Cohen. She said, "Peace with justice in Bosnia is crucial to defining a new Europe." He said it was more important to keep the promise to pull American troops out by mid-1998. In the end, Clinton sided with Albright, already sending signals that the troops may not be home.

Her belief in American activism is clearly a product of her own experiences as a two-time refugee, first from Nazism and then from Communism. Two-year-old Marie Jana Korbel fled with her family to England just days after the German army marched into Prague in 1939 and later attended a Swiss boarding school where she acquired the name Madeleine. Three years after her family returned to Czechoslovakia, they were forced to flee again as Stalin's forces moved in. Her father, Josef, who had been a high-ranking diplomat, got out at the last minute and brought his family to New York, where he worked briefly at the UN, and finally settled at the University of Denver, where he headed the graduate school of international studies. He never told his children, who were raised as Catholics, that their grandparents were Jews who had been killed in the Holocaust. All Albright knew was that they had died during the war and that her parents had twice protected her from certain death under totalitarian regimes, and that was enough.

Given her history and her own grateful feelings toward the country that granted her family asylum, it's no surprise that she refers to America as "the really, truly indispensable nation." The question, she says, is not "Is this in our interest?" but "Can we do good in the world?"—a complete reversal of the Powell doctrine.

On the fiftieth anniversary of the Marshall Plan in June she stood in the same spot at Harvard where George Marshall laid out his activist agenda for American responsibility in Europe. "Because of the Truman/Marshall generation, I have been privileged to live my life in freedom," she said. "Millions have still never had that opportunity. . . . It is not enough for us to say that Communism has failed. We too must heed the lessons of the past, accept responsibility, and lead." In a weakened and waffling post–Cold War America, she is not afraid to invoke America's superpower status. "There are people with all kinds of hang-ups from Vietnam about bringing power to bear," says retired diplomat Herbert Okun, who has known Albright for years. "She doesn't have those hang-ups." Albright herself is the first to say that unlike most of the members of her generation, her mindset is not Vietnam but Munich, where the West sold out Czechoslovakia for the first time, giving it to Hitler in 1938.

At the July NATO conference in Madrid, during a brief ceremony to celebrate the vote to include the three new countries, something she had fought hard for, Secretary Cohen introduced her as "someone whose life embodies what this week is all about." Afterward, the president thanked her "for bringing her personal life story and her vision into her work every day." When it was over, the speakers blared Louis Armstrong's "What a Wonderful World."

It's the schmaltzy touch the White House loves, but Albright's is a wonderful world these days. In Prague, just before her good friend Václav Havel presented her with the Czech Republic's Order of the White Lion, she said, "Of all the unbelievable things that have happened in the last ten years, the fact that I'm standing here, Czech-born, as secretary of state is a great privilege." Twenty-four hours later she stood on the sidelines of a softball game with Jesse Helms and looked equally thrilled to be there. Dressed in black jeans, black-and-silver sneakers, and a T-shirt adorned with the name of the State Department team, "the All-Brights," she stood with her arm around Helms, telling me, "He's my best friend." The senator, whose team is called the "Helms Hitbillies," wore a T-shirt she gave him when she went to his native North Carolina to make a speech, emblazoned with the message SOMEONE AT THE STATE DEPARTMENT LOVES ME. "Sometimes the devil gets in you, you know," the senator told me. "So when she gave it to me, I said, 'If you mean it, give me one'"—meaning a kiss. She did, and the lovefest continues. "I don't always agree with her," Helms says, "but she is not p.c. She is just honest; that goes a long way with me."

Despite the fact that her team is losing, the secretary is beaming, telling Helms all about her trip—which he does not approve of; he is against NATO expansion. "You must go to Prague," she tells him. "I'd like to," he says. Great, she responds; "We'll go together."

For Albright, it was a perfect thirty-six-hour period. In Prague, she ended her European trip triumphantly, despite the poignancy of her personal mission there. She welcomed the country of her birth into NATO, able, as the representative of the most powerful nation in the Free World, to undo an injustice, as she said over and over again. In Washington, she engaged in the old-fashioned politicking she thrives on, turning on her charm, paving the way for the upcoming Senate battle over NATO enlargement. She is equally in her element in both settings. "She loves it," says her sister, Kathy Silva, with whom she had dinner in Georgetown after the softball game. "You can tell by how she looks that she loves this job. She is at the top of her career, and she glows."

Albright's rise, says her close friend Senator Barbara Mikulski, has been "a 20-year overnight-success story." At Wellesley, which she attended on a scholarship, she decided she wanted to be a journalist, and spent one summer at *The Denver Post*, where she met Joseph Medill Patterson Albright. In 1959, three days after her college graduation, they married. While he was stationed at an army base near Rolla, Missouri, she worked briefly for the local paper there, but her fledgling career came to an abrupt end when the newlyweds moved to Chicago, where Joe went to work for the *Chicago Tribune*, which had been purchased by his great-great-grandfather before the Civil War. The paper's managing editor took them out to dinner and explained that it wouldn't be proper for them to work at the same paper, nor would it do for the young heir's wife to work at a competing paper. She went to work for *Encyclopaedia Britannica* instead. "The weird part," she says

now, "is that it was a blow, yet I didn't fight it. But it was 1960, and I'd
been married half a year."

The following year, her twins, Anne and Alice, were born six weeks
premature and spent almost two months in an incubator. Helpless, she
enrolled in an eight-week, eight-hour-a-day crash course in Russian to
take her mind off things. (When I say to her sister that I might have
delved into something a bit less grueling, like needlepoint, she replies,
"Oh, she did that, too.") When the twins came home, she had to feed
them three times a night. "Then I kind of sat there during the day, feeding them, watching soap operas, and I thought, I didn't go to college
to do this." The Russian course reminded her "that I really did like to
study"—so she enrolled in graduate school at Columbia.

By this time, the family was living on Long Island, where Joe was
being groomed to take over yet another family newspaper, *Newsday*.
Albright says she thought becoming a professor would be a good way to
keep herself busy while juggling the responsibilities of motherhood and
being "the wife of this person who was supposed to be the publisher."
During this period she was often described as a socialite because "I was
married to a man with four names," but it didn't last long. Joe's aunt Alicia Patterson sold *Newsday*, and Joe moved the family to Washington,
where he'd gotten a job as a reporter for Cox newspapers.

Albright had already earned her master's and was beginning work
on her doctoral dissertation on the role of the press in the 1968 reform
movement in Czechoslovakia. "It was fascinating and I loved it, but
Washington is not a very academic town," she says. I would spend my
time going to the Library of Congress and then I needed some people
activity." She got it when she was asked to join the board of her daughters' school, and though she says, "I had never raised a nickel in my life,"
she was put in charge of annual giving. Her fundraising cochairman was
another parent, who worked in the office of Senator Edmund Muskie.
He was impressed by her skills and asked her to cochair a Muskie fundraiser. "That's how the whole thing started," she says. When she got
her PhD, she took a job as Muskie's chief legislative assistant. He was
a mentor and her entrée into politics—in her State Department office

she hung his portrait where she can see it every time she looks up from her desk.

Albright has often been accused of collecting connections, of courting people who could advance her career, of being, well, ambitious. "It's funny that a word like *ambition* is used as a bad word, especially for women, right?" she asks me. "I liked foreign policy, and I love politics. I am determined and I like to work and I like people." Besides, she says, much of what she has achieved has not been the result of a grand plan but of "one thing kind of leading to another." Indeed, after two years with Muskie, she was offered a job on the staff of the National Security Council in the Carter White House—Zbigniew Brzezinski, the new Council chief, had been Albright's professor at Columbia.

After Carter's loss in 1980, she became a fellow at two Washington think tanks and taught international affairs at Georgetown, where she was voted best professor four years in a row. Even as her career took off, she managed to spend lots of time with her girls. (She and her husband had had a third child in 1967.) Though she admits she hates to cook, she says, "We baked on weekends in the country." She says her children agree that she did an admirable job of handling it all. It was other women who were hardest on her. "'How do you feel,' they would ask, 'when we're all in the carpool line and you're not?'" One suspects she felt just fine. "Madeleine," her sister, Kathy, says, "was never a housewife in mentality."

In 1982, after her husband left her abruptly for another woman, she kept their country house in Virginia, the spacious town house in Georgetown, and a hefty stock portfolio, and created another life for herself, as hostess of a sort of foreign-policy salon where the conversation was good and the food bad. "You did not go to Madeleine's for the food," says a frequent guest. "You went for the discussion."

If one step followed another, she took an important one in 1988, when she became foreign-policy adviser for Michael Dukakis. Then-governor Bill Clinton came to Boston to help prepare Dukakis for the debates, met Albright, and kept in touch. He asked her to recommend him for membership in the Council on Foreign Relations, and she did. When he won the presidency and promised to create a cabinet "that reflected America," she was the natural choice for ambassador to the United Nations.

It was at the UN that she first displayed her flair for talking in tough TV sound bites (she referred to CNN as the sixteenth member of the Security Council) and her considerable acumen in the realm of domestic politics. At the beginning of her tenure she called Boutros Boutros-Ghali someone she could "really admire." But after the ill-fated UN "peacekeeping mission" in Somalia, Boutros-Ghali became the symbol, especially to the Right, of an evil, meddling UN that Americans shouldn't be funding, and Albright led the charge to have him ousted. She is still criticized by many diplomats for her actions, but it could not have escaped her that the one line in Bob Dole's stock campaign speech that always guaranteed him applause was "When I'm president, America's foreign policy won't be conducted by Boutros Boutros-Ghali." "Decisions were made," says one British diplomat at the UN, "less by how they affected America's standing in the world, and more about how they played in Washington. It was never 'Let's stand up to Washington; this is an important issue.' It was 'How will Helms react? What will Congress do?'"

If that was the case, it certainly appealed to her boss, who put her on the shortlist for secretary of state when he won his second term and Warren Christopher made it clear he no longer wanted the job. Albright carefully avoided appearing to campaign on her own behalf, leaving the work to friends like Mikulski, who lobbied the White House tirelessly. She already had a powerful supporter in Hillary Clinton, whom she had accompanied to Prague in 1996, a trip that became known as the "Audition." It went well. News accounts of the trip included the tidbit that the First Lady, Albright, and President Havel burst into a rousing rendition of "Good King Wenceslas" as they drove together into Wenceslas Square, where the protest that sparked Czechoslovakia's "Velvet Revolution" had been staged.

Al Gore had favored Richard Holbrooke, and many agreed that Holbrooke was the more creative candidate. Then Gore was reminded that he would need the women's vote for his own race in 2000. In any case Holbrooke and Albright each promised that whoever didn't get it would recommend the other to the president. When Albright got word that she had won, she immediately commissioned an eagle brooch, which she wore at her swearing in.

Brooches are among her many trademarks. When she was still at the UN, the Iraqi news agency called her a snake, so she wore a brooch in the form of a serpent to her meeting with the Iraqi foreign minister. On her first visit to Russia as secretary of state, she wore the eagle pin topped with another one of Uncle Sam's hat in red, white, and blue. On her most recent trip, she favored a gold-and-diamond sunburst. She loves hats—especially the cowboy hat that aides tote on many of her trips—and gold jewelry. Around her neck, she often wears a thick gold choker; on her right wrist she wears two or three gold bangles, and on her left a half dozen gold link bracelets she is never without, not even when she threw the first pitch of the season for the Baltimore Orioles. She always wears heels and stylish clothes (a short-sleeved, red tweed Rena Lange suit she wore in Madrid was in the window of Prague's chicest boutique). Even when relaxing on her plane she wears silk trousers and matching blouses, and she paid attention when someone said her makeup was too heavy.

She says, "Until now, I always felt that there were many disadvantages to being a woman." For example, in meetings men always felt they could interrupt her, but she was scared to interrupt, so by the time it was her turn to speak (last), a man would have already articulated what she had wanted to say. These days, however, "I don't have to interrupt. When I raise my hand or a placard or my little finger, people listen." Being a woman now has advantages. "People are intrigued by the fact I'm a woman, and it helps get the message across. And I think people feel I'm more approachable."

Albright herself makes the most of her sex. When she met the State Department staff for the first time, she said, "You may notice I don't exactly look like Secretary Christopher," and makeup is a constant theme. When a *Time* reporter asked if her predecessor had given her any tips on how to "save time with her personal routine," she said, "He can't help me; I wear makeup." In a speech after she accepted an award from the Women's Legal Defense Fund, she said, "Now that I've had the job for about five months, I have decided that being a woman has several important advantages. One is makeup. If a 60-year-old male secretary of state has had a bad day, he has two choices—to look like a tired old man or to look like a tired old man with makeup." In St. Petersburg, when I told her how fresh she looked after what I knew had been a long night, she said it again: "Makeup." Her weight has been a constant problem. A friend reports how happy she was to have lost weight before seeing her ex-husband at their daughter's wedding last year. And she has lost more than twenty pounds since she was nominated for her job.

She loves to shop. On the agenda of a trip to Singapore is a hunt for black pearls. She has a good partner in her chief of staff, Elaine Shocas. In St. Petersburg, Shocas supplied the mirror and got the bargain—hers, a far more stylish hat, cost only $75.

Albright's daughter Anne says her mother "taught us that there was nothing wrong with being feminine." And she is certainly not above using her feminine wiles to court needed allies like Helms. At the UN one Valentine's Day she gave cards and candy to the other fourteen—male—members of the Security Council, and during tense negotiations on Haiti with the Chinese representative, she told him it was Sadie Hawkins Day, "the day men are supposed to do something nice for women." Protocol expert Letitia Baldrige is appalled by the fact that foreign leaders often greet her with a kiss. "Someone of her rank and dignity should be greeted with a handshake—a double-handed handshake if you're a good friend." But at sixty Albright is finally having fun.

Her father was a strict disciplinarian who drove her to her senior prom while her date followed in his own car. "It took a long time, but when he got mad he would send you to your room and then he wouldn't speak to you for two or three days," Kathy Silva says. "It was a very European upbringing." Albright herself tells me, "My parents were obviously very serious people, very oriented toward doing the right thing. They were passionate about Czechoslovakia and dedicated to doing what they could to improve things. They instilled that in me." They also put a high value on education. Albright attended, on scholarship, an intense private school in Denver, where there were only sixteen girls in her class. She was grateful that they wore uniforms—it meant one less thing to worry about in her quest to be like everybody else. When she arrived in her new country at age eleven, she spoke English with a British accent. "I spent a lot of time worrying, trying to make sure that I would fit in. I wanted very much to be an American. That was the big, defining thing of my life." America was viewed as the family's savior, which is why, she says now, "I have a hard time believing America is wrong."

She has an even harder time believing that her father was wrong. Her Jewish roots were discovered by a *Washington Post* reporter using documents that have only recently been made available in the Czech Republic. When the story broke, Albright says, it was a complete surprise, but even among those who believed her, there was the occasional insinuation that her parents were somehow dishonest, if not evil, in their choice to renounce their religion and raise their children as Catholics (the religious majority in Czechoslovakia), and their decision not to disclose to their children that their grandparents (whom only Madeleine had known, and only until she was two) had perished in the Holocaust. "I despise what was being said about our parents," says Silva. "They were incredible. What they did kept us alive. I cannot tell you how awful it was." It was particularly awful for Albright, who worshipped her father and is, says her sister, his carbon copy. In Albright's comments outside Prague's Jewish Town Hall, after she had been to see her grandparents' names on the wall of the synagogue where Czechoslovakia's Jewish Holocaust victims' names are inscribed, her most emotional moments came when she spoke about her parents. "They clearly confronted the most excruciating decision a human being can face when they left members of their family behind even as they saved me from certain death," she said in a voice choked with emotion. "I will always love and honor my parents and will always respect their decision, for that most painful of choices gave me life a second time."

Her brother, John, and sister, Kathy, had gone to Prague as the story broke last winter to look at the same documents the *Washington Post* reporter had seen and to visit the synagogue. It was their report back to Albright that enabled her to write her speech prior to her arrival in Prague—though she spoke of "the thousands of names carved on the wall," and in fact they are painted, the last names in red, the first names in black. "When we went to the wall and saw those names it was just undoing," Silva says. "I said, 'John, do you realize if they had not done what they did, their names and Madeleine's would be up here and we wouldn't be looking at it?'" Albright realized it as well. On the plane after we left Prague she tells me that she had always worked hard because "I somehow felt that I had been saved—I thought only from the Russians—in order to repay that debt, to repay the fact that I was a free person. I guess it's truer than ever now." She closed her remarks in front of the Town Hall by saying, "To the many values and many facets that make up who I am, I now add the knowledge that my grandparents and members of my family perished in the worst catastrophe in human history. So I leave here tonight with the certainty that this new part of my identity adds something stronger, sadder, and richer to my life."

Josef Korbel was certainly not the first immigrant to a new country to erase his painful—and dangerous—past and make a new start. In his books, he wrote that the family had been in danger from Hitler only because he was a known democrat—which was certainly true—and when his wife wrote an account of the family's experiences for other family members, she too made no mention of their Jewish background. This process has been called "historical amnesia." For Albright it was more a willed lack of curiosity. She would never have questioned anything her beloved parents told her, even after they were dead, even as she began hearing rumors of her background more than a year ago.

Albright was baptized a Catholic and, after her marriage, became an Episcopalian, which she remains. But, says James Rubin, her press secretary and close aide at the UN as well as at the State Department, "The religion she grew up with was the concept of democracy for Czechoslovakia, her parents' passion for Czechoslovakia. That was the construct of her life." She is a woman who fiercely protects her constructs. Just as she never looked beyond anything her father told her until she was forced to, she never questioned her twenty-three-year marriage. It was simply perfect until the moment it ceased to be, when her husband sat across from her in a chair while a snowstorm raged outside and told her he was in love with someone else, someone younger. That was it, over and out.

Not only were the two most basic truths of her life shattered in swift and brutal ways, but the whole world knows about it. After we left Prague, I tried to ask Albright if she resented having to respond to such private information on such a public stage, if she were nervous or angry or just plain irritated about having to face the press after seeing her grandparents' names for the first time, about having to defend her parents yet again. But she cut me off. "Julia, I made that statement because I'm not going to talk about that anymore." A question about whether or not she has been involved with anyone since her marriage broke up was met with much the same response. "I think it's pretty hard . . ." Pause. "I'm not going to talk about that part. A little mystery doesn't hurt."

The people with whom she does relax include two longtime aides—Rubin and Shocas, who have both worked with her for four years. They are able to be straight with her, to tell her when something's not working, when a speech is too weak, when a false note is sounded. As a result, Albright has the most consistent message in the cabinet. (She's also probably the only cabinet member who quotes T. S. Eliot—in a speech to the Czech people she used a passage from *Four Quartets*: "We shall not cease from exploration/And the end of all our exploring/Will be to arrive where we started/And know the place for the first time.")

Not only does their closeness make an effective working relationship, it makes a demanding life less difficult for all three. "She manages to make the people who work for her feel like a family in which she is both the mother and the father," Rubin says. "And she manages to do it in a way that inspires incredible loyalty and is also fun. There are very few people who have reached that level in public life who can create that kind of support system." It also makes the fact that "we work so hard and ruin our personal lives" bearable, he laughs. "We call ourselves—Elaine and Madeleine and me—the nuclear family."

She sees her own family as much as she can. The weekend after she returned from Prague, she went to Aspen to join twins Alice and Anne and her grandchildren. She sees Anne, who lives in Washington, frequently, and she is close to her sister, Kathy, a former assistant principal in the Los Angeles public school system who now works in the Department of Education. "She and I do not talk shop at all. We do movies, we do bills, we do closets, we go out to her farm," Silva says. "We go for sushi. We just veg out together. Sometimes I'll ask her something about work, and she'll roll her eyes and say 'Please,' because basically she needs that break."

But she doesn't seem to want too many. "I love all the subjects that are part of my day. I loved my last trip, and I'm looking forward to my next one," she tells me. "I have a lot of energy, and I like to work." The last phrase is one she utters four times in a single half-hour conversation. The word her staff uses most to describe her is *normal*, but it's not hard to see why a student in the audience at her speech at the University of Vilnius in Lithuania told me that "she seems very strict." Indeed, that very morning my attempt to engage her in some chitchat while on our way to the Catherine Palace ("Wasn't our tour of the Hermitage amazing? How many times have you been to St. Petersburg?") was met with "Well, are we going to get down to business?" The following day in Prague, during a press conference with Havel, she lost patience with the Czech translator, correcting him with a curt "not exactly" after one passage, which she then translated herself. At one point, the man, who was clearly terrified, literally froze. Albright was relentless. "Translate my answer." It is not the kind of mistake she would suffer well. "I pride myself on being able to explain things very clearly," she says. She attributes her own rise to the fact that, early on, from her first "job" as a fundraiser at the Beauvoir School, "I got the reputation of getting the job done. I have always believed—and I say this to my daughters, and I said it to my students—whatever the job you are asked to do at whatever level, do a good job because your reputation is your résumé."

She says she never dreamed her own résumé would include the title Secretary of State. On the plane home from Prague, our last stop, she comes back for the obligatory chat with the traveling press and tells a story about her first visit to Prague after the "Velvet Revolution." She had met Havel for the first time and she had sat with his advisers in a café drawing diagrams on pieces of scrap paper, trying to design the president's office. "I had worked in the White House, and they asked me what a president's office looked like—they had no idea." Later that evening, she says, "I had the closest thing I've ever had to an out-of-body experience. I was walking across the Charles Bridge and the snow was fresh and there was a full moon and I had just had this afternoon meeting with Havel. And there was this instant when I thought, I've spent my whole life preparing, I've learned all these things so I could help, so I could advise the Czech president. It was really weird."

As it happens, she was preparing for a bigger role than that. When I ask her later about her experience on the bridge, she laughs. "It didn't last long. I don't want people to think I'm Shirley MacLaine."

10

Sister Act

(2004)

t is Mother's Day, and Barbara and Jenna Bush, the president's twin daughters, are, fittingly, spending the evening in Manhattan with their mother. The First Lady's in town for official business the next day, and her daughters have some too, sort of: a photo shoot, their first ever, for which they're trying on clothes in a room at the Central Park South hotel where all three are staying. Barbara, who like her sister will graduate from college in two weeks, is a bit preoccupied—she has a long night ahead finishing a paper on Czech novelist Milan Kundera, and another to write the next day for the same English seminar at Yale. Still, she manages to find a shimmery fitted Zac Posen to step into, while Jenna goes straight for a pair of Joe's jeans and a white jacket that accentuates her tan. The girls, who call each other "Sister," are having fun rifling through the racks, approving or nixing each other's choices, but then they get to a flotilla of enormous debutante-style ball gowns. This is clearly not their preferred look—both arrived in skinny jeans and little tops; Barbara, the avowed clotheshorse of the two, says she "lives" in her jade-green, pointed toe Marni flats and is far more drawn to the elegant chiffon evening looks of Narciso Rodriguez and Carolina Herrera. But they are unfailingly polite and apparently good sports, so they agree to give the gowns a go. When their mother sticks her head in to say she's about to order dinner from room service, she takes in Jenna's poufy cream tulle: "That looks like what I wore to my seventh-grade dance." Jenna looks at her sister, whose tight-bodiced white satin number boasts a skirt better suited to a Velázquez infanta. "Mom," she asks, "do we look like cupcakes?" "Yes," says the First Lady, "you do."

They are laughing, but the image of privileged debutante—not to mention cupcake—is one that the sisters, with the help of their mother, have long tried to avoid. Unlike their first cousin Lauren Bush, a model who was presented in Paris at the Crillon Haute Couture Ball (in miles of Dior tulle) and who is represented by the Elite agency's celebrity division, they have shunned the spotlight and all the finery that it requires— Barbara doesn't own a long dress, and Jenna says her school uniform consisted of flip-flops, jeans, and C&C T-shirts. ("I wear Lela Rose," she says, speaking of the Texas-born designer both girls wore to their father's inauguration. "And I dress up when I'm in New York, but in Austin there's really no need.") College freshmen when their father was elected, they were granted privacy by the mainstream press largely because their parents worked hard to keep them from becoming fair game, not once using them in political ads or trotting them out on the campaign trail. When Jenna accompanied her mother on an official trip to Europe in 2002, the Secret Service shielded her from view as she emerged from Air Force One by holding up long garment bags on each side of her. And when Barbara joined her parents a year later on a five-country tour of Africa it went largely unreported.

Before they embark on their own careers, however, Barbara and Jenna are about to make a different kind of debut by joining their father's campaign. "It's not like he called me up and asked me," Jenna says. "They've never wanted to throw us into that world, and I think our decision probably shocked them. But I love my dad, and I think I'd regret it if I didn't do this." The president himself is naturally delighted. "The thing I'm most excited about is that I get to spend the last campaign of my life with two girls I love," he tells me in a June interview. "It's an experience we'll be able to talk about for years to come." Despite their enthusiasm, the girls also had to consider that any other job they might take would almost certainly be viewed through the prism of politics. Barbara, who majored in humanities at Yale, plans to sign up for a program in which she'd be working in Eastern Europe and Africa with children afflicted with AIDS; Jenna, who got an English degree from the University of Texas, plans to teach at a charter school. But neither wanted her choice to become campaign fodder. "We thought it would be better," Barbara says, with typical reticence, "to wait until after November."

So it is that in these months before the election, the country will get their first real glimpse of the First Daughters. Until now, they've been best known for their inevitable but sparse tabloid appearances and the much-mentioned reports of their 2001 run-in with the law for underage drinking. Into this void has stepped everyone from late-night talk-show hosts to journalists, all of whom have felt free—sometimes shockingly so—to define the twins themselves. The First Lady's unofficial biographer, Ann Gerhart, went so far as to condemn them for a long list of imagined offenses ranging from not showing "their faces at the White House" often enough to lacking "empathy toward the struggles and responsibilities facing their mother and father" (they are, she wrote, all "noblesse" and no "oblige"). This is tough, presumptuous stuff. "I'm sure it's annoying sometimes," says Jenna's close friend and fellow U.T. grad Mia Baxter. "But she just doesn't let it get to her. I don't think I could handle it as well, but she stays totally herself." In their new roles—which will include everything from pitching in at the Arlington headquarters of the Bush campaign to making occasional appearances on the trail— they will finally have the chance to define themselves. Many political observers think their presence may also help redefine their father, that the bright and unjaded First Daughters will serve to humanize and soften the image of a controversial wartime president. If it works, it won't be the first time. In 1969 so staunch an enemy of Richard Nixon as Norman Mailer was forced to admit that "a man who could produce daughters like that could not be all bad" after observing Tricia and Julie Nixon at the Republican convention. The elaborate White House weddings of Luci Baines Johnson and Tricia Nixon made the covers of *Time* and *Newsweek*, glowing coverage that stood in stark contrast to the batterings their fathers routinely received. Chelsea Clinton, who did not turn eighteen until the middle of her father's second term and was thus granted even more privacy than the Bush daughters, nonetheless served to put a brave face on the Clintons' family life: The day after her father admitted to the nation that he had lied about Monica, she became the literal link between her parents as they walked to the helicopter on the White House lawn. Karenna Gore Schiff did more than just make campaign appearances; she was an influential adviser, famously urging the employment of Naomi Wolf to turn her father into an alpha male. And this go-round, from the start of the Democratic primaries, John Kerry's daughter Vanessa and stepson Chris Heinz have traveled extensively to rouse the youth vote on the candidate's behalf.

There will likely not be any political advice from either Bush twin—they say they love their father, not the game—but at twenty-two, they should definitely be able to connect with America's young electorate. They drink soy lattes from Starbucks, and their favorite restaurants serve sushi; they are not averse to such adjectives as "awesome," and one of their highest compliments is that someone is "hilarious." They are far better traveled than their parents were at their age—on Barbara's graduation trip, she and three friends visited Moscow, St. Petersburg, and Prague; Jenna went with Mia Baxter to Spain, where they walked the Camino de Santiago de Compostela (the Way of Saint James), a five-day, seventy-five-mile segment of the spiritual trek through the Pyrenees on a medieval footpath. But both twins remain essentially all-American girls who grew up going to summer camp and public schools, who profess to "love" costume parties and Mexican food, who spent four years in college while their father was in the White House and still managed to come out well educated and unscathed. "Laura and I did everything we could to take the pressure off them, but they're the ones who handled it well," the president tells me. "They were relaxed about it. They made friends. They worked hard in school, and they enjoyed themselves. What I worried about most was if they'd be able to have a rich college experience, and they did. It was really their doing."

Of the two, Barbara generally has been viewed as the quieter, more bookish twin, while Jenna is seen as more boisterous and fun-loving—

the White House expressed irritation last year when the Associated Press revealed that her Secret Service code name was Twinkle. But their mother says that each shares some of the more obvious qualities ascribed to the other, and it's true that they often finish each other's sentences, falling out laughing when they do: "See, we are twins!" Barbara, says Mrs. Bush, "is also fun-loving and fun to be with, while Jenna loves to read and is a very good creative writer." In fact, both are described as "comedians" by their friends; it's just that Barbara is rarely first on the stage. "She is very self-deprecating and doesn't like a lot of attention," says Blair Leake, who spent a year with Barbara in Rome on a high-school study program. "But once she knows you and feels intimate with you, she can be really funny." Jenna, likewise, "is not one bit pretentious," says Baxter. "But she is the lively character of our group." Indeed, when Jenna hosted a circus-themed costume party at the family's ranch in May, she went, not surprisingly, as the ringmaster. "I hung out with the bearded ladies," she says, while Barbara opted for a Yale post-exam trip to Myrtle Beach, South Carolina.

"Jenna's more out there, more gregarious," says Regan Gammon, a lifelong friend of Laura Bush's and the godmother of Jenna. "She is not so guarded. Barbara, by nature, is going to think about it a little longer before she says it. Jenna is like her father and Barbara is like her mother—I think that's apparent to anybody who meets them."

Jenna Bush, named after her maternal grandmother, was born one minute after her sister on November 25, 1981, in Dallas. (Jenna Welch, whom Barbara refers to as "such a cute little grammy," is eighty-four and still lives in Midland, though she is a frequent visitor to the White House.) When *Vogue*'s photographer expresses "amazement" at the precise timing of their births, Jenna wisecracks that "it's not that amazing—it was a C-section." But their delivery was no joke. During Laura Bush's pregnancy she developed toxemia, a potentially life-threatening condition for both mother and child. In an interview during the last campaign the president told me he'd been beside himself with worry, but that his wife had given him confidence: "She turned to me and said, 'These babies will be fine; they will stay with me until they're big enough to emerge.' There was a determination and grit, an unbelievable will to protect the children."

In 1987, the young family moved from Midland to Washington, where George W. Bush worked on his father's presidential campaign. Two years later, when they returned to Texas, it was to Dallas, where Bush was part owner of the Texas Rangers baseball team. When the girls were thirteen, their father became governor, and they moved to Austin. Through it all, the twins say, they have remained "best friends," but as they grew older their differences sent them in different directions. When Jenna was sixteen, for example, she forwent camp in favor of a study program in Spain, where she lived with a family in Cádiz, learned Spanish, and met her friend Mia (after their recent Spanish trek, they traveled to the coast, where they had a reunion with other participants in the program). "The man was a soccer announcer, and I shared a room with their little girl," she tells me. "It was great."

At sixteen, Barbara, who also studied Spanish (she took it every semester at Yale), chose to spend a year at the St. Stephen's School in Rome, which made news during her father's first presidential campaign when it was revealed that the only European country the then-governor had ever been to was Italy—to visit his daughter. By the time Barbara rejoined Jenna at Austin High, it was already time to apply to college, so she applied to nine, including Princeton, Columbia, and, of course, Yale. She didn't yet know where she wanted to go ("I knew my grades were good enough that I'd get into at least some of them"), but she knew it wasn't home. "I love Texas, but I wanted a change. I like going to places by myself, and I knew so many people who were going to U.T.—all my friends from junior high and high school."

Jenna, on the other hand, was attracted by exactly what turned Barbara off. "I knew I wanted to go to a big Southern school. And at U.T., I had a great set of friends from high school and camp. I knew I'd have a built-in support system. Plus, I love Austin. Even now, after ten years, leaving is going to be hard. I definitely think Barbara and I both made the perfect choices. We had awesome college experiences."

"We were really happy that they were able to go to college and have pretty much of a private life," the First Lady tells me, adding that it never occurred to her or her husband to "use" their daughters during an election that was held during their freshman year. "All college freshmen want to be pretty much anonymous." While not anonymous—each has Secret Service protection, after all—they were aided immeasurably by the loyalty of those around them. "Their classmates were contacted [by the tabloid press], of course," says Mrs. Bush, "but they were both so lucky to have really good friends who shielded them." Their friends could protect them only so much, though, and when they did make the tabloids, they were portrayed as out-of-control party girls, barely restrained by the agents who guarded them. Rumors also flew that their grandmother Barbara Bush had given them a stern talking-to after initial press flurries; true or not, they landed firmly on their feet. Jenna proudly tells me that Barbara returned to Yale early from spring break this year to work on her senior thesis, that her sister took six courses in her last semester compared with her own three. "As far as their day-to-day choices, theirs are pretty much like anybody else's," says Regan Gammon. "There was never any 'You better not do that, because your grandfather's president or your father's governor or president.' I mean, I'm sure they were hoping that the girls would make good choices, but it was never held over their heads. It was normal parenting—here's what you can and can't do, and here are the reasons why." Gammon says they got through the rough patches much as their mother handles her own demanding role: "Laura's approach is 'Yes, it's stressful, but this is the task at hand, I'll get it done and still have fun.' Laura keeps things in perspective. You can see how much they're like their mother."

If the Bushes have achieved "normalcy" for their daughters, it helped that they themselves knew, as Mrs. Bush says, "what it is like to be the children of the president." When the twins were born, their grandfather was Ronald Reagan's vice president. "All their lives someone in the family was in public office. That's why we really wanted to give them a life of their own." It seems to have worked. "Strangely, politics and family life never crossed," says Jenna—which is all the more of an achievement since for the last four years family life has been conducted in the very political locales of the White House and Camp David, with occasional forays to the family ranch in Crawford. Their twentieth-birthday party took place at Camp David, less than three months after 9/11, during their Thanksgiving break. "We had twenty of our friends, and there was a really nice dinner and a karaoke machine afterward, and of course my dad had a sports tournament for the guys," Jenna tells me. "He's so competitive, so active. He was stressed out, I know, but we still had the party. People ask me if I ever see my father and I say yes, because he puts in the effort. He calls all the time to tell us he's proud of us."

Taking time for family is something of a tradition. "Most of our visits with our grandparents were in Maine," says Barbara, "and we were usually there with fourteen cousins. We had built-in playmates." (They also had "Ganny's" rules. Barbara says: "She's strict about some stuff, but she's hilarious.") "As a family, when we get together we've always managed to leave the politics aside and get on with our lives, our private lives," former president Bush says. "There are public demands, of course. But for the most part when we're together it's just us, uninhibited by outside pressures."

Bush 41 writes the girls "very, very sweet letters," Barbara reports, "and now he's into email." Their grandfather has one complaint: "It takes them a month to answer. They're very naughty girls."

The girls' frequent conversations with their mother (two or three times a week) are usually conducted by phone, and by all accounts it's an especially open relationship. "They're both just no-holds-barred in their relationship with Laura," says Gammon. And like most mothers, she bears the brunt of her daughters' teasing. Jenna says that proof of her parents having the "best marriage" can be found in the fact that "my dad thinks my mom's funny even though she's really not—she's cute, she has funny quirks." Such as? "When we were little, she'd say, 'Let's clean the third drawer in your bedroom,'" says Jenna, laughing. "I call her OCD [obsessive-compulsive disorder] to her face, but I'm glad now because some of it's rubbed off on me." Both twins remain highly amused that just after the sixth grade, when they were off at camp, she responded to their request for music by sending them Bob Dylan's *At Budokan*. "All our friends were like 'What is that?'" The future First Lady also took the girls to see Dylan in concert twice, and to a stop on Paul Simon's *Graceland* tour when they were only in the first grade. While still finding such things wildly funny, these days they appreciate their mom's musical taste. "Her record collection is awesome," says Jenna. "She's got Jimmy Cliff and Bob Marley. When we have parties at the ranch, we play them, and all our friends love it."

Their father has been known to do some teasing himself. "He has the best sense of humor, and he is very funny with boyfriends," Jenna says. "He's not the shotgun-dad type, he's the joking-around-to-the-point-where-he-scares-the-heck-out-of-them type." They all seemed to have survived it, since one of Jenna's exes is now a personal aide to her father, and three others showed up for the White House Christmas party. "I'm the serial monogamist, and Barbara's the dater. I'm the one that rushes into this long-term, two-year-relationship thing. I had a boyfriend all through college." But now the tables have turned. "I'm dating, and Barbara's got a great boyfriend"—a fellow Yalie whom she declines to name. For Jenna, at least, boyfriend material comes down to one thing. "He has to be funny," she says. "If not, *hasta luego*."

Now, as the sisters bid their own goodbyes to the mostly protected, private lives they have so far enjoyed, they are looking forward to being "independent and doing our own thing," Jenna tells me, adding that "for now, I think it will be great to do the campaign for several months where I'll work really hard and meet tons of people. I think it will help prepare me for the next phase of my life."

Neither girl's plans for that phase include politics. Barbara, who asked for a sewing machine when she was thirteen and made her own eighth-grade graduation dress, worked last summer for Proenza Schouler, the hot young design firm led by Jack McCollough and Lazaro Hernandez. "I wanted to work for someone who was just getting established," she says. "With someone bigger I don't think I would actually have gotten to do anything, and I feel like I did." A math whiz who, according to her mother, has always been fascinated by "the construction of everything," she has decided to channel her design talents away from fashion toward art therapy. On the five-country tour of Africa with her parents, she visited AIDS hospitals, and the experience made an impression on her. Children, she says, especially those who are sick or impoverished, can express themselves more freely through art. "Also, with art there is no language barrier." Jenna, who developed an interest in charter schools after spending the summer of her sophomore year working at one in D.C., says her "dream" is to start one of her own. In the meantime, she has interviewed for a teaching post in Manhattan, where she and her friend Mia have already found an apartment, and she may go back to school for a graduate degree. First, though, both girls will be players in a political drama they have only watched from the sidelines. "I'm just not political," Jenna insists. "I have opinions, but there's nothing about the process that has ever interested me. I'm twenty-two, and this is the first interview I've ever done in my life." It certainly won't be the last.

11

Winning Combination

(2005)

t is Veterans Day, a week and a day since John Kerry conceded the election to George Bush, and the president is in the Oval Office about to have his portrait taken with the First Lady. He is clearly comfortable in the sunlit room he's now occupied for almost four years. The walls are covered with scenes from home—turn-of-the-century oils of cacti and bluebonnets and the Alamo, and Remington's *The Bronco Buster* sits on a chest. But when he agrees to a request to take off his jacket, the audible gasps among staffers signal that this is by far the most comfortable he's ever gotten. It's not the first time he's been asked to pose in his shirt-sleeves, of course, but in the past he has always declined, citing respect for the office. This time, though, he doesn't hesitate, and White House communications chief Dan Bartlett looks at me and grins: "This is definitely a second term."

Well, not quite—the inauguration is still many weeks away. But it is clear that Bush is no longer the irritable, defensive candidate of the first debate; he's the relaxed, confident president who has just won reelection by three-and-a-half million votes—the first majority of the popular vote since his father won it in 1988. When I ask him how it feels, he all but shouts, "Good!" before adding, "It feels refreshing. It feels empowering to know that the American people listened to a long and serious debate and made the choice they did. I am invigorated."

He certainly seems so. Yasser Arafat has died the night before; Tony Blair is on his way to town; the fight for Fallujah has just begun; and he has a roster of other business before him, including the soon-to-be-announced appointment of national security adviser and close friend Condoleezza Rice as secretary of state. Still, he is loose, pumping hands and greeting the crew. He asks the hairdresser how he looks, and when she says, "Really good," he cracks, "Over 50 percent and they start saying 'Really good.'" When the photographer tells him she thinks his hair seems darker, he shoots back, "That's 'cause I won. Had I lost you would have said, 'He looks so gray and old.'" When she adds—voicing the opinion of millions still suffering from the "blue-state flu"—that the times seem darker, too, he doesn't miss a beat. "I don't see it that way. Where you see darkness I see light and freedom and hope." And then he's campaigning again: "It must make you feel good that an election was held in Afghanistan and the first person to vote was a nineteen-year-old woman."

If he tends to repeat the phrase *the people spoke*, you really can't blame him. Last go-round, after all, the people spoke by voting for his opponent—and the Supreme Court didn't rule that he'd won the electoral vote until well into December. In 2000, he won the contested state of Florida by a breathtakingly narrow 537 votes; in 2004 he won it by an easy 375,000. As the ballots came—slowly—in, the Bushes were joined in their second-floor private quarters by family (twin daughters Jenna and Barbara, his parents, and all his siblings except Jeb, who stayed home to monitor the Florida tallies) and five couples who have long been among their closest friends (including Chelsea Piers chairman Roland Betts and his wife, Lois, and Jan and Joey O'Neill, who introduced the First Couple at a backyard barbeque in Austin). Four years earlier, the same couples had gathered in a suite at the Austin Four Seasons for a victory celebration that never came. This time they all had rooms at the White House and dined on squash soup, mushroom tamales, and lamb chops.

"It was real friends and good tamales," says Regan Gammon, Laura Bush's lifelong pal, who attended with her husband, Billy. But as it became clear they'd be denied another immediate victory, "We were all on edge." When Gammon finally turned in at 3:00 a.m., the famously early-to-bed president was still awake. "That was pretty remarkable."

The next morning, the First Lady, who by then knew Kerry had scheduled a call to her husband, told Gammon it was "all over," but the evening had indeed been an edgy one, preceded by an equally edgy few days. During the weekend the campaign's own internal polls had shown Bush losing ground; former president Bush was so worried he'd been sick to his stomach for more than a week. On Election Day the Bushes and their daughters voted at home in Crawford and made a last-minute campaign stop in Ohio. After they boarded the flight home, Karl Rove started receiving the dismal exit-poll numbers: "I knew they were wrong, and I still got sick." When the president and his entourage landed late that afternoon on the White House lawn, Bush cautioned everyone to "look like you're happy" before getting off the helicopter. After Kerry's call came the next day, he didn't have to pretend anymore. Weepy with relief, he hugged his aides and thanked them.

He also thanked his wife, Laura, who enjoys the highest favorable opinion ratings of any First Lady in modern times, with the exception of her mother-in-law, whose ratings soared into the 80s by the end of her husband's term (her daughter-in-law's hover around the mid-70s). By the week before the election even 55 percent of Democrats said they viewed her favorably. "She's the reason I won," her husband tells me in the Oval Office. When someone in the room allows that the First Lady was with him "every step of the way," he says, "More important, she was on her own."

It's true that she had a solo schedule almost as grueling as that of her husband, an astounding fact when you consider that ten years earlier, during his first campaign for governor, she did not make a single public appearance. "She just wasn't comfortable with it," says Rove, who was the architect of that victory as well. "This time her staff would call and say the First Lady wants to add two more stops." During the final weeks, when Florida looked like it might be slipping, Rove dispatched her on a tour of the state. "She was spectacular," he said. "You could see the difference in him when she was traveling with him. He was looser, more energized. When he campaigned with the girls it was the same way—he was so much more at ease."

While the talk on the Kerry bus was of occasional marital squabbles and Teresa's often rambling speeches (at the end of one especially long day last August, a punch-drunk Kerry actually introduced his wife, without malice, as "someone who has made an art form of thinking out loud"), Laura stayed on message. On the plane she multitasked, poring over briefing books while picking out the White House Christmas cards.

It's not surprising that the Secret Service gave her the name Tempo. Her style, too, has remained steady and low-key. Although she has traded in the Dallas designer who made the clothes for her husband's first inaugural for such fashion luminaries as Oscar de la Renta and Carolina Herrera, de la Renta says that "no matter what she wears she is always herself. She is totally, totally natural." A few days after our meeting in the Oval Office, she took the twins and Lois Betts and her two daughters to a preinaugural planning session with de la Renta in his Manhattan showroom, and afterward the designer took them a few blocks down the street for lunch at a neighborhood Italian place. She wanted to walk, de la Renta tells me, and the group was "totally invisible" until people recognized her and began to clap. At the restaurant, a man approached with a photograph of his own twins, and the First Lady graciously wrote a long note on it. When they left the restaurant, the diners gave her an ovation—an especially notable turn of events in the bluest of blue states. Her seemingly unfailing ability to generate affection also serves her husband well overseas. During the height of strained relations between her husband and French president Jacques Chirac, a vocal opponent of the war in Iraq, she paid a call on him in Paris, a visit that began and ended with much showy hand-kissing. "She is all that is best about America," says de la Renta, who also dressed Hillary Rodham Clinton. "She's spontaneous; there's no fuss, no pretension."

To the campaign, she was valuable as "a link to what a lot of Americans think," says Rove. "She's sensible. She's what you'd expect of a former elementary school librarian with a sharp mind and her feet on the ground." Hence her sensible statement to *Good Morning America*'s

Charlie Gibson that she wasn't "really sure" about the gay-marriage amendment dear to many of her husband's supporters, much as her mother-in-law once tempered her own husband's hard-line abortion stance by hinting that she was prochoice. The president himself has indicated that he may not be interested in pushing the marriage amendment, but it's too early to tell whether, in his second term, he will move toward the center and govern as the "compassionate conservative" he ran as in 2000. He could well be liberated from the far-right elements of the "base," since he never has to face them again—at the very least he doesn't have to announce steel tariffs in an effort to court swing state Pennsylvania as he did in the first term (he still lost it by 2 percent). One senior adviser told me with a smile, "We're going to be far more reasonable than people think."

Whatever happens, his wife will continue to champion literacy programs and has said she is interested in focusing on the problem of rampant drug and alcohol abuse among juvenile delinquents (she is particularly impressed by a program in Dallas that gets kids cleaned up and teaches them life skills). She will also somehow find time simply to live her life. More than any other First Lady since Jackie Kennedy—who disappeared to Middleburg, Virginia, for weeks on end to ride her horses—she has managed to carve out a relatively normal private life for herself and for her husband, both at their chic-but-understated ranch house and in the White House, where she has imposed at least some of her personality on the private quarters. She covered President Monroe's Empire settee and chairs in Brunschwig & Fils luxurious tiger-striped silk velvet and hung Georgia O'Keeffe's *Jimson Weed* in the dining room, along with an enormous Helen Frankenthaler in the center hall. It's not exactly what you'd expect from a librarian from Midland, Texas, but she has a remarkable ability to somehow break the mold while also filling it perfectly. Though admired as a "traditional" First Lady, she's also a woman who sent her kids Bob Dylan tapes at camp—and is crazy about Ben Stiller. Above all she's never been anyone's pushover: When George introduced his prospective bride to his family, her imperious future grandmother-in-law Dorothy Bush asked her what she did. "I read, and I smoke," was the future First Lady's response.

Her "normal life" also includes the friendships she's never allowed political life to interfere with. Among her first guests at the residence in 2001 were the members of her Austin garden club. Each year she and several friends who all grew up together in Midland take a hiking trip to a national park. "We just laugh and talk and have a great time," Gammon says. "She's always been such a great friend. There's never been any agenda."

This time around, many people, including staff, hope that the official White House agenda will feature more public entertaining, and if Laura's increasingly glamorous wardrobe is any indication, there will be. She is considering wearing a black Herrera gown to the Texas State Society's inaugural week "Black Tie & Boots" gala, and says she may even wear cowboy boots with it.

As for the president's agenda, it includes, obviously, a war to fight and win. He has often said that history, not pundits or even his peers, will judge him, that none of what he is undertaking now can be accurately analyzed for at least a quarter of a century—and indeed the task the president has set for himself, to spread democracy in the Middle East, is not unlike the open-ended, "long twilight struggle" against totalitarianism that President Kennedy said he knew would not be accomplished in "the life of this presidency." But the telling busts Bush has chosen for his office do not include one of JFK. Instead, they are of Lincoln, Churchill, and Eisenhower. Prior to the Civil War, Lincoln was a minority president so unpopular he had to be smuggled into town so he wouldn't be killed. Churchill was the second choice of a party that distrusted him, and everyone assumed it would be General Marshall who got Ike's job as overlord. All three changed the world. The question is, If we're still here fifty or one hundred years from now, will an American president want the bust of George W. Bush in his office?

12

André Leon Talley's Deep Southern Roots

(2018)

On a clear and lovely Saturday evening last April in Charlotte, North Carolina, more than 450 guests gathered on the lawn of the city's Mint Museum for its annual gala, a black-tie shindig called Coveted Couture, a reference to the museum's dazzling show *The Glamour and Romance of Oscar de la Renta*, which opened the next day. André Leon Talley, the towering (he is six foot six) former *Vogue* editor who was a close friend of the late designer's and the curator of the exhibit, sat slightly apart from the crowd, bedecked in a stately Tom Ford cape made of black silk faille— "like those," he informs me, "of the bishops and cardinals." From his roost on a garden bench (where he was joined by Yvonne Cormier, a Houston anesthesiologist and philanthropist who has been one of Talley's close friends since their days at Brown University), he chatted with the likes of actress January Jones and gallery owner Chandra Johnson (who is married to NASCAR mega-champ Jimmie Johnson) as a growing group of fans circled tentatively in hopes of an encounter with the great man, who graciously obliged: "And what is *your* name? . . . Of *course*, you can take a picture . . . So nice to meet you . . . *love* the dress."

The event, a fundraiser cochaired and envisioned by Laura Vinroot Poole, owner of the fashion-forward Charlotte boutique Capitol, also made the almost infinite list of what Talley is prone to call "moments," intensified occasions invested with special excitement or emotion that could range from, say, the sight of me in the lettuce-green Scalaman-dré silk Carolina Herrera wedding dress he all but designed ("It was a moment, I tell you, a *moment*") to the deep, deep pride he felt when he dressed and profiled Michelle Obama for *Vogue* ("I only wish my grand-mother had been alive to see it"). This particular moment was especially significant because it marked a meeting of Talley's two worlds: North Carolina, where he was raised by Bennie Frances Davis, the beloved grandmother he called Mama, during the dark days of the Jim Crow-era South, and what he refers to as the Chiffon Trenches, the rarefied world of high fashion where he has toiled for more than forty years as an editor, curator, commentator, and behind-the-scenes adviser and muse to countless designers, including de la Renta.

"To have the prodigal son come home after all his years in fashion and curate such a spectacular show in a changed South from the one he left felt important to me and, I think, to Charlotte," Vinroot Poole told me. "We are so proud of all he's accomplished, and I loved the opportunity to truly thank him for all that he has done."

Talley, too, was proud—"I was proud to be in my state." Though he grew up in Durham, just 142 miles away, he had never been to Charlotte until he spent weeks at work on the show, but he came away "impressed" with the city's "beauty and Southern grace" as well as the "refined" gala with its "off the charts" Southern food and "extraordinary" flowers. "I was very, very happy," he says. "I felt good about Charlotte and I felt good about the upcoming film."

The film is *The Gospel According to André*, which had its Los Angeles opening just days after the gala and which has by now been shown in cities across America as well as in England, elsewhere in Europe, and Israel. An illuminating documentary by Kate Novack, it has precipitated an ongoing major ("major, *maaa*-jor") moment and serves as what Talley calls the "gateway to the final chapter of my life"—one that is almost too big and too complex for a single film to capture (though *Gospel* tries mightily and is something of a mini-masterpiece). "It absolutely has shown the world who I am in a very emotionally honest way," he says. "The love from the audiences has just been amazing."

Of course, it could have gone the other way. "He's courageous. He couldn't know how the film would be received," says his great friend Deeda Blair, the über-elegant fashion icon and medical philanthropist who has been at the forefront of cancer research for the past fifty years. "This film was a creative act. He's an extraordinarily imaginative, creative person."

That imagination and creativity were evident from his earliest days in Durham, where his grandmother worked five days a week as a maid cleaning the Duke University men's dorm rooms. Like his affecting and beautifully written memoir, *A.L.T.*, the film begins with his childhood. As he once told *New Yorker* writer Hilton Als: "You know what one fundamental difference between whites and blacks is? If there's trouble at home for white people, they send the child to a psychiatrist. Black folks just send you to live with Grandma."

Thus it was that he arrived at Bennie Davis's doorstep at Christmas in 1948, less than three months into his life.

It was in his grandmother's pristine house—always cleaned and polished to the nth degree—that he learned the values he says have helped him navigate and survive the often "tortured" world of fashion, and though they were never forced on him, they were clear: "I learned how to live just by watching her work, pray, and go about the business of making a home for me." It was also where he learned the true meaning of luxury—boiled, perfectly ironed sheets and starched white Sunday shirts; a well-tended rose garden and latticework piecrusts; "the beauty of ordinary tasks done well and in a good frame of mind." They were lessons that never left him. "André has always understood that luxury provides distinction," Blair says. "It's all in the details. It's not consumerism. He's always talking about sheets."

"My childhood, by anyone's standards, was a rich one," he says, adding that he took umbrage at a recent piece in the *Guardian* in which the writer referred to his "poor" upbringing. "Honey, we were not poor and I wanted her to know," Talley says. "We were not on welfare, and we were not on food stamps. Wealth is based on values and traditions. I had food and unconditional love. I knew nothing about poverty."

On Sunday mornings the tradition included a pan of his grand-mother's biscuits and the elaborate process of dressing for church. He remembers pulling on his starched and pressed boxer shorts, his grand-mother's handkerchiefs "folded as neat as a letter," and, always, her hats. "Going to church, the way you dressed, you learned how to be," he says. "In the black South, the church culture was almost like a finishing school."

He excelled in actual school, but life was not without trauma. After church each week, he walked across town to Duke's newsstand to buy the magazines that provided a window into a dramatically different world. On one such trek, a carload of students assaulted him with gravel. Then, as now, he remained undaunted. If the real world was cruel, fashion seemed kinder—or at any rate he could create his own fantasies. He installed a fake-fur bench in his bedroom; the pink walls were papered with the pages of *Vogue*, at the time edited by the brilliant Diana Vreeland, who would become the second most important woman in his life. At the public library he checked out Marylin Bender's seminal *The Beautiful People* and *The Fashionable Savages* by John Fairchild, publisher and editor in chief of *Women's Wear Daily*, where he would eventually work. During a visit home, his mother refused to walk through church with him wearing a navy maxicoat he'd procured from a flea market, but his grandmother never once wavered in her support.

He swears he became enamored with all things French by watching Julia Child on TV, and he couldn't get enough of the subject in high school. At North Carolina Central University, he majored in French literature and spent summers in Washington, D.C., with his father, something of a "hepcat" who worked by day as a printing press operator and by night as a taxi driver. Talley himself earned spending money for the school year by serving as a park ranger at the Lincoln Memorial and splurged on fine gloves for his grandmother at the city's haute department store Garfinckel's. He made the local newspaper by winning a full scholarship to Brown, where he wrote his master's thesis on Baudelaire and where he could finally spread his wings.

He and his friends from the nearby Rhode Island School of Design had extravagant dress-up parties. He wrote the social column in the RISD newspaper and bought a set of Louis Vuitton luggage with the money he made as a teaching assistant at Brown. Says his friend and former classmate Yvonne Cormier: "Even then, André just thought it was good manners to look wonderful."

He left school for Manhattan after earning his master's, sleeping on the floors of apartments belonging to some of his fancier school friends. When one of their fathers wrote a letter of recommendation to Vreeland, who had recently taken over the Metropolitan Museum of Art's Costume Institute, he won a slot as her volunteer assistant. They immediately became as thick as thieves—DV's emphasis on the importance of maintenance and her habit of having the soles of her shoes polished with a rhinoceros horn were not so different from the polish that marked his grandmother's house; Vreeland had an entire walk-in closet with floor-to-ceiling shelves of miraculous sheets.

From the Met he got a paying job at Andy Warhol's *Interview*, where he finally met the people he'd been reading about all his life. He danced every night at Studio 54 but never succumbed to the nightclub's infamous sex-and-drugs scene (in the film, Fran Lebowitz describes him as "the nun" of the group). He interviewed Karl Lagerfeld, who became a lifelong friend, and hobnobbed with Naomi Sims and Pat Cleveland, the groundbreaking black models who had given him hope when he'd seen them on the pages of *Vogue*.

During a long stint in Paris at *WWD*, the thin and beautiful young Talley cut a flamboyant swath at the fashion shows, but he also possessed a knowledge of fashion and its historic influences that was almost shocking in its depth and breadth. "André is one of the last of the great editors who knows what they are looking at, knows what they are seeing, knows where it came from," declares the designer Tom Ford in the documentary. Or, in the words of Talley himself: "I got here because I had knowledge. As Judge Judy always says, they don't keep me here for my looks. They keep me here for my power. Because knowledge is power."

Upon his return to New York in the 1980s, he remained devoted to Vreeland, whose eyesight and health were failing and to whom he read almost every night. In 1988 he joined Anna Wintour when she replaced Grace Mirabella at *Vogue*, and in the following year both Vreeland and his grandmother died, only months apart. It was an enormous blow. He installed a granite obelisk carved to his exact height at his grandmother's grave to signify his watching over her, and was the only non–family member at Vreeland's funeral other than her two longtime nurses.

Though he is no longer on the *Vogue* masthead, he was inextricably linked to the magazine for almost thirty years, taking his seat alongside Wintour on the front row of every fashion show, escorting her to (and quietly dressing her for) almost every big-deal fashion event. The film, then, is the first thing in a long time that is his and his alone. "Finally," he says, "it's about me. It's not about *Vogue*."

Still, it was in the hallways of the magazine that we first met and formed an instantaneous bond deriving from our mutual devotion to our innately elegant grandmothers, our memories of the food we so loved growing up, and our early obsession with the magazines that took us to the wider world. During projects together, he would jokingly refer to our employer as the Slave Ranch, and it is true that we worked extremely hard on stories ranging from the first-ever *Vogue* cover picturing a man—Cindy Crawford and her then-husband Richard Gere in Malibu—to a feature on John Galliano just after his first, earth-changing show. (We took the designer to lunch at Paris's Caviar Kaspia, where Talley translated not just his often-slurred French but also the brilliant references that informed his clothes.)

We never failed to have a blast together, but it was on one of our trips that I also understood the racism and the slights that he had so long endured, despite his achievements and stature. We were tasked with producing a huge spread on Estée Lauder—she'd been furious about a piece called "The New Beauty Queens" in which her photo had been relegated to a page with her dead contemporaries Helena Rubinstein and Elizabeth Arden. When she threatened to pull her advertising from all of Condé Nast's titles, including *Vogue*, we were dispatched to Palm Beach, but not before André hand carried some hastily whipped-up couture gowns from Paris for the shoot. Since there was a direct American

Airlines flight from Charles de Gaulle to Raleigh-Durham, he planned to spend the night with his grandmother, who was battling leukemia, before leaving the next morning for our assignment. Upon landing, he was taken aback by the appearance of two of Lauder's armed security guards—she had no intention of allowing her clothes to stay in the house he'd bought for Bennie Davis for even a single night.

Ironically, it was in Paris that he endured the worst of it. A woman at Yves Saint Laurent dubbed him Queen Kong. One of his bosses at *WWD* told him his unparalleled access to designers must obviously have stemmed from the fact that he jumped in and out of all of their beds—which was patently untrue. "I was either a gay ape or a black buck servicing every designer in town," he says. After the latter comment, Talley sought refuge in La Madeleine—the same church, in a detail that only Talley would insert, where both Marlene Dietrich and Coco Chanel were eulogized—and thought for a long time before tendering his resignation. Even so, he says, "I bottled it up and internalized it. It hurt me very deeply." But he was determined to make like his grandmother, to carry on doing the work with dignity rather than carry a placard: "I have fought quietly to impact the culture." When in 2017 Edward Enninful became the first black man to lead British *Vogue* (or any mainstream fashion magazine, for that matter), Talley wrote him a note of congratulations. Enninful replied, "You paved the way," a sentiment Talley described at the time as "the proudest moment" in his long career.

In the film and the many pieces that surrounded its release, he is more open than ever about the racism and loneliness he endured and the fragile friendships that exist in such a competitive, ephemeral world (Wintour is supportive sometimes, not so much at others, he says; Lagerfeld, for the moment, has gone dark). His friends applaud his bluntness. "I'm glad he's doing that," Deeda Blair says. "I don't know why he hasn't been more out there before now."

What the film doesn't always capture is Talley's effervescent sense of humor and his boundless generosity and energy. There's the obvious theatrical exuberance—and Lord knows he's had to trot it out repeatedly over the years—but it's infectious because there's such a deep layer of genuine exuberance and delight underneath. After I gave him my grandfather's silk top hat from Lock (who else on earth could I have given it to?), he faxed me an effusive note of thanks signed, in his large, loopy script, "Love, André, top hat on my head!" This was his period of nonstop faxes so brilliant in their almost stream-of-consciousness commentary that Wintour asked him to do a column based on them, and *Vogue*'s wildly popular StyleFax was born.

He is also a true-blue friend. When I tied the knot in my hometown, he helped plan every inch of my wardrobe and descended into the Mississippi Delta for five days and nights. At one point during the festivities, the local bookstore hosted a party and a signing for the newly released *A.L.T.* that was so heavily attended by the locals that the mayor himself ended up directing traffic and Talley landed on the paper's front page. Exhausted from the marathon, he fell asleep at the wheel on the way to catch his plane from Memphis and was discovered in the middle of a cotton field in his overturned rented Cadillac, still snoozing and suspended upside down by his seat belt, by a gobsmacked farmer. The nice man managed to get him on the plane to D.C., where Deeda Blair was hosting a book party in his honor, but most likely did not understand the supreme urgency of not keeping "Mrs. Blair" waiting.

As a thank-you for the party, he gave Blair a pair of Manolo Blahnik shoes, "black with gray and white embroidery," she says. "André realized I needed them. I still have them. I'll have them always." In addition to such thoughtful gifts (when I got my first garden, he sent me two of his favorite brand of watering cans; when a dear friend wanted to see a Chanel show, he not only got the two of us some of the best seats in the house, but also plucked the hand-painted camellias right off the models' lapels and pressed them into our hands), he is big on sharing his famous "moments" with those he loves—or indeed, creating them. Blair recalls a long lunch in Paris after which he took her to see Lagerfeld in his studio for a tour of the designer's beautifully curated bookshop, which she hadn't known was there. "We spent a magical afternoon with Karl," she says. "I'd known Karl, of course, but it was sort of a heightened moment. And a heightened moment for André too—between two friends, a moment in time."

Now, in his current moment, Talley says he hopes the film becomes "a good legacy piece for the ages. . . . It can be shown in high schools, colleges, churches." There is no question that his life and his accomplishments could provide inspiration to new generations, not least because he has always, always embodied the principles his grandmother instilled in him. His upbringing "was aristocratic in the highest sense of the word," he declares on-screen. "You can be an aristocrat without being born into an aristocratic family."

During much-needed downtime spent in his gracious white two-story house in White Plains, New York, he takes solace in that sentiment, in knowing exactly who he is and where he came from. He also revels in his garden full of boxwood and hydrangeas and dozens of enormous shady trees, in watching the birds and the resident rabbits from his front porch. As he wrote in *A.L.T.* fifteen years ago: "At the end of the rainbow that has led me to a successful career in the world of fashion . . . I find that the things that are most important to me are not the gossamer and gilt of the world I live in now, but my deep Southern roots . . . what matters is a sense of place, a sense of self."

PART 4

Adventures

13

Diary of a Spa

(1992)

feel," McGee says, "like we're in an insane asylum." We have on beige terry-cloth robes and rubber shoes, and everybody else we see is wearing beige robes and rubber shoes. Also, they have that serene look that usually comes from Thorazine, although I guess it could come from a lot of exercise, a general sense of well-being (as alien to me as Thorazine), or maybe just plenty of sleep.

Though it may have been more appropriate, we are not in fact in an asylum. We have committed ourselves instead to the Doral Saturnia International Spa Resort in Miami for four days of detoxing, defatting, pampering, and rest. Not long, but maybe long enough to kick-start us into better lives than the ones we have been leading.

McGee, my most willing traveling companion and adviser in all matters pertaining to beauty (she once plugged some Clairol Kindness curlers into the cigarette lighter of a car so she could roll up her hair on our way to go duck hunting), has just returned from a month in Europe with her family—not a relaxing bunch. In addition, her husband is a wine importer, and they are in the middle of buying, or trying to buy, a house, which is keeping her up on those nights when she isn't already up drinking copious amounts of very fine wine. I myself have been in about fifty airports in the last month (Miami alone eight times), am trying to conduct not a bicoastal but a bicontinental love affair, and cannot remember the last time I had more than five hours of sleep in one stretch. It is high time to purify—if not our souls, at least our bodies.

I am worried that I may not have chosen the right companion. McGee advises me on beauty but certainly not on health. When we were eight, she sold beer at our lemonade stands and smoked cigarette butts she found on the side of the road. On the other hand, when her mother ran out of cigarettes at parties at our house, she knew to look for more under my mattress. Apart we are not strong on discipline; together we are hopeless. The last time we were in Florida together was ten years ago in Key West, where she drove our hotel bill into the thousands by teaching the bartender to make a Goombay Smash, a mixture of several exotic and apparently very expensive rums she had sampled at a University of Georgia frat party. We are at a place where rum is not on the menu. This will be a test.

DAY ONE: We land in Miami at noon, starving, but we resist the temptation to go straight to the airport hot dog stand (a wise move since we later learn that one hot dog without the bun contains 140 calories and 13 fat grams, more than half the fat we are allowed to have per day). We also forgo the spa's stretch limousine with tinted windows for a rental car, not because we are embarrassed but just in case we need to escape. We pass a Checkers hamburger stand, hard to find and so delicious, and experience another moment of weakness, but press on to the clinic of clean living.

Arrival is promising. Our suite is huge and quite grand. We have a Jacuzzi and a bedroom apiece. There are three TVs, a VCR, a bar (albeit one stocked with water, plain and fizzy), a balcony overlooking a golf course, and the latest Sotheby's auction catalog. No ashtrays. We immediately ask for whatever is left from lunch to be brought to the room: butternut squash soup (60 calories and 0 fat grams, or "points," in Doral-speak) and pasta shells in tuna and olive paste (240 calories and 4 fat points). Terrific. We applaud our remarkable discipline for not eating the hot dog or the hamburger and go off to get our robes and gym clothes.

The fact that they give you clothes is to me, a person who hates to pack yet has to all the time, one of the best things about the Doral Saturnia. All you need in life is a toothbrush, a nightgown, and workout shoes. They give you the beige robe, the rubber sandals, a pair of cotton shorts, and a T-shirt. There is plenty of bath stuff in the suites and more in the ladies' locker room. You do not have to dress for dinner (it is perfectly OK to show up in the robe), and there is absolutely no point in putting on makeup (but if you feel the need, for $35 they'll do it for you). Feeling liberated, we put our stuff in our tote bags and head off to see the nurse, who takes our blood pressure (low) and our cholesterol (high). We tour the premises: a beauty salon, the treatment rooms, the gym, the lap pool, the exercise pool, the "recreational pool." McGee, a complete hedonist and massage junkie, sits down to schedule as many massages as she can cram into three days, and I go to my body polish, highly recommended as a treatment upon arrival.

This is extremely overrated since I do more exfoliating with a Buf-Puf in the shower, but at least I get to lie down. A very nice woman covers me with a scrub, loofahs it off, and sprays me with oil. Sensing perhaps that I did not thoroughly relax during this treatment, since my neck and shoulders are in a giant knot, she tells me I should go straight to the "Cascades." The Cascades, adjacent to the recreational pool, feel like a million pounds a minute of water free-falling from eight feet above, your choice of hot or cold. I lean against the tile underneath the hot Cascades, head down, and let the water pummel my neck and shoulders. At this moment I cannot remember ever having felt anything so good. I stay until I am a prune, swim a few laps, and meet McGee, who had found the nude sunbathing deck, for dinner.

The dining room is very swish—I have a Bill Blass coat from a few seasons back made from the same leopard print that covers the chairs. We sip Pellegrino from wine goblets while the waiter explains the menu, which has a calculator glued to it. At our place settings are pencils and a scratch pad with "suggested meal totals" at the top. If we are going for the Spartan 1,000-calorie/22-fat-point-a-day program, we are allowed 400 calories and 11 fat points for dinner. This is tricky. The waiter suggests

blackened swordfish with brown rice and vegetables—it may have only
215 calories and 5 fat points, but, he points out, at least it's not bland.
This way we also get to have chilled tomato vegetable soup (35 calories,
0 fat points), sorbet (40 calories, 0 fat points), and, most important, a
glass of white wine (70 calories, 0 fat points). The soup tastes like cel-
ery, the swordfish is spicy and delicious, the wine comes in the tiniest
glass I've ever seen, the sorbet is actually very creamy and comparatively
decadent. The waiter asks us if we want anything else. McGee says yes.
"Another plate of swordfish and another glass of wine." He mistakenly
thinks this is an attempt at humor and walks away. It is eight thirty. We
have two options: attend the lecture by the resident shrink called Living
Again (for the First Time), which will teach us "how to get your life off
HOLD . . . and establish your goals & dreams and make them happen!
Now!" or watch *Mrs. Doubtfire* on pay-per-view. The lecture is clearly out
of the question, and we are too tired to stay up for the movie. What has
happened to us? I tell McGee I can actually feel the effects of the puny
glass of wine. She says, "See, that's that clean living." I remind her that
we've been living clean for less than six hours. I get in bed and read *Fit
or Fat*. On my pillow there is a thought for the night engraved on spa
stationery: WHAT IS POETRY? AN EXTENSION OF VISION,
AND MUSIC IS AN EXTENSION OF HEARING. Jesus.

DAY TWO: We skip the 7:00 a.m. walk and the 8.30 a.m. stretch class
and wait for room service to bring out dry seven-grain toast (wonderful,
actually, because it is the only thing on the menu that tastes like it has
salt in it), fresh orange juice, and papaya halves. They are not big on caf-
feine here, but they let you have it in the morning, thank God. There is
only so much I can cut out of my life on short notice. With that in mind,
I schedule a manicure and facial for the morning and the hard stuff for
the afternoon. In between I have lunch (crudités with mustard dip, 135
calories, 1 fat point; lentil and brown rice soup with tomato, carrot, and
fresh herbs, 85 calories, 1 fat point; and dill shrimp salad with cucumber and chopped egg whites with creamy dressing in whole wheat pita

with red leaf lettuce, 150 calories, 3 fat points) with the public relations woman for the resort, Kathy Casper. She is very thin with good jewelry. She wants to know if I loved the body polish she had scheduled for me. I do not tell her that I do that for myself every day in a lot less than twenty minutes and for a lot less than $35.

She tells me that many "famous writers" come to work here, that an overweight Brazilian girl came for four months and lost sixty pounds; that some guests come to do nothing but sleep till noon and have a massage a day. "Weight loss is not number one," she says. "To de-stress is the biggest thing. We get a lot of people from New York, a lot of type A personalities." Indeed, Barbara Walters and Linda Wachner have just left. "The key thing is you really don't have to think. The biggest thing you have to worry about is, What time is my facial? We call it spa brain."

She doesn't have to hard-sell me. I'm sick of thinking, and I am in fact crazy about Doral Saturnia's format—I could never make it at Canyon Ranch, where you are hauled out of bed at dawn to climb mountains and commune with higher powers. I want to stay in a plush hotel suite, take a morning walk if I want to and have my toenails polished if I don't. There is no way to go seriously wrong, because unless you leave the premises, you can't ingest much more than 1,500 calories, even cheating, and there is nothing alcoholic to be had but the miniature wine or champagne. I tell Kathy I'm having a lovely time when the manager comes by to say hello. He has a paunch. I have not yet had my one-on-one workout with Stefan, or I could tell him: "Remember, you have not successfully worked your abdominals until you cannot physically perform one more crunch."

Stefan has already had McGee in the morning. She is extremely fit and, like all McGees, completely muscle-bound, and Stefan has got her so fired up that she has already called her husband to tell him how much money she is getting ready to spend on free-weights. I warn Stefan that with me, however, he has a challenge. When I'm not traveling, I do manage to swim every day, but I walk straight past the weight room to the pool, and I have never been on a treadmill or a StairMaster in my life. I ask him to show me enough so that I won't look like a fool at the gym.

Stefan is a stud with a perfect body, shaved legs, and blond hair. He is also, thankfully, patient and sweet. He prescribes twenty to forty minutes of StairMaster or treadmill five days a week and shows me how to turn the machines on. I am crazy about the treadmill. The StairMaster will take some getting used to, but fortunately I have been given a head start by my fourth-floor walk-up in New Orleans. Next I try the chest-press machine, the pec deck machine, and the rotary deltoid machine. I do three sets of fifteen repetitions on the lat pull-down and move on to triceps pushdowns. I do arm curls and leg curls. I press one hundred pounds with my legs, and I do abdominal crunches, like Stefan says, until I physically cannot do any more. I suck down about a quart of lemon water mixed with diluted strawberry juice, my new favorite drink, and feel like Arnold Schwarzenegger. Stefan promises to give me a take-home program complete with pictures and instructions.

Having finally worked up a sweat, I feel entitled to my next appointment: Terme di Saturnia Neck, Bust, and Décolleté Treatment, a "highly advanced treatment utilizing specialized formulas for one of our most forgotten areas . . . to help establish epidermal elasticity, toning, and firmness." This costs $60, and they want you to buy the "breast contour cream," for $77, to be used daily. Once in the chair, I realize why Kathy Casper has told me that I would find this treatment "interesting" and "a hoot." After I am lathered down with the cream, the technician employs a "pneumatic" massage technique, which basically feels like she is playing patty-cake with my boobs. Finally I am left alone, wrapped in warm towels from the waist up, and free to wonder why on earth I had this treatment when I could have been watching *One Life to Live*. To wash this sticky crap off me, I hit the lap pool, which is always empty.

McGee has had a far more satisfying afternoon having a shiatsu massage and foot reflexology, which is supposed to do all kinds of things for your internal organs by stimulating the pressure points on your feet. Whatever; it feels great and she is totally blissed out. We get around to reading the morning paper, eat all the fruit in the fruit basket, and go to dinner.

We decide our first workout entitles us to splurge. We get some breadsticks at 20 calories apiece and a glass of wine like civilized people instead of demanding immediate food, as is the norm. They know everybody is starving, so there is an average wait of about two minutes between ordering and eating. Next to us is a table full of women. They all have on Doral sweats that they have bought in the spa shop, except for one who has on a black suit and black sheer stockings and black platform shoes. She looks ridiculous. We wait at least seven minutes and order the seafood soup (75 calories, 3 fat points). It is full of shrimp and scallops and red snapper and is out of this world. McGee gets a huge plate of stone crab claws with mustard yogurt dip and a baked potato (350 calories, 9 fat points), and I have the grilled beef fillet with vegetables (425 calories, 10 fat points). We order a second glass of wine and the sorbet for dessert. We cannot finish the second glass of wine. This is phenomenal for a known wine head like McGee, and I myself was spotted just a week ago draining the last swallow of Lafite Rothschild straight from the bottle. We pass on the Meditation and Motivation lecture as well as *Mrs. Doubtfire*. Tonight the message on the pillow reads, SEEK THE BEST! IN YOURSELF! IN OTHERS! IN US!

DAY THREE: We are fired up now. We eat our toast and make the 8:30 a.m. stretch class, at which we are the only students. Limbered up, we grab some lemon-strawberry water and hit the gym. Stefan has told us that we can do weights only three times a week, every other day, so we do the treadmill for twenty minutes and climb on the StairMaster. McGee puts me on a program called Pikes Peak. I feel like I did after our first skiing lesson when she made me go down the expert slope— sure I wouldn't make it alive. I did. To show off, McGee gets on the rowing machine, where she stays eight boats ahead of the boat on the screen. Outside the gym is a vegetable basket. Raw cauliflower has never tasted so fabulous.

Next we have an appointment with the nutritionist, Alix Landman. Outside her office is a sign that reads, POSITIVE THOUGHTS ARE CALORIE FREE, and inside on a table with plastic beans and broccoli is a very disgusting plastic replica of five pounds of fat. We are supposed to have filled out a form describing what we eat in a normal day. I can't—I have no normal days. McGee fills in hers but doesn't mention the minimum of four or five glasses of wine she has every night. She is diagnosed as a carbohydrate junkie who needs to eat more fruit. I am diagnosed as a mess. Until this week I have never eaten breakfast in my life. This, says Alix, is a no-no. So is drinking as much wine and whiskey as we finally confess to consuming. Alix tells McGee to tell her husband to quit bringing home all those open bottles of Latour and Lafite left over from wine tastings. McGee looks skeptical. All right, says Alix, but to make up for all the extra calories, you'll have to have an aerobic workout every day. We agree, but at this point we can't even get through a second glass of wine, so it seems a moot point.

Alix gives us 1,500-calorie-a-day low-fat sample menus with recipes; a guide on how to eat in every known kind of restaurant, including Scandinavian (yes to limpa bread and poached fish, no to Swedish meatballs and *Isler flot*); a calorie count and nutritional breakdown of everything from so-called lite products to Kentucky Fried Chicken legs; and an admonishment about our cholesterol. We explain to her that it's probably high due to the fact that we eat at least one meal a year at the best restaurant in our hometown in Mississippi, if not in the world, Doe's Eat Place. The only things on the menu are fried shrimp, spaghetti, garlic toast, french fries, hot tamales, and steaks. They are unquestionably the best steaks on the planet, but you have to eat them real fast before the pan drippings harden into white. Alix, a vegetarian, looks like she is going to throw up. Instead she recommends some vitamins designed to protect against free radicals and to rev up our metabolism. I go buy about $200 worth.

We have lunch in the room so I can watch *All My Children* on the big-screen TV. The waiter watches it with us even though he tapes it at home. We have the best food yet: hot-and-sour Thai soup with shiitake mushrooms and tofu (35 calories, 1 fat point), grilled dolphin fillet topped with papaya relish, with steamed vegetables and brown rice (240 calories, 5 fat points), and peach bread pudding (95 calories, 2 fat points). The soup is basically warm vinegar, which I happen to like, but the fish is perfect, and the peach bread pudding sends us into spasms of ecstasy. I don't even like bread pudding and neither does McGee, but she is on the phone to the kitchen requesting the recipe. Is it that we are deprived or is it really good? Who cares?

After a brief pummeling in the Cascades, I go off for a massage and meet McGee afterward for a golf lesson. The Doral Resort and Country Club is adjacent to the spa, and it offers a free clinic every other afternoon. McGee is convinced that we should learn to play. It is fantastic, she says. I ask her how she knows this. "I played one time," she explains, "and after I finally made contact with the ball, it was great." Thank God we are late and the guy takes one look at us in our workout clothes and jogging shoes and tells us, basically, to forget it. We take a fast walk around the enormous golf course, ignore the disdainful looks of the very serious golfers we pass, and soak up the intoxicating scent from the hundreds of huge gardenia bushes planted along the trail.

We have pedicures and decide to dress (i.e., put on some actual clothes) for dinner since our toenails are painted pink and we feel festive. I want to hang out in my own personal Jacuzzi before dinner, but McGee is starving to death and our fruit basket is empty. She had told Alix that fruit "is the last thing in the refrigerator" she reaches for, and now she's begging for a plum. I tell her to order some crudités and calm down, but she drags me off to the dining room anyway. It is 7:15 p.m. Neither of us has ever eaten this early in our lives.

It's our last night, so we go for it. We get breadsticks and a salad with vinaigrette (35 calories, 3 fat points). Then we split polenta lasagna with smoked chicken, spinach, sliced tomato, and red sauce (180 calories, 6 fat points). I wonder how a huge thing of polenta can possibly be only 180 calories until I taste it. Never eat polenta with no butter, oil, or salt. The waiter tells us that the special, veal marsala with wild mushrooms (330 calories, 8 fat points), tastes the most like "real food," and he is right—it even tastes like good real food. For dessert we try two things we've never had, pumpkin crème brûlée (80 calories, 1 fat point) and chocolate madeleines with fresh berry puree (90 calories, 2 fat points). Both are swell and both are in the cookbook, which we buy to take home.

Tonight's lecture is Chatting: Italian Style. We are so curious we almost attend but entertain ourselves instead with hilarious and unprintable conjecture on exactly what chatting Italian style might be. We don't even consider *Mrs. Doubtfire*. Tonight's message: KNOWLEDGE IS LIFE WITH WINGS.

DAY FOUR: It is our last day, and I am unspeakably sad. Spa brain has finally kicked in. I have had three nights of real sleep and have been reminded of what it is like to wake up free of stress, hangovers, lethargy, bad attitude. McGee and I have a nostalgic breakfast on our balcony and go to stretch class. We work out for an hour, and she goes off to get encased in fango mud, "to exfoliate, nourish, smooth, and hydrate skin," and I opt for the foot reflexology since I will soon have to hit the ground running. For our last treat, we have a makeup application so that we can face a world in which most people don't wear bathrobes. We look like sluts, but we don't care—we are so thrilled to have cheese with our final meal, an open face turkey-and-aged-Swiss(!) sandwich with tomatoes and alfalfa sprouts (240 calories, 6 fat grams). I sip an elixir made of three berries and look out over the golf course. I can't believe I'm thinking it, but I could easily stay here for another two weeks. I have yet to go horseback riding, take underwater calisthenics, get up for the early morning fast walk. I never tried the porcini risotto (390 calories, 8 fat points) or the mango mousse with berries (65 calories, 1 fat point).

The real world beckons, but I am a changed woman. My new life will include daily workouts clutching Stefan's program, less fat, breakfast, aerobic atonement for booze, nights on which I will do my damnedest to go to bed before 2:00 a.m. I will probably not take up golf, but I have yet to smoke a single cigarette. McGee is armed with info on how many pounds she and her husband stand to gain if they continue on this wine binge. I tell her, "Knowledge is life with wings." She tells me to go to hell. It's not engraved on a card on my pillow, but it will have to do for my thought for the night.

14

Fountain of Youth

(1992)

I t was on the plane that we decided to have the injections. I was flying, quite comfortably, drinking champagne in business class with Courtney, an old friend from boarding school, the only kind of friend I could ever have talked into something like this, a mad jaunt in search of eternal youth and newfound beauty. Specifically, it was a jaunt to Clinique La Prairie in Montreux, Switzerland, and the Hotel Flora in Bucharest, Romania, where a host of treatments and the injections of serums promised—depending on who was doing the talking—to prevent cancer, cure cancer, increase sex drive, decrease depression, enable you to wake up without an alarm clock, achieve a general glow, and, of course, to add years to your life. My mission was to find out if any of this might possibly turn out to be true. I had intended merely to observe, but the champagne changed all that.

Why not? Courtney said. I felt a bit guilty about Courtney, like I did that time during our junior year when I taught her how to smoke cigarettes. On the other hand this might make up for it. We'd been reading the literature on Clinique La Prairie, the famous clinic founded in 1931 by Professor Paul Niehans, inventor of the "elixir of youth," actually "intramuscular injections of live fetal cells" from the wombs of "strong and sturdy black sheep" raised high in the Alps and given cesarean sections. No joke. We remembered Gail Sheehy's profile of Margaret Thatcher in *Vanity Fair* that gushed about her then-glowing skin, and now the PR package was coyly suggesting that La Prairie's sheep embryos were responsible. I'd wanted glowing skin all my life, and I could certainly use the "increase in mental and physical ability" promised in the brochure. Better still there were La Prairie's Beautymed Services: an ozone shower that promised to "relieve metabolic disturbances, rheumatic symptoms, obesity [!]"; something called the corpofit unit "to make the face look fresher, brighter, more relaxed"; the corpolux unit that uses different colors of light to treat everything from stress to acne (why didn't my dermatologist know about this?); and the absolute best yet, the corpo-trim unit that came with the breathtaking guarantee that "laying down for seventeen minutes gives you the same results as one hour of aerobics and can trim and tone you up to five centimeters." My God. Courtney and I couldn't wait to land.

Arrival in Geneva was as promising as the literature. A gray Mercedes stretch limo awaited, *Herald-Tribune* neatly folded on the seat, to whip us up the road to Montreux. At the clinic, which possesses a stunning view of Lake Geneva and the Alps, we were met by Armin Mattli, owner of Clinique La Prairie since 1976 and himself a remarkable advertisement for its services. I had been told we would find him in a wheelchair since he had only recently emerged from a seventy-eight-day coma, the result of a brutal mugging. Instead, he greeted us on his feet with a glass of beer (it was about eleven o'clock in the morning), bet me a thousand dollars that Ross Perot would be the next president (this was June), gave me a lurid kiss, and took to calling me his "little criminal."

Once ensconced in our suites, it was clear that, despite the divine cotton damask sheets and enormous black-tiled bathrooms with their huge sunken tubs, we were in a hospital and not a grand hotel or spa. Nurses came and went from the rooms without knocking, the beds were hospital beds, with call buttons affixed to every possible surface.

Whether you believe in them or not, there has to be a limited market for sheep cells, especially at $7,000 for a week's worth, but Mattli is a smart businessman. Since he bought Clinique La Prairie, cosmetic surgery in the United States alone has increased by almost 70 percent, so next to the original *clinique*, a rather austere Swiss chalet, he built the ultramodern and luxurious facility where we were staying and where rather more concrete treatments of aging can be performed: plastic surgery, orthopedic surgery, dental work, ear surgery, eye surgery. An enormous operating theater is being completed, and a doctor who specializes in sports medicine, Thierry Wälli, has been brought in as chief physician in charge of developing the new services. A phenomenal French chef has designed three menus: regular, low-calorie, or high-protein (to lose weight fast), all served in your room or in discreet dining rooms where waiters pour wine and lift silver domes. There is an exercise room, a terrific pool, saunas, and Turkish baths. What Mattli is aiming for is the plushest, most private hospital in the world.

What Courtney and I were aiming for was "the general feeling of well-being and health" from the injections, not to mention the loss of five centimeters from lying down for seventeen minutes. However, the road to well-being and svelteness is not always smooth, even in swanky Swiss clinics.

The first jolt came when I got to my room and scanned the list of famous people who had taken the injections—Noël Coward, Greta Garbo, Winston Churchill, Somerset Maugham. An impressive lineup, but they were, after all, dead. Then I found the live clients, the ones I could look to for proof of the benefits. Mmmm. Johnny Cash and Rod Steiger. The discovery was not unlike an experience I'd had earlier in the day when Mattli introduced me to a repeat customer, another Ross Perot fan from Pebble Beach, California. "How old do you think he is?"

"Eighty-one," I said, confident I was about to be given the amazing news that he was really 110. He was eighty-one.

The second jolt came when I was awakened at seven o'clock the next morning by a nurse holding a carousel of test tubes in one hand and a large syringe in the other. "I have come to take your blude," she informed me. It was the first in a long line of procedures patients are put through before being allowed the pleasure of the sheep placenta: an electrocardiogram, a chest X-ray, a skin test. By injection time, Courtney and I were really hoping our skin tests would act up, giving us a gracious escape from the traumas to come. It was not to be. "Roll over," said the nurse, and we were injected.

The third jolt came when I interviewed the profoundly humorless Wälli, who rather shockingly told me that while it was possible the injections increased immunity to disease, I was too young for them to do much good and that their best use was that of "any placebo. It's like going to the drugstore and buying ginseng. You take it for a month and you feel good because you think so up here." He tapped his head.

Now, I'd already interviewed Otto Westphal, a doctor at the clinic and professor of biochemistry and immunochemistry who had known Professor Niehans, and he had assured me that the injections can do everything, including slowing down or stopping the growth of cancer cells. Which was it? Why had I just tortured myself if I could've stayed home and popped ginseng? But I knew what Wälli was up to. Westphal gives the rap of the glamour days, when Marlene Dietrich and Charlie Chaplin checked in for embryonic miracles. Wälli is the good cop, whose role is to give the new medical facilities credibility. Besides, he said, the injections might have been worth it. I might feel less depressed and get fewer colds next winter.

The most jolts came in Beautymed, where Courtney and I were stripped, strapped down, and outfitted with electrodes literally from head to toe. The first zaps, or "electroimpulses," were rather mild, designed as they were "to stimulate the lymphatic system, thereby draining impurities and excess water from the connective tissues." They were stepped up a bit for corpoform, which "firms and tones buttocks, arms, thighs, and breasts," and cranked up like a cattle prod for corpofit, enough so that I realized finally why it was possible to lose the famous five centimeters. The electric shocks forced otherwise unwilling muscles into strenuous, isometric exercises. Even Wälli insists this stuff works, and it does— for the same reason that lying down and contracting all your muscles for three hours works. It's the lazy man's dream exercise. There's that satisfying soreness afterward, even though you never actually move a muscle yourself. Turn it up, we screamed. By the end of the second day, Courtney swore to me her entire body had changed. This may have had something to do with the fact that we hedged our bets with laps in the indoor swimming pool, steam-bathed ourselves half to death, and signed up for the low-calorie menu (divine fennel soup, grilled shrimp with thyme in a reduced crayfish sauce), but I prefer to think not.

Had I known what lay ahead for me in Romania I wouldn't have opted for the low-calorie menu, and I would have taken a few extra doses of the corpolux tranquility light (blue). Eager to get back to Palm Beach and show off what she was convinced was an entirely new face and body, Courtney deserted me, but I figured I was fine.

I had an itinerary that told me, reassuringly, to go to the "ONT information desk" to meet an English-speaking guide who would accompany me throughout my visit, and that at the Hotel Flora I would be met by Drs. Manu, Marcu, and Pepenel. No problem, except that the airport had no roof (most of it was on the floor), much less an information desk with an English-speaking guide waiting to meet me. Crude cutout letters taped to the broken windows exhorted me to "enjoy health and happiness *sur la mer* 365 sunny days of the year." Rather touching, but I was far more interested in the letters that told me about the next flight out. There were none.

In the taxi I decided to cheer up. I was, after all, going to one of the world-famous clinics of Dr. Ana Aslan, inventor of Aslavital and Gerovital, which, according to the clinic's material, can be injected, infiltrated (infiltrated?), taken by tablet, applied to the skin in creams or to the hair in tonic, and which will cure everything from ulcers and asthma to Parkinson's disease, as well as improve memory and "depressive hypermotivity conditions." Besides, it was a hotel and I could get room service; it was hot and I could go swimming.

A whole lot of stuff messed with my resolve to be cheerful. One, the hotel was obscured by about fifty Mack trucks, the drivers of which appeared to sleep in the lobby when not making lewd gestures toward the female guests. Then there was the problem of no doctors Manu, Marcu, and Pepenel. The pool had been drained. Though it was almost one hundred degrees outside, the air conditioners no longer functioned. I checked out the restaurant and knew instantly that I was going to subsist on bottled water and my lone piece of chocolate from Lufthansa for the next three days. I looked at the bed and knew I would be sleeping in my clothes, including my shoes, for the next two nights. The light bulbs in the lamps were broken, as was the water glass in the bathroom. At least there was a TV—I could watch the French Open. Nope. I could watch a Romanian guy read the news in Romanian for twenty-four hours.

With a flashlight I read about Aslavital and reached another certainty: If and when the doctors did show up, I would not be taking their injections, which turned out to consist primarily of procaine, a form of Novocain, which, according to Ana Aslan's obituary in the *New York Times*, not only causes numbness but serves as an antidepressant when given to older people. This was a serum I could have invented—everybody feels young when they're both numb and perky.

After a long night fending off spiders and being kept awake by the howls of one of the packs of wild dogs (no kidding) that roam through Bucharest, I remembered this was where Dracula had come from. I also got to meet with one Dr. Munteanu, who was not Dracula at all but very sweet and eager to please, so I gushed my way through my tour of his rather tiny and slightly filthy facilities. Ashtrays were everywhere—there was even a cigarette burn in a prehistoric Jacuzzi. There were the same Beautymed-style machines, except that they were at least thirty years older than the ones at La Prairie, as were the exercise bikes and bathtubs in which the good doctor, perhaps sensing that I was not thoroughly relaxed by my stay in his country, suggested that I enjoy an herbal bath. He explained to me in lengthy and incomprehensible scientific terms why Gerovital and Aslavital worked, and that post treatment, patients could "do ten problems in one minute." At this point, the man could have offered me eternal life, but I was not taking those injections.

Since there were only two fat Romanian women on the premises of the actual clinic (one was getting massaged by a blind person, because blind people, according to Munteanu, give superior massages), I figured I was not alone in declining the "cure." I decided to change my ticket and get the hell out of there. Nothing doing, said the Romanian lady at the Delta office. Given no choice, I then decided to find out what was up with the dozen Aslan clinics scattered throughout the country. For this I needed my nonexistent English-speaking guide, but by luck I found another—Mike Cioca, my cabdriver, an unemployed computer programmer and hereafter the most wonderful person in the world, who had learned almost impeccable English through a high school course and a host of Kevin Costner movies. His mother happened to run a leading Romanian cosmetics factory; he told me she had gone to school with Ana Aslan. We toured Bucharest, my savior and I, and he showed me another clinic, now empty. What was going on here? My brochure said a million people a year visited Romanian spas. I finally figured out that Aslan had been yet another stooge of Ceaușescu, the clinics had been well financed and publicized by the government to lure tourists who'd spend lots of foreign currency. Now Ceaușescu was dead, Aslan was long dead, the clinics were falling apart, and cash-rich tourists didn't want to sleep in their clothes and fight off truck drivers.

I am given a tour of Mike's mother's factory, which, owned by the Romanian Beekeepers' Association, makes products using royal jelly, an ingredient I feel sure is far superior to procaine. I am laden down with piles of products and am at last convinced that my trip has been worthwhile. I tour Ceaușescu's legacy: the unbearable pollution, the overgrowth of vegetation and waist-high grass in the middle of the boulevards, the concrete-block high-rises for the poor that replaced the "nonmodern" houses he insisted on razing, the grotesque, enormous, half-finished billion-dollar buildings that were to house his bureaucracy. I realize that this was a country run not by a mere communist but by a truly insane person. I tour the countryside (Mike wants me to meet his mechanic, since what I am so happily paying him is going to pay for the repair of his aging Romanian car), and I see the oxcarts and horse-drawn wagons on the superhighway Ceaușescu built from Bucharest to his massive country estate. I see Gypsy families begging on the roadside and flimsy lean-to taverns where the cherry pickers drink beer and listen to staticky French pop music, and suddenly I want tourists to come to the clinics, to spend money anywhere, to give joy, anything, to these people.

Now, a month later, I am watchful, not for signs of improvement in poor old Romania but in my travel-weary body. So far not a whole lot is happening except that every time I have an itch I think I'm dying from a fatal reaction to sheep placenta. Not only does my skin not glow like Maggie Thatcher's, but even Maggie Thatcher's skin no longer glows like Maggie Thatcher's. I venture a guess to a reporter who covered her when she was prime minister. Maybe, I said, she hasn't been to Clinique La Prairie in a while. (The older you get the more patch-ups they recommend.) Maybe, he replied, she hasn't been in 10 Downing Street for a while. What? It wasn't the injections that made her glow, he explained, it was power she got off on. Jimmy Carter aged ten years in office. George Bush has aged at least twenty, but Thatcher looked so good, everybody thought she was checking into La Prairie once a month. I am gravely disappointed. After all this, thousands of miles, humiliation at the hands of stern Swiss nurses, near-starvation in Romania, I find it can't be done with a quick poke of a needle after all. The secret of youth lies in being elected prime minister—and staying there.

15

Accidental Africa

(1994)

My lifelong friend McGee and I found ourselves in Africa, two entirely accidental tourists, because my father told my mother he had seen all the animals he wanted to see on the Discovery Channel, and my mother asked me to go instead. Then my poor mother, who as a child harbored ambitions of being a missionary in Africa, could not go herself, and since she is not the type to buy something as practical as travel insurance, she grandly gave her ticket to McGee, who will go anywhere. We were grateful but not beside ourselves. I frankly wished that my mother had wanted to be a missionary in, say, Venice, but I figured I'd get some rest at least and spend some pleasant days looking at the scenery. And then we went. And Venice and just about every other place in the world seemed sort of tawdry and confined and even just a little silly compared with this grand, wild, passionate, still place we had come to.

"It gets you, doesn't it?" said an acquaintance, an old Africa hand, upon my return, after I'd gushed on for hours about the wonders of a continent he'd been to a hundred times. He was laughing, pleased not so much that I had enjoyed Africa, but that it had somehow, inevitably, gotten me.

I have to say that this did not seem likely at the start of the trip. We were part of a group of fifteen—some of whom were from our hometown in the Mississippi Delta and some of whom we had never seen before—on a whirlwind safari covering four game parks, including the enormous Serengeti, in two countries, Tanzania and Kenya, in eight days. We were to be transported in three Nissan vans, with extra shocks and pop-up roofs, under the guidance of Charles, our hyperefficient and ever-grinning guide, who told me at the end of the trip that he intended to be Kenya's next minister of tourism, and by that time I believed him. When we arrived in Nairobi, which looks like every other Third World capital, with bad traffic and pollution and Eastern Bloc modern architecture that's already falling down, Charles gave us the first of many lectures: Don't pay the Maasai (the native herdsmen of Tanzania and Kenya) to have their pictures taken—it will encourage a beggar's economy; don't eat any food unless it is OK'd by him; stay in the vans on game runs—the animals are cute but they will kill you.

Charles also taught us how to say "no problem" in Swahili and assured us that we would have a wonderful time, but it was all starting to feel a bit too much like camp, with the group and the buses and the rules, not to mention the troop leader. But then we piled into a low-flying Cessna and looked down on Hemingway's wide-open "gray-yellow" plain, stretching from Nairobi to Arusha, Tanzania, where we landed, and I knew that this glorious landscape would overpower any number of tourist entrapments.

When we landed, there was a brief bureaucratic entanglement—since McGee was a last-minute traveler, her yellow-fever vaccination was six days old instead of the required ten—but Charles entered into heavy negotiations with the customs officials, who, he informed us, were all drunk, and we got McGee back but lost all our cases of bottled water. Then we got into our vans, five in each (McGee and I and three other particularly festive folks from home), and met our driver, Edward Salali, and took off, cold beers in hand, down a red clay road, and I felt like I had come home. McGee and I had spent every summer between boarding school drinking beer and driving too fast down dirt roads, and now more than 7,000 miles and a decade later, we were about to spend a week doing the same thing. I was thrilled.

Our first stop was Mountain Village, a group of thatched cottages outside Arusha, in the shadow of Mount Meru. The whole place was overgrown with jasmine and plumbago, huge bushes of poinsettias and screaming purple flowering jacaranda trees. For breakfast we had fresh mango and papaya juice and deep red bananas with buttery, pale pink flesh, and then we headed off for our first game run, in Lake Manyara National Park, 123 square miles on the edge of the Great Rift Valley.

Lake Manyara was where we saw the only real forest of the trip— massive fig and mahogany trees, sausage trees with their sausage-shaped gourds whose insides the Maasai make into a sort of tequila. But my favorites were the acacias: the thorn acacia, which starts as a scrubby tumbleweed of thorns; the umbrella acacia, which looks just like its name; and the gorgeous yellow-barked acacia, nicknamed yellow fever. Lake Manyara was also where we saw our first animals: some typically exhibitionistic baboons who exposed themselves to us at the gates; a pregnant giraffe (they are pregnant for fourteen months and then drop the babies six feet down onto their heads); a pool of at least sixty hippos, all of them resting their chins on each other's behinds while sand plovers and egrets perched on their backs, picking at the bugs that light there. Eddie shouted the names as we drove: zebras and wildebeests grazing beyond the hippos (they migrate together because they eat different grasses); black-faced monkeys and bush babies in the trees; a beautiful Bohor reedbuck, which looks like our deer but bigger; fish eagles perched at the tops of thorn acacias; ostriches mating with a frenzied flap of their enormous wings.

I realized early on that McGee and I were looking at the animals in entirely different ways. She was reading *Out of Africa* and all about Karen Blixen's rather wonderful life on a Kenyan coffee plantation, failed though it was; and I was reading "The Snows of Kilimanjaro" and "The Short Happy Life of Francis Macomber" and all about bitter relationships and people living lies and things you don't even recognize when you read the same stories in high school. Also, the great majority of the animals Hemingway wrote about were dead. So when we saw a gazelle, McGee thought of Blixen's sweet house pet Lulu, and

I thought of a freshly shot "Tommy" (Thomson's gazelle) made into a broth for the dying Harry in "Snow." When we saw the Cape buffalo, she thought of them happily grazing in the Ngong Hills surrounding Blixen's farm, whereas I heard Francis Macomber's bullets shattering their huge handlebar-mustache horns as they charged and saw them moving across the plains "looking almost cylindrical in their long heaviness, like big black tank cars . . ." We saw the impossibly graceful impalas, and I thought of them as Macomber's shots sent them into a gorgeous frenzy "bounding wildly and leaping over one another's backs in long, leg-drawn-up leaps as unbelievable and as floating as those one makes sometimes in dreams."

It was starting to get weird, so I put the book down and decided to try to look at what I was actually seeing, an activity made easier by the fact that I was not taking pictures. McGee and our fellow passenger Bob were the camera jockeys in our van, toting around bags of film and a dozen lenses, knocking each other down for a shot of the seven-hundredth giraffe. (By day two we had quit shrieking at the sight of them, but they never ceased to charm us with their curious, long-lashed eyes and necks that swiveled toward us.) All that constant picture-taking seemed like too much hard work to me—I knew we'd have two sets of slides, and besides, I had to concentrate.

McGee had announced on the first night that we should all pick an animal with whom we could identify in order for the trip to be properly spiritual. I chose a Grant's gazelle, not because—as anyone who knows me will attest—I move with remotely that much grace, but because as soon as I saw one, there was something about his eyes and long face that reminded me instinctively of my own, and I knew he was looking at me, too, a soul mate at last. It did not hurt when Eddie told me that they were the most independent and intelligent of all the antelopes, and I was also heartened by the fact that the poor smaller Thomson's gazelles are caught and eaten a lot more easily than their larger cousins.

I had assumed everybody would want to be a lion, with their mating habits that reminded me of one of those intense hotel-room affairs, the kind where you lock the door and don't come out for a week and order room service maybe once. A lion goes off with a lioness and does little but mate for seven days, up to eighty-four times in twenty-four hours, hunting only if a zebra happens to wander where he can be easily gotten. We actually viewed this phenomenon in progress: the lioness swishing her tail in front of the lion's face; the lion mounting, biting her neck; the lioness tossing him off and rolling over to scratch her stomach, a feline smile of perfect ecstasy passing over her face. The whole thing takes about twenty seconds, but eighty-four times a day is still a mighty impressive thing.

Perhaps exhausted by the thought, all the men chose instead to be cougars, who are fast and shy and brave, with great square shoulders and slightly too-small heads. They are not solitary or even vaguely malevolent like the leopard, but Eddie chose to be a "lay-o-pard" anyway, because he said he was greedy when it came to eating meat. (Leopards are said to be the only animals who kill more than they can eat, who hunt just for the hell of it, hanging their kill like so much washing from the branches of fig or sausage trees.)

On roughly this same theory, McGee flirted with being a leopard, because she always overbuys at the grocery store, but the rest of us voted her a baboon due to her penchant for exhibitionism and strong capacity for making mischief. But everybody in the bush hates baboons—"They are very, very bad," said Eddie—so she finally settled on an elephant, hardly a modest choice, but fitting. Elephants are sweet to one another; they can sleep standing up (I'd certainly seen McGee doing that); they all have a kind of sixth sense (they can transmit low-frequency calls across miles of wilderness and are thought to be the only animals besides humans who can anticipate when they are going to die); and, wrote Peter Matthiessen in *The Tree Where Man Was Born*, they command "the silence ordinarily reserved for mountain peaks, great fires, and the sea."

I felt the same way the first time I saw the Serengeti, our second game park and the essence of Africa, with its seemingly endless bands of color we ran out of names for and blue-green mountain horizons and umbrella acacia silhouettes and sunsets that fill up the whole sky. There is the highest concentration of game animals in the world on its 5,600 square miles of open plain and occasional woodland. Ten minutes into our first game run we saw a pride of lions, a leopard lounging two feet from the road, and hundreds of giraffes and zebras and wildebeests and gazelles. Eddie's eye was amazing—we would never have noticed the lions, who, though not ten feet in front of us, are the exact color of the grass; or the leopards, who look quite exotic and shimmery and gold in the zoo but who are the same gray and white as the bark of a tree when lolling in its branches. He could tell us "ume" (male) before we knew what we were looking at, and he pointed out which trees were merely dead and which had been trampled and devoured by elephants.

At the end of the day we watched the sun go down from our glass-walled room at the extremely swanky Serengeti Sopa Lodge (hair dryers and bidets in the bathroom) and later that night heard the elephants wreaking havoc outside our window. The next morning we saw another leopard munching on a gazelle in the branches of a sausage tree, his tail indistinguishable from the gourds hanging down, and a family of chee-tahs sunning themselves under a spindly acacia.

We saw trees full of the nests of weaverbirds, who fill up the branches with nests to attract countless females, and dozens of waterbucks graz-ing on the banks of the Mara River. We stopped for lunch under a mas-sive fig tree and sat on our metal coolers eating cold roast chicken and drinking cold Tusker beer, guarding our food against the kites swooping down from overhead and gazing out toward the zebra one hundred feet away. The only sounds were the laughter of the drivers and the breeze blowing through the trees, and I don't think I've ever been so content in all my life.

If the Serengeti is open and endless, the Ngorongoro Crater is like the inside of a dome—on another planet. The light is strange and the sky is so dense, it looks like water, like the sky just before a tornado rips through it. The crater is the largest collapsed volcano cone in the world, nine miles across and 2,500 feet deep, covering 102 square miles. It is breathtaking approaching from the rim—but nothing like being inside beneath that still, blue-black sky, while soda mists rise from the lake bed. It felt so prehistoric that I expected to see a dinosaur cross our path, but we saw black rhino instead, a sight almost as amazing, with their magnificent horns and lordly presence. The rhino is hunted by no predator but man. He is one of what game hunters call the Big Five, along with the elephant, the lion, the buffalo, and the hippo, all of which we saw within an hour. The hippos this time were surrounded by flamingos, bright pink from the carotene in the algae they eat, which in turn can feed off the hippos' dung. Much to Charles's distress, we ate watercress growing on the banks of the hippo pool and stood waist high in the gorgeous bright green elephant grass. And then we headed up the narrow road back to the Serengeti Sopa's sister lodge in the crater, where we were protected from all that we had just seen by Maasai tribesmen wielding spears and stationed outside each of our rooms.

The next morning we deserted all the lushness and luxury and bombed back up the road through tiny towns with single water pumps and juke joints and concrete-block buildings painted bright turquoise that reminded us all of the Mississippi Delta. We passed through make-shift shopping centers painted with zebra stripes, where we traded our T-shirts and shoes (McGee thoughtfully brought some silver evening sandals she turned out not to need) for Maasai belts and bowls and fly swatters made from wildebeest tails. The others disparagingly referred to our van as the jet set because of our proclivity for shopping (Eddie persuaded some Maasai selling bracelets on the side of the road between the Serengeti and the crater to accept our traveler's checks and left his own belt there to be beaded) as well as our penchant for drinking the most beer and having the most fun.

It was an occasionally alarming point of pride for Eddie to always be way ahead of the other drivers, so we called him Fast Eddie, and he called McGee Mama Maridadi, which means "beautiful mama" in Swahili, and she certainly is, and he called me Mama Roho Maisha, the "mama of all enjoyment," and I certainly was enjoying myself. I was beginning to like this Swahili business, a beautiful language Eddie swore he would have me speaking like a native in three months. I longed for three months to give, but we were heading back across the border to Kenya, to Amboseli Maasai National Park, our last stop.

Were it not for the large numbers of elephants and the breathtaking sight of Mount Kilimanjaro, Amboseli would have reminded me of Kansas, it is so dusty. More water than usual came down from Mount Kilimanjaro several years ago, pushing salts farther up into the soil and killing off most of the trees, but there is still plenty of vegetation, attracting more elephants than we had seen anywhere else. We watched them make their early morning pilgrimage from the wooded area where they sleep leaning up against the trees to the watering holes where they feed, and then we watched them lumber back again at the end of the day, the lower halves of their bodies black from the water. We watched them eat, which they do a lot of—shoveling the grass into their mouths with their trunks. We saw a three-month-old who had not quite gotten the hang of the grass-shoveling technique and had to be helped by his mother. They all looked so wise and mysterious and serene, and big as they are, they make no sound as they move, and I knew why Peter Matthiessen wrote that "I can watch elephants (and elephants alone) for hours at a time, for sooner or later the elephant will do something very strange such as mow grass with its toenails or draw the tusks from the rotted carcass of another elephant and carry them off into the bush."

That night we stayed in our most rustic spot to date, the Amboseli Lodge, with charming fifty-year-old cabins surrounded by baboons and vervet monkeys who played on the roofs at night. In the morning, before the clouds set in, we had incredible views of Mount Kilimanjaro, and in the afternoon we lay by the pool in the sun. We also had our most successful shopping outing, at a nearby Maasai village. We had seen lots of Maasai in their bright red-plaid robes herding their cows and goats through the Amboseli and the crater, where they are allowed to graze but not live, but we had never been to one of their villages. They live on a mixture of cows' blood, which they draw off into beaded calabashes, and milk, and sometimes porridge; and they live in huts made of mud and cow dung. The men are circumcised without the benefit of anesthesia in a ceremony when they are eighteen, and, despite Alice Walker's best efforts, the women have clitoridectomies. However, they are quite sophisticated when it comes to negotiating—the price of admission to the village is $50 per van.

We were met by a young man who, in addition to his rather skimpy red robe, wore brown socks and shoes, a digital watch with a traditional beaded band, and a pink nylon money belt. We did not disappoint him, as we bought loads of necklaces and bracelets and calabashes, though I noticed that in some of the huts they had abandoned these in favor of empty Evian bottles. The children were in school under a tree on whose trunk was nailed a blackboard, and they recited the ABCs and the months of the year and sang "Yes, Jesus Loves Me." I gave them all my paper and my pens, and one of the children made a telescope out of a roll of film and peered at me, delighted, and I wondered what would happen to these people in their circle of huts, now circled almost daily by Nissan vans.

Hemingway used to stay near our hotel, and on our last night I thought about him drinking his beloved beer (he expounded at great length in *Green Hills of Africa* on what "a bloody marvel" beer is, and I have to say it seemed even more marvelous in this particular spot) and roasting his gazelle tenderloin on a stick here in this very same dark, and I remembered what he wrote after his own first trip, the one that had "gotten" him: "I loved this country and I felt at home and where a man feels at home, outside of where he's born, is where he's meant to go."

He wrote of coming back to "really live. Not just let my life pass," but of course he blew his brains out instead. His stories set in Africa evoke the place completely, and I was feeling very sad for him and for me too as we flew back to Nairobi, where we would spend our last hours. I was already plotting my next trip and missing Eddie and wishing that I had seen just one more leopard in all his majestic indifference. And then, as we drove from the little airport into the city, whizzing by factories and hordes of people walking to work, the driver suddenly stopped and pulled over, and there, on a branch extending slightly over the first real highway we'd seen in a week, was a leopard, his tail hanging down for all the world to see. I hadn't known that one of the best game parks in

Africa is right on the edge of Nairobi, and we were driving right past it, and damn if Charles hadn't spotted the leopard at sixty miles an hour. "Ume," he said, grinning, and I thought of Eddie and his "lay-o-pard"-like self and his sly sense of humor and his fast driving and his moods after he had stayed out late at night, and I knew I would be right back.

16

Our Girl in Havana

(1994)

At the end of my first week in Havana, a military jeep pulled up in front of our hotel, a tiny place well off the official tourist track in the old part of the city. This in itself was not unusual, my presence in the capital having by now aroused such great interest in all quarters of the vast Cuban officialdom that I had been accused of being a CIA agitator, and almost everyone with whom I had come into contact had been arrested or at least questioned about my activities. The driver, wearing combat fatigues, mirror lenses, a muscle shirt, and a wad of gold chains, jumped out and came in, flanked by two mirror-lensed but plainclothes colleagues and quickly followed by "the fat man," our regular spy from the Ministry of the Interior, who happened, as always, to be outside. But it was not me they wanted. They went straight to the tiny bar off the lobby, the driver engaged in a heated discussion with the barman, until finally the barman, a sweet soul who had previously made me a frozen daiquiri topped with green crème de menthe and an olive, threw up his hands in disgust. He stomped off behind the bar and emerged with two handfuls of swizzle sticks. The driver grabbed them, he and his cohorts jumped back into the jeep and drove away, the fat man went back outside, and the barman stuck out his wrists as if they were handcuffed to demonstrate his fate had he not capitulated. I looked in disbelief at the desk clerk, who had watched the entire brief episode without changing expression. He shrugged, deadpan: "It's *Cooba.*"

Yes, indeed, it is: "Cooba," a 43,000-square-mile anachronism held hostage by a sixty-eight-year-old megalomaniacal crazy person, brought to its knees by the loss of its annual $5 billion subsidy from the former Soviet Union, and further crippled by an absurd American policy controlled by about a million Cuban Americans a little more than 180 miles away in Miami. Our "closest enemy," a place where since 1962 it has been a federal crime for American citizens or corporations to spend a single dime despite the fact that the day I left for Havana we dropped the embargo against Vietnam and, on the advice of Jimmy Carter, have since given a reprieve to North Korea, a country that may well possess a nuclear bomb. In the meantime, buildings implode and spirits languish, everything that is not stamped MADE IN THE U.S.S.R. is 1950s vintage American, and the only currency worth anything is the good old capitalist dollar, legalized for use by Cubans last summer on the thirty-fifth anniversary of the revolution (and not coincidentally the date Castro's own economists predicted collapse), in hopes of luring some family cash, known as *fulla*, from the archenemy to the north.

It is not even 1994 here but the thirty-sixth Year of the Revolution, a revolution that has failed so miserably that it has come full circle— the week I left, the police were rounding up truckloads of unemployed men in Havana and sending them off to camps to cut sugarcane. Prostitution has been restored to its 1950s prominence, except that now the girls turn tricks for some soap and a shower. Electricity is limited to a few hours a day, with few exceptions the telephones simply don't work, people get married to get the two crates of beer (down from five) that the government still provides as a wedding present (a touching souvenir from the days of Fidel the Benevolent that now fetches about $24 on the black market). For the first time, ordinary Cubans will speak openly but very quietly about their frustration with Fidel, to whom they now refer more often as Castro, a far less affectionate moniker, or El Terminador: el Ultimo Capítulo (the Terminator: the Final Chapter), the most derisive of all. El Comandante has wisely held off on the umpteen-hour speeches out in the open and risky air, and entertains himself lately by presiding at the ribbon cuttings of chicken restaurants for tourists and receiving the likes of Pierre Cardin and Mort Zuckerman in one of his six lavish guesthouses. He produces "beautiful dinners" for anyone who might still buy his act or give him some money, most recently a group of Americans under the auspices of the Center for Cuban Studies, which gets around the travel ban under the shaky guise of academia (journalists, academics, and a handful of others can travel if approved by the US government). The most recent group included a young filmmaker, the head of a modeling agency, a handful of socialites, and a writer for *Vanity Fair*.

Meanwhile Cubans are forced to buy back cooking oil stamped GIFT OF THE ITALIAN PEOPLE TO THE CUBAN PEOPLE in state stores and spend hours a day scrounging for simple staples like black beans on the black market. Sugar, still the number one crop in Cuba, though the harvest last year was little more than half what it was the year before, has not been available for months, and cheese has not been available for more than two years. (It was explained to me that "you just have to forget it exists.") Che Guevara is the most visible image (much more romantic than Fidel—better-looking and dead after all), though no one mentions that he renounced his Cuban citizenship two years before he was killed leading an insurrection in Bolivia. It is no wonder that Charlie Chaplin is the island's most popular unofficial icon, and that shakedowns for swizzle sticks don't warrant so much as a raised eyebrow.

COOBA, LAND OF THE ABSURD. Fidel is trying so desperately to lure tourists, maybe he should adopt that as his new slogan. It's a whole lot catchier than SOCIALISM OR DEATH, though the neon version near the Hotel Inglaterra is halfway burned-out and says just DEATH in enormous red script. Death is not very catchy at all but a route that a rapidly increasing number of Cubans take, as they bet their lives with one-in-four odds in inner tubes cast off Cojímar, Heming-way's favorite fishing spot, hoping to make the treacherous ninety miles across the Straits of Florida.

"Meet me in Havana," Peter had said, an irresistible invitation really, and so I did, traveling without a visa, flying through Cancún, arriving in pitch so black I could not fathom how the Chilean pilot landed the plane: Peter, who has a British passport, was taking pictures of houses, crumbling balconies, a handful of architectural treasures preserved as museums, the odd private dwelling—museums, too, in their way, con-taining the chipped and tattered relics of a different time that the fam-ilies so carefully preserve and display. I wanted to have a look at this country that has loomed so large for so long in the American imagi-nation. I wanted to witness Fidel's last act, the final chapters in a saga that began before I was born, or indeed before the majority of Cubans were born, when Fidel and his small band of revolutionaries landed in a yacht called *Granma* and defeated Fulgencio Batista and his army after a two-year struggle, ultimately taking over the government on January 1, 1959, and nationalized all the property, including the substantial amount owned by America. I wanted to see the effects of our embargo and learn the answer to the question every single Cuban exile I met asked me once I returned: "Is it about to blow?"

I did try briefly to acquire a Cuban press visa, but it is a process that can take months or even years, and more than anything, I wanted to avoid the Fabulous Fidel tour that invariably produces pieces that describe his "long, elegant hands," his proclivity for giving interviews at three in the morning, and the kiss that is always bestowed on his almost invariably female interlocutors. So I chose the route taken by a grow-ing number of American tourists and businessmen on the sly—through Mexico or Canada or the Bahamas.

"It is fabulous," a woman who had been on the Center for Cuban Studies trip told me before I left. "Even the poor people live in fabulous houses." She had, she said, "fallen in love" with Fidel, with his "brilliance," his unique grasp of history. "When you ask him a question, he gives you a perspective that you never thought about." Caught up in his particular perspective, she had, therefore, not noticed the willingness of some Cubans to risk their lives to escape such a fabulous place. Indeed, why should they? "Everybody has free HBO and CNN."

"Take some food," advised another recent traveler, who had not enjoyed the benefits of Fidel's personal attention. "And some toilet paper . . . and some soap."

"If I were writing this story," said a Western diplomat to whom I had been given an introduction, "I'd say I was welcomed to Havana by the Ministry of the Interior." It was the end of my second week, and despite the fact that I had come to realize that nothing in "Cooba" is what it seems, I was not yet convinced that the theft of my handbag containing my passport, my plane ticket, and several thousands of dollars in cash (American traveler's checks and credit cards cannot be honored per our Trading with the Enemy Act) had been the premeditated act of the department of the Cuban government in charge of state security.

The theft occurred on Sunday, my first morning in Havana. We had been driven out of the Hotel Inglaterra by the hordes of hookers and the German tourists and the cold showers and the salsa band that played on the roof until 4:00 a.m. With us was Emily Hatchwell, a thirty-year-old Leeds University grad from the Cotswolds who had first come to Cuba in 1990 to write, with BBC correspondent Simon Calder, the aptly named *Travellers Survival Kit to Cuba*, and who had returned due to her attachment to the country and her friendship with Roberto, a twenty-five-year-old black Cuban drummer. She was our translator, guide, and savior, and she was walking with us to the Valencia, a tiny hotel in old Havana owned by a Spanish firm in partnership with the government (the Cuban government owns at least 51 percent of every foreign operation, though desperation has made it increasingly flexible about terms of investment). On the way we stopped at a beautiful but burned-out church, and a thug with an earring followed us in, which sent us quickly out, and a few blocks later he grabbed my bag and got away because he had a bike and we didn't.

There was nothing to do about it really, so we decided to have lunch. But we had more company. "Pssst" is the national language of Cuba, honed by a society in which everybody is watching you—the regular police, the secret police, the neighborhood CDRs (Committees for the Defense of the Revolution), who report everything they hear on the streets, outside the always open windows and doors, on the packed and polluting "camels" (a ridiculous amalgamation of a truck and the shells of two Hungarian buses), in the endless lines for food. A sigh of impatience in a bread line can get you a black mark on your government-kept "secret" records, or worse. So Cubans (none of whom are referred to here by their real names, except for a police officer, a government official, and an entertainer) tend to speak in sounds and sideways expressions even when they don't have to, even when they're ordering a cup of coffee. Because "pssst" is also often followed by requests for money or "shicklay" (Chiclets for the children) or offers of a deal on Cohiba Cigars, I was inclined to ignore the sound coming from somewhere on the sidewalk because my money was now in considerably short supply. But he is not to be ignored.

His name is Ramon, and we are about to embark on a long and expensive and rather tragic relationship. He knows who has my purse, he says. He will meet us with the names and addresses of the thief and his accomplices at our hotel at five o'clock, and in the meantime he'll alert a friend of his in the police department. This seems a bit suspect to me, but Emily tells me that's how she got her bag back when it was stolen, that people survive by passing and receiving bits of information on the sly: who stole what, what food is in the state stores, if the eggs really did come in as promised, if the police have been seen at your door.

I have nothing to lose, and Ramon's as good as his word. We take his bits of paper and I give him $50, touched by his helpfulness and his bravery. He kisses us, and Emily and I march off to the nearest police station, leaving Peter behind on the theory that two women will arouse more sympathy. They're expecting us. Outside a young policeman in

uniform asks Emily if I have lost a lot of money. She says yes and he tries
to guess how much. "One hundred? Two hundred?" At three he has to
stop, incredulous. Any more than that was literally beyond imagining. I
am reminded of something an economist had said to me after her visit:
"We don't realize how deep the isolation of the Cuban people is—from
options, from everything. There is an incredible gap with the rest of the
world. You have to relocate your brain to where they are. The limitations
are beyond our comprehension." The young cop is still wide-eyed. At the
black-market rate of 120 to 150 pesos to the dollar, $300 translates to
roughly one hundred times the average monthly wage. What I had in
my purse, about $8,000, is about a thousand times the amount of pesos
per capita circulating in all of Cuba at any one time.

Inside the station, the stairwell smells like a latrine. We're escorted
past holding pens and policemen's bunks into a room decorated with
a tattered poster of Che and a photograph of Charlie Chaplin. In the
corner on the floor is an ancient tin hot plate, on which an equally ancient cop is making coffee, a task he will undertake exclusively for the
next forty-five minutes until he decides, after many, many machinations,
that it is exactly right. On the wall is a chart titled "Crimes Against
Tourists." I am the second casualty of the day. Emily tells me that two
weeks ago a Cuban was shot and killed by the police for robbing a tourist outside the Inglaterra.

At the table we tell our story to a uniformed guy and a couple of
plainclothesmen, even though they already know it. The thief was white,
very Spanish, with dark hair, no mustache or beard, a gold loop in his
left ear. We proudly hand them his name and address and those of his
cohorts. They tell us they've already been by the houses to search and
there was nobody home. They will have to wait until the thieves come
back. This is hilarious. I am touched by the sudden concern of Cuban
policemen for the rights of the accused. I hadn't known they had Mi-
randa laws. I tell them all I want is my passport back and get up to go.
Nothing doing. We have to fill out a thousand official forms.

A kid named Nemesio is in charge. He has on a white T-shirt, tight
brown pants, brown lace-up shoes with no socks, and a smartass expression.

He wants us to show him exactly on the map where the robbery took place. He wants to know exactly what my bag looks like, a description that takes a full twenty minutes after his many questions about the handle, the closure, the color, the weight, exactly how I was carrying it, until we finally move on to the contents. "How much money did you have?" I tell him. He looks at me. "What were you planning to buy?"

I describe for him my wallet, my passport, my plane ticket, my notebook, what was written on each thing. I write out words like *Chase Manhattan, Ladeco Airlines, Passport United States of America.* He is either fascinated or just cruel. "How big was the hairbrush?" I show him with my hands. "What did it look like?" I draw it on a piece of paper. "How many lipsticks?" Two. "Are you sure?" Yes. "What color?" I tell him I think one was called Sublime. He writes it all down in Spanish, has me write it in English, has Emily write what I write again in Spanish, has Emily write her own version in English and in Spanish. Everybody signs and we drink the much-fussed-over coffee.

During the many gaps in this three-hour process, Emily tells me about her life here. How Roberto had gotten stabbed in the head the week before, trying to keep her bicycle from being stolen. How emotional contact is so important in a place like this, where pain and poverty and repression are all around you, where every day is a literal struggle for survival and "there is no letup." How all the Cuban television shows are historical because "they couldn't possibly deal with modern issues." Indeed. Roberto's mother throws pots at him because she thinks it's his fault Emily hasn't married him yet and rescued him from this place.

Roberto is a gifted drummer, but he has not been able to play because he has been the victim of a mysterious eye disease called optic neuritis caused by malnutrition, which has afflicted tens of thousands of Cubans and left some blind. He has almost recovered, but work is scarce. You can't just pick up your drums and play them. Most of the clubs open to Cubans have been shut down, and playing unofficial venues could get you arrested. A Cuban who wants to be a musician must first be evaluated by the state. You must have documents proving that you have completed high school and you must register with the *empresa,* the company that decides whom you can play with and where you can play. The *empresa* used to provide instruments and sheet music, but they came from the Eastern Bloc and are no longer available even in the conservatories. The state decides what music can be played—primarily salsa and some Afro-Cuban music (jazz is now heard almost exclusively at Havana's biannual jazz festival)—and once a year groups are evaluated and rated on a scale of A (which earns you a salary of 350 pesos a month, or about $2.50) to D (126 pesos a month). Emily tells me that one of Roberto's friends, a successful singer for fifteen years, failed the music-theory part of the evaluation and is no longer allowed to perform with his group. I ask her what he's doing now. "He's not doing anything," she says. "Like most Cubans."

Finished with our business, we join Peter for what would become our usual dinner: chicken with sort of brownish gray meat (no matter what the cut) or an incredibly chewy frozen lobster tail, cabbage, rice, a limpid tomato slice, and beer. The Cuban brand is Hatuey, named after the Arawak chief who in 1511 managed to resist the conquistador Velázquez and his first group of settlers for three whole months. He was finally captured and offered salvation in exchange for becoming a Christian, but he turned them down for fear heaven was full of Spaniards. We toast to Cuba's first revolutionary and receive the first of numerous visits from our friends the police, designed to reassure us of the gravity with which they are treating the matter of my stolen bag.

It is ten thirty at night. Could we come down for a lineup? Absolutely. The three of us trudge off through the unlit streets and are told not to worry, the suspect would be behind two-way glass. At the station we are taken to a tiny office off the lobby, wait about fifteen minutes, and are finally told to peer around the corner at the people in the lobby we just walked past. On the way out we pass a terrified-looking young black man with a mustache who has obviously been rousted for this occasion. Next to him his mother is sobbing uncontrollably. On the street, Emily heads for home and we go off to the hotel bar. Thank God dollars will get you Scotch. I have been in Havana only twenty-four hours.

The next morning the cops are back with pictures of the same black man who was in the lobby and two others. He is not black, I tell them again; he does not have a mustache. At this point I have doubts about these guys producing my passport, so I decide to try my luck at the non-embassy. The US Interest Section, an enormous green-and-white tower along the seawall, or *malecón*, is the ugliest building in town with the exception of the old Soviet embassy, which may soon be converted into a luxury hotel. Though we have no formal diplomatic ties to Cuba, we do have a ninety-nine-year lease and the largest diplomatic staff (thirty-four) in town, and we are currently spending $20 million on a general face-lift as well as to repair the damage done to the building during the Storm of the Century, a devastating hurricane that hit Havana in March 1993.

By the grace of God, I found out two days before I left the States that an old friend from boarding school is a vice-consul at the Interest Section. I had intended to call her up for dinner, but now I use her name, Sophia, to get past the hundreds of people standing in line to get inside so they can stand in line some more to discuss their applications to visit the United States. The applicant has to convince the officer that he will come back. In 1993, 27,304 visas for travelers were granted and 43,000 requests were turned down. I am told that before the hurricane there had been a backlog of more than 100,000 applications. While still in Havana, I manage to get my hands on a *Miami Herald* in which unnamed "diplomats" attribute the new streamlined backlog of "probably less than 10,000" to "new procedures."

Sophia is not particularly surprised to see me. Even though it has been at least ten years, she's been in Cuba for two of them, after all, where people sprinkle Santeria powder at her interview window ("Why are you doing that?" she asked the first time, and the woman replied, "Because you should approve my visa") and accost her in the streets, even at the beach: "You're the one who didn't let my wife go to Miami." She tells me she fears she is becoming irreversibly cynical—her job is to doubt people and their over-the-top stories all day; she is surprised by nothing. She steers me to a junior officer to solve my passport problem. He gives me a passport application to fill out, just like the one at the post office at home, and has me raise my right hand and swear that everything on it is true. He hands me a photocopied form with all the places in Havana where I can get my passport picture taken, tells me it'll be ready in a week unless I need it sooner, wants to know if I need any money. I am astonished. I'm a journalist but I came as a tourist, and even journalists are barred from spending more than $100 a day on anything other than research materials. What about the ten years in jail and $250,000 fine? He grins. "Hey, this is the State Department. We are not a law-enforcement agency." Then he arranges for me to have a few thousand dollars from the States wired to me so I can spread some more money around Havana.

In the car I speak English with Lorenzo, who is to be our driver for the next few weeks. He is very amused by my current plight. He says he spends all his time driving around mean Europeans who won't talk to him and don't tip. I, on the other hand, am screaming and hollering and being sort of generally animated, and have already promised him virtually all the money I'm about to have wired. Emily found him through the official state taxi service, although any Cuban with a car and some guts is available for hire (my favorite gypsy cab was a knockout marigold yellow 1955 Chevy with a bloodred-and-black interior). Enterprising Cubans can make enough to keep gas ($4 a gallon) in their cars plus a little extra, although the government recently began a heavy crackdown on these budding entrepreneurs. Lorenzo drives a red Russian Lada with the shocks and ride of a Russian tank, but like every other Cuban, he can spot the year and make of every American car on the road from a mile away: 1958 Buick, 1942 Dodge. Just in case I am interested, he negotiates the sale of a huge gray 1948 Plymouth at a stoplight for $600.

Lorenzo is sixty-five and has a mischievous sense of humor and the lined face and rough brown hands of somebody who has worked hard all his life. He also possesses the sort of wry calm that comes from knowing that things have been better and things will get worse and how to get along—and even entertain himself—either way. He picked up his rudimentary English in Miami, where he lived from 1953 to 1961 and where he drove a truck and worked in construction. He left Havana in the first place because "I had no work. There were many problems. The police were killing people in the streets." He came back—in a year that did not see a lot of movement from Miami to Cuba—"because I am Cuban." Later I ask him how he feels about Cuba now. "I think everything is going to be better in a few years. They are making changes in the government, a change of ideas. We have to wait a few years, a few times." Pause. "Of course, it could be many years, many times."

Peter and Emily are much impressed by the extraordinary helpfulness of my hypocritical government, so we decide to celebrate at the Nacional, a grand, well-manicured pile. During the Havana Film Festival, all the movie people set up camp here; serious European businessmen are the hotel's most steady customers. Security is tight and the hookers are provided by the hotel, so there is no loitering in the lobby for pickups. Outside on the terrace, two Italians with bulging briefcases and beautifully monogrammed fine cotton shirts are poring over taxes. We sit down at a wicker table and order three daiquiris. The waiter rolls his eyes. "No daiquiris." Why not? "The machine is broken." The fabled Cuban bartender is not what he used to be.

That night Emily calls me at the Valencia. She wants to know if I would like to talk to Jorge, an acquaintance who was jailed a few months earlier for *peligrosidad* ("dangerousness," a broad-based excuse for controlling "antisocial" elements for which the most common sentence is two to four years in an agricultural camp). He has bribed the guard for one night out—his daughter had turned three the day before. She and Roberto bring him to the hotel, and we sit in the courtyard (Cubans are not allowed in rooms anywhere except the government-run "love hotels," where couples go for an hour of privacy not available in the average overcrowded dwelling). We drink beer and pretend to talk about music. Jorge tells me he was imprisoned once before, in 1986, for distributing "enemy propaganda." At the time he had been active in the PNP, the Partido Nacional Popular, a small group campaigning for democracy in Cuba and for economic support for the cause from abroad. After his release he distanced himself from the party, kept a low profile, and tried to get work as a trumpeter. He doesn't know why he was jailed this time, only that someone from the SUVP (Sistema Único Vigilancia y Protección), yet another group composed of civilians and the military who pass along information to the police, turned him in, and that he was arrested standing in the doorway of his own house. He was brought to the police station, interviewed by the *jefe superior,* "chief civilian spy," and put in a cell. After two days he was shown a *denuncia,* a file of information listing his supposed activities, which included unnamed "clandestine acts against the government," typed up and signed by the *jefe superior.* Eleven days later, he was handcuffed and escorted to his trial, "a piece of theater" at which he was introduced to his lawyer, a young man just out of law school. The *denuncia* was read, Jorge repeated his original statement of innocence, the court countered by reading a list of his activities from 1981 to 1986 for which he had already been jailed, and he was told to sit down. Within fifteen minutes, six more people were tried, and, after a five-minute break, the verdicts, all guilty, were read. Jorge got two years and the right to appeal.

The appeal was a replay of the first trial, except this time the same lawyer represented eleven people whose appeals took three minutes apiece. In the cell beneath the "tribunal" that day there were 170 people waiting to be tried for the same crime. Everyone went to prison and all but two were black. Castro makes much of the racism in America and told a reporter just a few months ago that he has always "struggled against discrimination against the blacks," but this, Jorge says, is what happens to black Cubans.

He has the look of a studious Ivy Leaguer in his khakis, horn-rimmed glasses, and clean white shirt. He is also amazingly composed for a man who has to slip back into a jail cell before dawn, who is facing another year and a half imprisonment, and who could get another eight years just for sitting here talking to me. I tell him so, and he tells me he has "come to terms" that "far worse could have happened" to him. He didn't tell the authorities about his high blood pressure, so he could work outside in relatively lax conditions. He and his fellow inmates, again predominantly black, cultivate food at a prison farm outside Havana for the enjoyment of the bureaucrats in the Ministry of the Interior. Though punishment for political activity in prison is another ten to fifteen years, he says he has tried nonetheless to get fellow inmates interested in what is happening to them. "It was like beating my head against the wall. Ninety percent were completely uninterested." He uses the words robotic, numbed, separate. "They had questions that showed they didn't have any idea of what I was talking about. They have no concept of what democracy is." But it is no different on the outside. "Most Cubans don't know what to do. People know more about the risks they run by acting on ideology than the benefits, and the system, obviously, encourages that. . . . Most people try to get on with their lives outside the political system."

It ain't easy. The next morning we are summoned for another lineup, a big deal this time, at the main police station. We are taken to an office on the second floor where we sit facing a cop wearing a Chicago Bulls T-shirt. I recognize him from the day Emily and I made our report, but he says nothing. On the wall is another photograph of Charlie Chaplin. We sit. After about twenty minutes, Emily asks him what we are waiting for. Nothing, apparently, because he immediately jumps up and takes us downstairs. We violated, says Emily, the first rule of survival in Cuba: Never sit down.

The suspects are lined up in a courtyard, and we are told to look at them through the slats of louvered shutters. "The guy you want," says the cop in charge, "is the one in the middle with the green pants. If you don't want him, you want the guy on the end in the shorts." Thus instructed, we are assured that we won't have to be present for the trial. Given my conversation with Jorge, I have to laugh out loud. We look through the slats. No one remotely matching the description we've given is standing there (four of the five are black), though the guy in the green pants and the guy in the shorts looks distinctly jittery. Later that day Peter sees the real perpetrator outside the same burned-out church. He vanishes instantly, of course, but it's a funny place for a guy with a bankroll, a passport, and a plane ticket to Mexico to be.

Outside, near the station, people are lined up for tickets that will entitle them to a single hamburger, for which they will then have to stand in another line on another day. A hamburger is nothing short of a miracle, and the line goes on for blocks and blocks, a common enough sight. But then I see a guy coming down the street, past the line, through the filth and the rubble and the listless, mangy dogs, carrying with one hand, high above his head like a sprightly waiter, an enormous, lavishly decorated sheet cake with shiny icing and bright pink-and-turquoise roses. Speechless for about the fifth time that day, I look at Emily, who explains that in the benevolent tradition of wedding beer, the government still provides birthday cakes for kids under ten.

Peter goes off to photograph the Casa de la Obra Pía, now a museum, part of which is dedicated to Alejo Carpentier, Communist Cuba's most famous novelist. His Volkswagen Beetle is on display in a room on the first floor along with some of his manuscript pages and his raincoat, which is rather stylishly thrown over his old desk chair. The rest of the house, built in the seventeenth century, is stunningly beautiful and extremely well kept, an oasis in the middle of crumbling buildings held up by leaning scaffolds. I go off to the Museum of the Ministry of the Interior, unquestionably the most entertaining place in Havana. In the front rooms there are the weapons and even the Dopp kits used by Fidel et al. during their successful landing, but that is not the point. The point is the room dominated by an enormous CIA seal with huge cartoon darts stuck in it. It is a shrine to the ineptitude of American intelligence. There are countless photos from Cuban intelligence featuring the hapless American CIA agents hiding fake logs filled with film in wooded areas, and countless photos of the equally hapless agents who come to pick them up and can't understand why there is nothing inside. On display are wooden train sets, shoe trees, clothes brushes, fake rocks, and trick briefcases, all meant to hide things and all with their hiding places exposed. There is a cupboard with a briefcase in the baseboard and a transmitter that was hidden in the briefcase. There are cameras that look like Bic lighters. And there is my favorite: an entire display case devoted to the agents' confiscated sport shirts, bearing the familiar logos of Fred Perry and Izod Lacoste.

At the end of the day, we compare notes. While Peter was taking pictures, a class of primary-school children had come in in their red jumpers with matching pioneer scarves. Until they reach junior high school age, the young students wear these uniforms and recite every day that "we are pioneers for Communism; we will be like Che." The teacher asks Peter shyly if they can watch, explaining that she has taught them about photography. Peter says sure but warns that he is taking long exposures, movement will ruin them, so thirty nine-year-olds stand frozen for an hour watching him work, while the teacher explains why he takes Polaroids first, the difference between a Hasselblad and other cameras. At one point she asks the class, "If the speed is a thirtieth and the f-stop is eight, what would the f-stop be if the speed was a sixtieth?" A little boy raises his hand: "Five point six." Of course, he has no camera.

The hotel had seemed safe enough for Jorge's visit, so in the afternoon, Emily and Roberto arrive with Lazaro, a very different breed of disaffected Cuban. ("Cuba attracts extremes," says Emily. "That's why it's so problematic.") We drink more beer and pretend to talk about more music. I have been reading *Trading with the Enemy*, a boring and fairly sympathetic account of a year in Havana by Tom Miller, and it is on the table. Lazaro is dressed in $150 Converse high-tops, a souvenir from his days in America, where he went in the Mariel boatlift, the largest single influx of Cubans to the United States. He had been one of the original 10,800 Cubans who stormed the Peruvian embassy and refused to leave for fifteen days, prompting Castro to let them go—along with another 118,000 of their countrymen, many of whom were inmates from prisons and mental hospitals. If Lazaro wasn't a criminal before he left, he made up for lost time in America. After his arrival in 1980, he ended up in Detroit, where he noticed that crack dealers were living better than Ford Motor Company assembly-line workers, which he happened to be. He made a career change that landed him in penitentiaries in Michigan, New York, and Georgia before the US government provided him with his return trip to Cuba. He is currently trying to get back to the States the only way he can, by boat. He made an attempt with two others in an inner tube last January but was forced back by the weather. One of his friends drowned. Now he is paying "little by little" the $150 fee that will go for a seat on a motorboat (passage on boats can be provided by fishermen, exiles from Florida, or even drug runners heading back to the States). He says that if he makes it this time, he intends to behave himself. "When I go to the US, I was twenty-six. Now I am forty-one. I have learned."

Lazaro is very bright and very funny and very desperate. His conversation is peppered with references to American status symbols like Johnnie Walker and Hennessy. He says his sneakers are falling apart, he has lost what minuscule rights he had as a Cuban because he is an *excluible*: He has been deported from America. "I feel like an alien," he says, so for a dose of the promised land he listens "every day" to R&B on AM 1040 from West Palm Beach. Weeks later I visit the Cuban American National Foundation in Miami (CANF, the largest and by far the richest and most powerful of the exile groups, considers itself the Cuban government in exile and is more or less treated as such by the administration). The staff show me their own radio station, which broadcasts to Cubans renditions of the latest atrocities: how many were beaten in what jails, who was killed trying to escape, the latest medical and food shortages, all information gleaned from refugees and phone lines rigged from Cuba to Canada and back to Miami. It is not hard to understand why Lazaro—and everybody else in Cuba—prefers pop radio. Lazaro picks up my book and looks at the price on the inside jacket nap. "Twenty-four dollars. Shit. I could tell you everything in this book." I ask him if he is frightened, referring to the impending boat trip, but he is thinking of something else. "Yes," he says. "I have no job, and I could get thrown in jail. I want only one thing, to arrive in the United States or die."

Not twenty minutes after he leaves, Emily returns, breathless, to tell us that Roberto and Lazaro have been stopped by the police and threatened with imprisonment. They are told that I am with the CIA, that they know there was "propaganda" on the table where we talked, that they have a tape of the conversation, which is doubtful because we were outside on the second-floor balcony and anywhere outside in Cuba is incredibly noisy. What I realize they do have is a description from the maid who doesn't speak English but who had taken a keen interest in cleaning the room nearest to where we were sitting. Back at the hotel there's a guy on a bike who says he found my passport in a trash can and that he has left it at the Habana Libre (formerly the Havana Hilton) for safekeeping. This is too much. I tell him I am ill and to come back tomorrow.

The next day the passport man, dressed in Italian designer jeans and wearing lots of gold jewelry, is back and I ask him how he found me. He says he went to every tourist hotel in Havana until he got to the Habana Libre, where the desk clerk advised him to leave the passport as it was too dangerous to carry around. I still don't know how he got to the Valencia, but Emily and I meet him at the hotel anyway, I give him some money, and we are thrown into another nightmarish journey inside the Cuban bureaucracy. The desk clerk tells us yes, she did have the passport, but now it is at the central immigration office in Miramar: the Beverly Hills of Havana, home of the embassies and diplomatic residences and Fidel, though no one knows which of his several houses he is in when. We go to immigration, and they have no idea what we're talking about. We go back to the Habana Libre, where I threaten to kill the desk clerk, who has become totally unresponsive, until finally she directs us to the immigration office in the hotel about two feet away. The man there says another man does in fact have my passport and that he had intended to be here with it but his child has been hurt and is in the hospital. He swears the man will bring it to me in the morning.

The next morning there is a knock on the door at dawn. I go down with a bag of candy for the kid and condolences for the man. I am an idiot. The guy who hands me my passport looks very familiar. Right. He is the guy who has been standing around our hotel since my arrival; he's the guy having the friendly chats with Lorenzo every morning and with the desk clerk every afternoon. He was with the police when they questioned Roberto and Lazaro; he works for the Ministry of the Interior— our MININT man. In his almost nonexistent English he finally gets across to me what he wants to know: "Why are you talking to Cubans?"

Because, I tell him, they are such nice people and I am extremely interested in the music of this wonderful country.

Every day I have gone back to the United States Interest Section to pick up my money (which means I've had my picture taken another dozen or so times), but I have not been high on the State Department's list of priorities. All I am waiting for is a cable saying that my office has wired money to Washington. It finally arrives, and I take it to the Interest Section's bank and the teller hands me some cash. While I'm there, I decide to tell my helpful young non-law-enforcement officer that I no longer need a passport. He is looking a bit worse for the wear. When I ask what happened to him, a secretary tells me that he had "TV duty" before he can stop her—"That's classified." Too late. I find out that everybody in the place, even the top honchos, have to spend about one night a month riding around Havana—in his case on a bicycle—from 3:00 a.m. until dawn "assessing the effectiveness" of TV Martí, the TV station developed at the behest of CANF, paid for with $10 million a year of taxpayers' money and beamed on a signal that can be received by Cuban television sets only in the wee, wee hours. So far, after months of "research," no one has ever been found watching the station, except those who are applying for tourist visas. The only place it is watched is on the big-screen TV in the giant waiting room of the US Interest Section.

Emily has to fly to Cancún to renew her visa, but before she goes she introduces me to Pedro, a draftsman who has agreed to help Peter find some houses that people actually live in. His dedication to this task is almost embarrassing in its generosity until I realize that he is dying for something to do. He is well educated but has very little work and no outlet for his creativity (much has been made of the revolution's great strides in education for all the people, and it's true, but so what—kids know about f-stops but have no access to cameras, draftsmen have nothing to draw); he is gay in a country that persecutes gays (early on Castro said a homosexual could never "embody the conditions and requirements of . . . a true revolutionary"). The first thing Pedro says to me is "I have heard that the newspapers are very good in America, yes?" In Cuba, of course, there is only one, *Granma*, named after Fidel's famous yacht, and Fidel is de facto editor in chief. He asks me if I like Cuba. I tell him yes, very much—it is, after all, still his country, and I am a visitor here—but he laughs quietly. "I don't like Cuba. It is very difficult to live here." Later he wrestles with more words: "Everything is very scarce here, both materially and spiritually. You cannot have the friends you want."

He takes us first to a small modern apartment building in Miramar. He is nervous and proud and explains that he has heard that these are "some of the most beautifully decorated houses in Cuba," meaning they are decorated with things produced after 1959. They are the homes of people of privilege, members of what is left of the Communist elite, people with connections to the government. However, during this "special period in peacetime," as Fidel likes to call it, the connections don't seem to be worth much anymore. In the upstairs apartment, I am shown batik-covered sofas and chrome tables and the ubiquitous photo of Charlie Chaplin. "We like him very much." Pause. "Would you like to buy some lamps?" Downstairs, an obscene amount of produce—cabbages, peppers, and onions, which I hadn't seen—is piled up in baskets all over the place, a badge of prosperity for the visitors. An architect who has been allowed to travel freely to America—once to an art exhibit in "Dallas. Dallas, Texas"—lives here with his wife. They have a canary in a cage, a Goldstar VCR, a Sony stereo with Mozart playing, fake Tiffany lamps. To be polite, Peter takes a picture. How can we tell them their house looks like an upscale seventies dorm room? In return for the photograph they ask for $20. "We don't have economical problems now but . . ." On the drive back to Old Havana I see a billboard: BEAUTIFUL CITY, BEAUTIFUL LIFE.

In Emily's absence we have also acquired Omara, a Naomi Campbell look-alike with a close-cropped Afro, blue eye shadow (everybody wears it—the makeup stopped in the fifties too), a tortured expression, and flawless English. Omara works for an international company involved with cultural exchange. More than anything she wants to go abroad to continue her education, an arduous process that requires an invitation from someone abroad who will also pay your way, and an endless wait for permission and a passport from the state. She accompanies us to the 1830, a ludicrous place on the *malecón* built in the twenties as the private home of a rich Cuban, and now a restaurant complete with an elaborate grotto made of shell and coral, and a cage that houses a baboon. While Peter takes pictures of the grotto, Omara looks at the houses he has photographed in *The World of Interiors* and cries. "This is an impossible dream."

Meanwhile Peter has gained an assistant, Luis, eleven. I know this because he takes his identification card out of his tiny pants pocket and views it through the camera. It is probably his only possession. Like Pedro, he is thrilled to have a project—he throws away empty film packets, points out the prettiest coral patterns, gets the attention of the baboon, whose name, he informs me, is Niño, meaning child. The baboon has even more produce in his cage than the commie architect. Lorenzo, Peter, Omara, and I have the usual tasteless lunch in the dining room, where the band features a grand piano, an accordion, and castanets. By now Lorenzo is used to the good life—Peter had remarked earlier in the day that before long he would be driving while Lorenzo and I sat in the backseat smoking his cigarettes—but we have to force Omara, who is as skinny as a rail, to order more than a tiny appetizer. She is terrified of doing something wrong.

Next we go to an apartment where two spinster sisters have lived for forty-seven years. It was the home of their great-uncle, who was a dentist and who had bought all the fine things in the rooms. I had been, unannounced, to see them earlier in the week. They had been having lunch—black beans and rice, the awful pale tomatoes—alone in the kitchen on fine old china. Their hair had been in curlers though they seldom leave the house. Now their hair is curled and down; they have put on lipstick and made tea to receive us. We tell them how beautiful their home is, but they are embarrassed. "It used to be very beautiful, but we don't have any materials to repair it now. It is in decay." The canvases of the oil paintings have worn through to the wall, and the upholstered furniture is covered in deeply yellowed plastic, which they lift to reveal pristine white damask. They pose and then the elder sister takes me to the bedroom and points to the soap I had given her a few days before. She speaks no English, but she has been rehearsing: "Thank you so very much," she says carefully, and kisses me on both cheeks.

Upstairs, the neighbors' entire apartment has fallen in, and the young couple and their son who live there are forced to camp out in the kitchen. The kid just turned six, so they bring down what is left of his birthday cake courtesy of the state. He has on a Monte Carlo T-shirt and is too shy to pose for the Polaroid his mother desperately wants taken of him. He lets me tickle him and in return he gives me affectionate bites on the stomach. When we leave he says, "Please don't leave us. Why do you have to go?" On my previous visit I had brought him a heart full of candy, and now he wants to give me something back. He whispers to his mother, runs upstairs, and returns with a carved pair of palm trees on a base that says CUBA. "You have to put it on top of your TV." At Lorenzo's it is the same. He has asked Peter to take a picture of him with his grandchildren. When we're done, his daughter-in-law comes running out to the car and presses a frozen lobster tail into my hand.

All this goodwill from these suffering people is about to kill me. Earlier, the maid at the hotel had taken four days to muster the courage to ask me for an eyebrow pencil she had seen in my room. I know she spied on us, but she had no choice—it is the fact of life in the current Cuba. When I gave it to her, she literally cried with joy. But for people who allow themselves to dream of something more than a Shiseido crayon, life is almost unbearable.

When Emily returns, she is very tense. She was grilled at the airport for two hours about where she had been staying in Havana—they are only happy to have foreigners if they are spending money—so she has had to check into a fleabag hotel in case she was followed. Lazaro has been picked up again, and the police have come by Roberto's mother's house looking for him, so he is afraid to go outside. On top of that, she has seen Ramon in the square trying to sell his guitar, the last thing he owns, because his wife has just had a baby.

I decide this is a good time for all of us to get out of town. I want to go to Varadero, the beach resort that is supposed to save the Cuban economy. A German company called LTI has put up two enormous hotels, which are already at full occupancy, and a third is under construction. (In reality, tourism is little more than a salve. Only 460,000 tourists visited Cuba in 1992, compared with the 705,000 who went to Costa Rica, which has only one-quarter of Cuba's population. Many come out of curiosity and don't return, and the industry must spend so much importing the simple basics tourists demand that profits are small. Moreover, there is a tourist apartheid bitterly resented by the Cuban people.) We set off, past the hideous smokestacks of the refineries billowing clouds of jet black smoke, past what used to be the Havana Country Club and the finest golf course in all of Latin America, where they now practice military maneuvers, past one of the old rum distilleries that was confiscated and that now produces Havana Club. In Matanzas, birthplace of the rumba, we stop for lunch. The sign welcoming us to the city depicts a giant-size Fidel in a tank, but there aren't even any cars around. In the Hotel Louvre, full of Spanish antiques and untouched for at least a half century, we eat black beans and rice, all they have, and watch the birds fly around the courtyard.

Varadero looks like an Olympic Village circa 1969. Thousands of German and Canadian tourists are crammed into hotels whose lobbies feature geometric orange furniture and gift shops that sell the Spanish celebrity gossip magazine *Hola!* and *Tomorrow Is Too Late*, by Fidel Castro, and purple baseball caps that say VARADERO BEACH and statues of the ever-present Chaplin. By the pool, people eat spaghetti Bolognese and crinkle-cut french fries and peach Melba and sign up for volleyball and Ping-Pong and dance to "Guantanamera" (we hear that song no less than a half dozen times a day, and every time I flash to Vanessa Redgrave singing it in full combat fatigues at London's Royal Albert Hall as a gesture of support for Fidel—one of those indelible sixties images like Jane Fonda at the controls of an antiaircraft gun in Hanoi). A bridge over the pool spells LOVE in big yellow letters. An LTI official, an Irishman who speaks with a German accent, tells me that Fidel showed up for both ribbon cuttings, and that his biggest problem is that his workforce, all these "people trained to be engineers or lawyers or whatever, who now find themselves superfluous . . . have no concept of food and beverage management." We could be anywhere but Cuba until we pass some lone official graffiti: DURING THE SPECIAL PERIOD WE MUST PROVE WE ARE CARRYING OUT THE WISHES OF FIDEL.

On the trip back, dozens of people emerge from the brush holding up something to sell. Squash, two for a dollar. An enormous stalk of bananas, $2.50. The sellers appear and disappear faster than lightning—this is extremely illegal—but I feel like we are driving from aisle to aisle at the Winn-Dixie. In the end Emily and Lorenzo decide to share a ten-pound bag of black beans, which are rationed in the stores and rarely available anymore, even in the tourist restaurants; a bag of tomatoes for $2; and the bananas, enough food for a month. Lorenzo nixes the chicken a woman holds up by its hind legs and offers for $5. "Maybe if it was killed and plucked and cleaned . . ." The last billboard before Havana says, COUNTRY BEFORE EVERYTHING.

Before Peter leaves, I check into the newly renovated and much less intimate Sevilla. At the Valencia one of the clerks is spying now with such gusto that it is starting to irritate me. Even Lorenzo, who has not shut up for two weeks, has ceased to speak. Pedro has told me that he saw the MININT man in the car with Lorenzo, which explains his silence—we've been bugged. I hate this for Lorenzo far worse than for me. He asks me what my room number at the Sevilla is and he can hardly bring himself to get the words out. He drives us to the airport for Peter's flight home, and when I return, there is a note from Ramon (the Valencia has sent him here, although I certainly didn't tell them where I was going). His mother and his newborn baby have been hit by a bus and he is desperate to see me. They need medicine and he has no money.

The next day Ramon shows up with his prescriptions and I give him some money, which still may not get him what he needs. Like the educational system, the health-care system is held up as the great achievement of the revolution. However, now there are very few antibiotics available, no painkillers, not even aspirin, and abortion is the number one method of birth control (so much for the much-vaunted great strides of women).

I wish Ramon luck and head to the Habana Libre, where I run into Sam, a producer for an upcoming BBC documentary in which an interviewer will talk to "real Cubans." Emily has been helping him, but he has given me a wide berth because he is terrified that he will be tainted by association with the agitator, and I don't blame him, but at last we meet in the hotel phone room, where everyone in Havana who needs to make a phone call ultimately ends up.

Sam "loves a good show," so we go check out La Maison, the "house of fashion" that the "fabulous house" lady had told me about. It is basically a state-run whorehouse where female tourists come to shop in the sort of duty-free stores in the complex and the men sit outside and eat lobster and watch the "fashion show" on the runway and choose their girl or boy. We go to Tropicana, which is not as tawdry as I expected but quite spectacular, and El Floridita, "cradle of the daiquiri," where Hemingway propped up the bar. But the best show in town is well off the tourist track, a "nightclub" on the edge of the black ghetto known as Colón.

It is run by a woman named Yoya, an older Tina Turner look-alike whose pictures adorn the walls of the club, which also happens to be her house. There is only one room, and the bar consists of a door on some sawhorses. A guy who must be one hundred years old pours some unbelievably powerful homemade rum into an assortment of chipped mugs and glasses for $1 a shot. But the music is the thing. The group of people crammed into the room take turns doing what they are otherwise hard-pressed to do—they play and sing. A man with a fiddle held together by wire and glue plays it like a guitar. A deeply beautiful girl with jet black hair and pale white skin plays the bongos; another plays the trumpet. Behind the bar, the only place where there is space, is a guy with an enormous bass, also cracked and wired together. Yoya gyrates and sings while her son, Papito, a singer and a dancer, literally swings from the rafters. She is larger than life and bombed out of her mind. She tells us we are honored guests and dances with Sam. When she makes us write in the "comment book," there are simply no words.

Lorenzo's still not talking, so I give him the day off and meet

Orlando, a "private" driver Sam found in front of the Habana Libre. Orlando is the former chairman of the Havana Chamber of Commerce, but he has just spent an entire month's wages for a single part for his car—a fifteen-year-old steering column switch that still doesn't work well. He shows us photographs of his time in London, where he went in the seventies "on a trade mission to procure parts."

There are shots of him in front of Buckingham Palace, in front of the Tower of London, and at Karl Marx's grave, where he felt, he says, "great emotion. I could hardly believe I was standing on Carlos Marx's grave." He proudly shows me his tattered twenty-year-old business card and I begin to copy his full name. He grabs it back. "Please don't write my name. I want to continue working when you leave." We are having lunch out of town with Emily and Roberto. I ask Roberto if he, too, would feel great emotion at Marx's grave. "I would put a bomb under it." On the way back into Havana we are overtaken by Fidel's motorcade—three identical black Mercedes that constantly switch positions, with Ladas in the lead and in the rear.

After lunch Sam meets Rafael, chief press attaché for the state, who has said he will arrange for some Cubans to go on-camera: "Some very nice leaders of the CDR in some very beautiful neighborhoods." (Rafael himself declines to go on-camera because he is hoping for a posting in Rome.) Back at the hotel, Ramon is waiting. I'd already given him more money outside El Floridita, where he'd materialized the night before, but he says he needs to talk to Emily and me someplace neutral, so we meet at the Don Giovanni. Our presence here is certainly not suspect—we have eaten lunch here every single day because Lorenzo gets a percentage when he brings tourists. Ramon has on two-toned red-and-white wing tips that he has achieved with Mercurochrome and informs us that he knows who has the stolen money: Nemesio. Ramon's friend in the police department has seen it. Emily looks at me: "This is irresistible."

We have not been called for a lineup since the last charade, but I was finally shown photos of the real guy. After that we heard nothing and it has been more than a week, so we march into the main police station.

No one stops us so we go upstairs and demand to see Nemesio. We are told he is in a police-training class, so Emily writes him a threatening letter. A French tourist comes in to complain that all his money has been stolen from his room in the same hotel Emily is in. We go back to check on hers, and it is gone, too.

When we return, Nemesio is waiting with "his lawyer," who locks the door to his office once we are inside. I tell him that we have it on good authority that Nemesio has the money. The "lawyer" takes a leather strap from his drawer and begins to slap it against the palm of his hand. He informs me that I am in very big trouble, that I could be sent to jail for "defaming the police department." (Defamation is a serious crime in Cuba—María Elena Cruz Varela, who won her country's 1989 poetry prize, was dragged out of her house by her hair, forced to eat her manuscript, and jailed for a year and a half on the grounds that her poems "defamed state institutions.") I smile at him and tell him he can beat me or throw me in jail if he likes, but the MININT man outside will grow concerned about my whereabouts—he won't have anything to do if he can't follow me. Nemesio and Emily are looking very nervous. The "lawyer" backs off and asks me if I still plan to leave on Sunday, although I had never told him my departure date. I tell him I have no plans to leave at all until all the money is returned.

Outside, however, I figure it may be time to split. So I start my rounds of goodbyes. Pedro asks me to send him an American flag and magazines on architecture and parapsychology. "I love you very much. Please do not forget me." That night Sam and I have a drink with Sophia at her apartment. Outside, the entire neighborhood is lined up on folding chairs—their electricity is blacked out and Sophia has a generator. We are the show.

I pay a call on my diplomat, the one who laughed at my early innocence. He tells me that the United States must drop the embargo or suffer the consequences. That trade would lead to economic choice that would wake Cubans up to social and political choice they don't even know exists, and it would be Castro who would become superfluous. That unless we put down some economic roots and stem the tide of petty crime bred by the black market and motivate the Cubans to be reliable players, teach them accountability, there will be a vacuum when Fidel finally goes. That CANF relishes the vacuum because the argument that they should be the ones to fill it will be stronger—they know Cuba, they are close, etcetera—but their presence would likely lead to civil unrest (I've never met a single Cuban who welcomed intervention from Miami in any form but money) and that Cuba would fall prey to organized crime and drug running. "People with the real power will be the guys with the tommy guns and the bucks. Those people who had been hoping to make a constructive contribution to Cuba would be discouraged. If something like that does happen here, the drugs and the human flotsam will go straight to your country and that will be directly attributed to a failure to try and put in place an economic base." The only hope, he tells me, is to "make Cuba legitimately strong in economic terms while Castro still provides stability."

CANF argues that to spend a dime in Cuba or to send a dollar over is to "prolong the agony of the Cuban people," that the embargo forced Fidel to legalize the dollar, and the negotiations can only begin if Fidel is gone. But Castro is not about to depart because we say so, and having seen the "agony of the Cuban people," I must agree with the diplomat. Our embargo is not only dated and shortsighted in terms of our own interests, it makes Fidel a martyr, it gives him an excuse to crack down even harder on internal democracy movements and to deny civil rights, and it is simply cruel. "We wonder how much of the mistakes made [by Castro] are attributed to your embargo," an artist—a Communist, even—said to me. "I think the authorities like it. They say everything is the embargo's fault."

I do not relish the prospect of returning through Cancún, and I have no plane ticket anyway, so my buddies at the US Interest Section tell me to get on one of the twice-daily charter flights from Havana to Miami. Show your business card to the people at the charter desk, they assure me; there will be no problem. They've been right so far, but I should have known this was too simple. I have nothing saying it's OK for me to be here—they will get in trouble from the other side. I lie and tell them I had a visa but it was stolen and produce the police report. I am making headway. They want to know if I have anything besides a business card to prove I am a journalist. There is a half hour before the flight. Emily and I race back into town and get a *Vogue* that is at Roberto's sister's house. It has my picture in it. It doesn't help. I am not getting on that plane, but I'm actually relieved. I don't want to go. I can't bear to leave Emily in the fleabag with Roberto on the lam, and Lorenzo is even starting to speak again. On the way to the airport we passed the insane asylum and he told us to "look at the crazy peoples."

Two days later, after much money has changed hands, I am on the plane at last. In the back a man sings "Guantanamera." There is no escaping it. The woman behind me holds her head in her hands and sobs for the whole hour.

Back in America, the overwhelming sensation is one of boredom. Being in Cuba is like being on a drug. It is surreal and addictive. I miss the enormous affection and stunning dignity of the people and the strong bonds so immediately forged. I miss the sense of living inside a drama unfolding, but it continues without me. Sam sends me word that Roberto has had to leave Havana, that he was finally arrested but managed to escape. I get a letter from Emily saying that many more cops are in the streets, that Fidel has launched a huge crackdown on all black-market activity, that at night in targeted areas like Colón people run from doorway to doorway, knowing they could be picked up for any reason. Sophia sends me word that 119 people have camped out in the Belgian ambassador's residence demanding asylum and that twenty-one more crashed the gates of the German embassy, but that "the people are still not bloodthirsty. The police state is too secure."

I read in the paper that the head of the Havana Film Festival is seeking asylum in the United States and that Jorge Mas Canosa, the Miami-based head of CANF, has met with the Colombian president and convinced him not to sell much-needed oil to Cuba. There is a rumor that Fidel is dead, and I heard through the grapevine that Mas Canosa is already talking about an interim government. I meet with a man at CANF, a Cuban American who refers to Mas Canosa as "the Cuban leader in exile," and to the Cubans in Cuba as "them." He tells me that he knows "these are jovial people who like to dance and drink rum," even though he himself has never been there. I meet with an American economist who has met with Castro's representatives in Havana. "They are ready to sit down and negotiate with no preconditions, which is hardly outrageous." But candidate Clinton wanted to carry Florida and promised CANF that would never happen. Anyway, Cuba is very low on anybody's list of foreign policy priorities, though it will ultimately affect us a lot more directly than Bosnia or even Haiti. We will continue to impose unspeakable suffering on the Cuban people in hopes they will finally rise up in arms against the only leader most of them have ever known. This is absurd and irresponsible, but the way it is. "Something will happen within the next five years," says the economist. "It's just a question of whether we are there or not."

Anyway, anybody with enough energy or strength to rise up and do anything opts to leave. The coast guard reports that as of June 1994, 3,854 refugees had already landed in Florida this year compared with 3,656, the total for all of 1993. I go see a man in Key West, a Cuban who houses and feeds refugees until they are picked up and processed and delivered to family or jobs or whatever. His office wall is completely covered with thousands of bits of paper—the names of the people who did not make it all the way, gleaned from the people who did. At 3:00 a.m. he calls me: Two sets of boys, thirteen of them in all, have just washed up. I speak to Albert, who is twenty. He had tried to leave once before but turned back due to bad weather. He was arrested and lost his job. It took him six days to get here; he lived on boiled eggs and sugar water. Now he wants to work and finish school, a goal worth leaving "my mama, my sister, my brother" for. He has on brand-new Keds and a Budweiser baseball cap from the "transit home" closet. I ask him if he was scared. "Oh yes, we lost our oars and fell in the water every time a big ship came. But I called to God." And suddenly I think of cagey Lazaro with his dreams of new sneakers and Johnnie Walker and wonder which of his two stated options God dealt him: death or salvation.

17

Slow Train to China

(1995)

When I was too young to be in charge of my own destiny, I spent four summers at camp, and after that, for two years I went to boarding school. Since then I have planned my life very carefully so that I never have to be in the company of more than one hundred women at one time. And then in August, two weeks before my thirty-fifth birthday, I find myself on the trans-Siberian railway with 150 feminists bound for Beijing and the United Nations Fourth World Conference on Women.

It is called "Femmes en Train Pour Pékin," and it was organized so that its passengers, women participating in the Non-Governmental Organizations (NGO) Forum held in conjunction with the conference, can conduct "dialogs" and write songs and stuff in preparation for the fantastic femmes fest ahead. Everybody kept telling me how funny it would be. I did not think it would be funny. I'd spent most of the summer watching Barbara Boxer's self-righteous self raving about the pathetic antics of Robert Packwood on television every night and getting deeply depressed over the newspaper every morning as the UN systematically abandoned "safe areas" it had promised to protect in Bosnia. I am sick of women, and I am sick of the UN, and I've never understood the purpose of conferences except that they make the people who attend them feel very important.

Last year the UN held a conference on population control in Cairo at which the delegates pledged to spend $17 billion on family planning in developing countries by the year 2000. And now it's staging a $30 million women's conference in a place where family planning consists of murdering girl citizens before they get to be women. For months before the conference, women from all over the world met in New York to draft a "platform for action" that says really earth-shattering stuff like "girls are the women of tomorrow," and which advocates "government action" to "promote a positive, balanced, and non-stereotyped portrayal of women in the media." So much for freedom of the press. The declaration almost never mentions the word *sex*, referring instead to the female *gender*. According to the head of the newly renamed Gender, Population, and Development Branch of the UN's Fund for Population, "Gender refers to socially constructed roles, and gender roles change. Sex does not."

Since I have no intention of ever, on purpose, being around people who get paid to talk that way, I am not actually going to the conference. I am just going to ride the train. And not, thank God, the official United Nations train, but one organized by a group of young women based in Paris. They weren't so pompous as to dub theirs the "Peace Train," but they did state their intention to donate all the resulting literature from the train "experience" to a library in Sarajevo. Of course they didn't count on the UN abandoning the heavy-weapons exclusion zone around Sarajevo before they got back, or the Serbs shelling the place to smithereens.

In my bones, I know this is not a good idea. But like Hillary Clinton, I decide to go anyway.

Although the trip began in Paris, with festive stops in Berlin and Warsaw for local entertainment and visits to female coffeehouses, I am scheduled to get on in Moscow for "Phase 2: The Trans-Siberian Workshops." This is not as easy as it sounds, due to the fact that UPS has lost my Russian visa and British Airways takes a very dim view of passengers going to Moscow without one. I lie and insist that I have a visa waiting on the other side, and, it turns out, I do, as soon as I start waving big wads of crisp American dollar bills around. Dollars are the currency of choice in the frontier city, and the most visible woman is Cindy Crawford, whose face is emblazoned on hundreds of billboards advertising

Flex shampoo. I'm not interested in Cindy; I'm on the lookout for my feminists, and at the train station I finally catch sight of them: the only women in Moscow wearing multicolored Alain Mikli glasses and yellow and lavender whistles around their necks. The whistle wearers are German, of course, but there are others, from Holland and Poland and Italy and Spain and Belgium and Portugal and Canada. They are waving red balloons around to help identify themselves and madly chattering in French.

But then I hear a voice behind me, an American one. "Are you from the States?" Yes, I say, beaming, thrilled at the thought of a compatriot. She's beaming, too—she's from CNN and thinks she's finally found an actual American participant in this lunatic exercise. I tell her I'm working, too. "Are you getting on the train?" I ask, desperate to know. She looks at me as though I am crazy.

I may well be. As I step onto the train I am given my berth number and a brochure, which, I note with horror, lists me as a "*participante*." What if someone sees this? There is also a list of celebrity "supporters" (as opposed to benefactors who actually gave money) including Germaine Greer, Alice Walker, Kate Millett, and Floria (*sic*) Steinem. I wonder what they did to "support" the train, since they certainly don't appear to be on it. Neither are any representatives of the numerous print news organizations listed. There's Ana from a Lisbon daily; Marie from a French weekly; two women from *Paris Match*; Souâd, who writes for French *Elle*; and me.

Souâd tells me that the first five-day leg had been a nightmarish journey in which the things that always happen when a lot of women get together happened: hostile cliques, general bitchiness, the rush to judgment, and the laying of blame at each glitch along the way. The more militant women are furious that nonmilitants were allowed on and make this known loudly and often. I am profoundly grateful that I am due to disembark two days later in Novosibirsk ("New Siberia"), toward the edge of Mongolia, four full days before the rest will arrive in Beijing. Christine, a funny young woman who works for the German travel company in charge of logistics, shows it to me on the map. "You are so lucky to be getting off," she says with genuine envy. "They are like children. I could tell you enough stories to fill books already."

But Maya, the young coordinator who conceived of the trip in the first place, is determined to put the best face on things. "Since there was no time to talk about issues during those first few days, I thought the women would get closer, just making small talk, but they didn't. The worst happened, and now they have to work it out. That's a lot like life in these communities. Women have to come together." (The women, of course, didn't quite come together in Beijing, either. Despite exercises in solidarity like mass hand-holding, a Muslim organization called the lesbians "sick"; an alliance of the Vatican, Muslim fundamentalists, and American conservative women complained that the platform's language denigrated motherhood; and there was a protracted dispute over the really important issue of whether the word equality or equity was more appropriate.)

The first indication of women not coming together here comes from the ladies from *Paris Match*. They had paid for an entire compartment (each sleeps four) so that they wouldn't have to mingle, an impressive show of foresight that enrages the others and makes me hideously jealous. When I arrive at my own compartment, I am met by three gray-haired French women who simply say "Non" and refuse to let me in. At last I find the one free bed left in the place and thank God I'm no longer at the mercy of the ladies in compartment 28. "They are Parisian," Linda, a Swiss radio producer, says to me later. "What can you expect?"

I sort of expected a shower, but there is none—just a metal sink and a metal toilet that opens over the tracks. Everybody tells me repeatedly that the official UN train has a shower, the implication being that somehow the UN itself has kept us from having one. But even I can't blame the UN for our primitive latrine, or for the fact that Maya did not manage to rustle up the satellite dish and computer hookups they promised, and which the UN train has. "If you hear the whole story," Linda tells me ominously, "it seems like the UN wanted to stop this train. They are afraid there are too many free women. Some women are from organizations, but not all by any means."

It is the free women, those who came of their own accord, who are, in fact, the most interesting. Linda herself, though a journalist, came to "be with women." She is friends with Marie-Françoise, a "professional feminist" who brought her daughter along as a present for her university graduation. Marie-Françoise says she came to quit smoking, but she also hopes to regain some lost energy—both her own and that of the movement. "The women's movement in Europe is very weak right now. We're not creative enough anymore."

In the bunk above me is the very beautiful Françoise, who teaches writing workshops in Paris. She has been working with a group of fishermen's wives from the South of France who want to tell their story. The wives are my favorite women on the train, and they insist on being called "wives . . . absolutely not fishers." Though they work alongside their husbands every day, and they are the ones who actually sell the fish at the markets, they are not recognized as workers by the French government and are denied benefits. They tell me they won't receive a pension and are not allowed to send their children to state-funded day care. This is their first trip away from their husbands, the first time they have ever had passports. "We feel very small in the middle of women who have much more problems," Dominique, forty-four, modestly tells me. But I think they have the best reason to be on the train: If they are recognized in China, they hope to receive recognition in their own home villages. Dominique says shyly that there is no greater love than that between a fisherman and his wife, except maybe between a fisherman and the sea. "Please say our husbands support us a lot for making this trip."

Also in my cabin is Pia from Milan, who is very sweet and trying desperately to improve her English. She manages to tell me she went to America once, to a women's conference in Cincinnati. I respond that she must come back and visit a less dull place, but I am reprimanded by our fellow cabinmate Farrah, who demands, "Isn't that a stereotype?" I must admit that it is, and I vow to keep an open mind about all regions of my country.

Farrah is Iranian, but she has lived in Paris for several years with her children and her abusive husband. When her daughter was about to turn thirteen, Farrah realized she must set a different example for her only female child. She went into therapy, started working out, enrolled in university classes. "I read the books and the magazines; I study psychology so I know how the men arrived at this point in history, this patriarchal society." She started making her sons help around the house ("They call me the Ministry of Work"). And though she loves him very much, she finally left her husband. Now they are back together, but he hasn't changed, she says, only the relationship. "He is very nervous and fat," she says. "But he is rich. That's good for me. I need money."

The first night's dinner is Russian salad, pickles, and sardines, served by the only men on the train. The women love that they are served by men. I fall asleep reading *Smilla's Sense of Snow*, and Farrah tucks into Catherine Ponder's *The Dynamic Laws of Healing*. The next morning we have a twenty-minute stop on the platform in Kirov, where we are welcomed by a delegation of women who give us bouquets of marigolds and dahlias and roses. A German woman with a crew cut is so moved by this that she clutches her dahlia, crying. There are members of two singing groups, Zarmazones and Mafucage, on the train, and they lead everyone in a sort of Indian war whoop, the kind you used to do as a child, which seems to be the official chant of the trip. A woman who bears a striking resemblance to Leonid Brezhnev, had he been a dyed blond, makes a speech. "We are continuing our struggle against the men," she says in Russian, which is translated into English by a very chagrined male translator. "Ah, not against the men," Farrah murmurs next to me. Brezhnev continues, "If any men try to bother you, you must strangle them." The translator dutifully accompanies his translation with a strangling motion to his own neck.

After the stop we attend the morning meeting in the conference room, an empty train car with no seats whatsoever. It is hard to follow because almost every sentence is repeated in at least three languages, but one thing that's clear is that the Germans and the Italians are not getting along very well. The Germans complain about the lack of punctuality. The Italians call them Fascists. At one point Souâd interrupts the German who has taken charge, and she tells Souâd to shut up. Souâd explains innocently that it is her nature to interject. The German is unmoved. "You be quiet and keep your mouth shut." Among the topics is whether or not journalists will be allowed into the workshops. Never mind that we have been invited on the train for that express purpose; we are told that "sometimes in our work we will go very deeply, and we may not want it expressed or written." I have no intention of fighting with these people, but the brave Souâd protests. She is told that she must decide whether she is there as a journalist or a woman, whereupon she lifts her T-shirt, grabs her breasts, and says, "These are always the same."

After the meeting, a suggestion sheet goes up for workshop topics: "I'd like to make a briefing on Chinese and French nuclear testing." "I would like to do a workshop with other lesbians about our strategies in Beijing." "What can we do about women and Bosnia?" And "Has anybody bought body oil? Then I can offer a massage workshop." The afternoon schedule calls for a sing-along led by Zarmazones, who have helpfully posted some lyrics: "Trash, trash, trash all the nations/We are the feminist generation/We destroy Fascist nations/We blow up US bases/Bombs 'n' guns 'n' evolution/We're gonna make a revolution/We're gonna start an insurrection/We're gonna find a new direction."

To get some idea of what that direction might be, I have lunch with Maya. We eat an incredibly wonderful clear chicken broth with a hard-boiled egg and stare at some unidentifiable meat served with frozen french fries that have been partially thawed and drenched in cooking oil. It occurs to me that this is not a bad place to lose weight. Maya is pretty, with shoulder-length dark hair, turquoise eyes, and rimless glasses that make her look very serious. She has three rings on each finger and one on her thumb, and seems an extremely unlikely force behind this trip. She says in perfect English that she is Spanish, was born in Ireland, studied visual arts in China, left after Tiananmen Square, and got a Fulbright to Rutgers. In America she had been active in women's groups, but when she moved to Paris she was shut out by the more established organizations. "They were suspicious; they were not action groups," she says. "I wanted to harness the energy of younger women and start a dialogue between the two, to find an excuse to get women working together." The idea of the train to Beijing was born. But when the French government was slow to fund the train, the older, more "theoretical" feminists objected to Maya's lining up sponsors. "They didn't want to enter a market economy."

Maya found new allies and raised the money. "I had never coordinated anything before. I have a lot of conflicts with power. I can't accept it, so that was very destabilizing. So I had to accept myself." Now that she has, what does she hope to achieve with this expedition? "I think the train is what I wanted to achieve." Right, but what do you think the women on the train—or off the train, for that matter—should be trying to actually accomplish? "Women should be communicating. There should be more communication." Fine, I say, desperately trying to communicate. But if you objected to the older groups because they were not "action groups," what action do you think the younger women should take? (I realize I'm starting to talk like people do when they are addressing someone who does not speak their language, very slowly and really loudly.) "Well," she says again, "the train is action." I give it one more try and ask if there's anything she'd like to see come out of the conference in Beijing. "If you are fair to every woman, it's a better world," she says. "When there is less injustice, it's a better world."

This is an inarguable point, but at this moment I would sacrifice a better world for one lone cigarette. But like Marie-Françoise, I have quit smoking, so I go to the sing-along instead. The pretty young singers are explaining how to make the war whoop. They stick out their tongues and move them very quickly back and forth and up and down. Then they teach us how to hold a high note for a long time "like Algerian women." They teach us an American Indian song, they sing the "bomb the US bases" song, which makes me very nervous, and then they put everybody in groups to do a French round. "What are they saying?" I ask someone.

"'I have good tobacco in my purse; you will not have it.'" This makes me think of cigarettes again, so I leave.

In the late afternoon I talk to the head of a German group called Lesbenring. Their manifesto is posted on the door to their cabin, next door to ours. "The lesbian way of life is an alternative for women to live independently and free of male domination. . . . If a woman's erotic choice extends further, she weakens the patrimony and becomes a political actor. . . . We want the Christian churches to expressly state that lesbians are welcome to work in church institutions." That last one is their big issue. Monica, Lesbenring's leader, is a professor in a Protestant university. When I ask her if she believes in its teachings, she says, "I believe only in the feminist hierarchy. I don't believe any longer in the father in heaven, the men in heaven who say what's good or not good." (Later, when I read that the Chinese government has advised the residents of Huairou, site of the NGO forum, to wear bug spray because flies might transmit AIDS carried by lesbian women, I decide these women ought to thank their lucky stars that their biggest enemy is the German church.)

That night a porno flick is on Russian TV, and a crowd gathers to watch it in the dining car. In the conference room the Zarmazones girls are playing drums and a bass, and there is much dancing. Everybody is drinking vodka, and even Souâd is in the spirit of things. In our cabin, Farrah frets that the women are going to be sick from the vodka and the jostling of the train. "People will write that we are all lesbian, that we drink too much and watch pornographic movies." I reassure her, and she goes back to her reading. Tonight it's *Psychanalyse et Féminisme*.

When we wake, no one knows what time it is. We have passed through three time zones, but the Moscow-based train staff refuses to change the clocks. By the time the train gets to Beijing there will be a four-hour difference. "We'll be the only people in history to ever get jet-lagged on a train," says an American girl named Kathryn Turnipseed, who used to be a commercial banker at Barclays Bank in New York and now runs a group called Electronic Witches, based in Zagreb. She teaches women in Bosnia to ease their isolation by communicating with one another electronically. Today she is leading a workshop on email even though we have no computer hookups or phone links.

In the class there's a French woman named Simonne, who looks exactly like Charlotte Rampling. She runs a group called S.O.S. Re-membrement, which opposes a law in France dating from the Vichy government designed to redistribute farmland into larger, more efficient units. In addition to being unnecessary in today's economy, the law has been corrupted by government appointees and regional landowners who take the choicest land for themselves, destroying more than a million trees as well as people's property rights and livelihoods along the way. I completely agree with Simonne. I think she's so attractive, and I'm so impressed with her work. But when she shows me her clippings, there's one that stops me, the one about her inclusion in the *Guinness Book of Records*. She had parked her car outside the local prefecture in her Nor-mandy village and lived inside it—for more than two years.

I'm starting to get nervous about my instincts. Thank God I'm due to get off the train soon. When word of my imminent departure spreads, my German next-door neighbors give me letters to mail; Farrah gives me a letter in Farsi to fax to her husband. Even the militants who have glared at me for two days come to stroke my hair and tell me, "You are great." I feel like I'm at camp again and maybe I should get them all to sign my pillowcase before I leave. At dinner I buy everybody beer.

As the train pulls into Novosibirsk, Françoise and Farrah see me to the exit. Sweet Farrah cries and takes the Iranian silver chain from around her neck and gives it to me. She tells me that God has sent me to her to hear her story, because I have been telling her how brave and strong she is, how happy her life will be. Françoise and I laugh and em-brace. Christine and one of the waiters get off with me to find a taxi to my hotel. It is two o'clock in the morning, but we find a guy with a car and run toward it through the pitch-black night. Simonne is running behind me, begging me to take more letters, which I do. Finally we get to the car and I am left alone. I am thinking this may not be the best position I've ever been in, but I get in and I give him some dollars as incentive to get moving. He holds them up to his face, inhales their new-money smell, and kisses them. Then he turns on the radio. "Phil Collins," I say, uttering the only two words I can say that he will understand. "Yeah," he says, and grins. "Phil Collins."

At the hotel I take the longest, hottest shower I have ever taken in my life. By the time I get out it is time to go to the airport for the plane back to Moscow. The Novosibirsk airport defies description. The closest I can come is the Houston Livestock Show. It is chaos; every sign is written in the Cyrillic alphabet; I have no idea where the plane is or when it leaves. No one speaks English, and everybody seems to be carrying everything they own, including their dogs and cats and chickens. Finally I see an extremely well-dressed man who looks reassuringly like Tom Hanks, and I ask him if he speaks English. I had seen him in the hotel elevator. He does, in fact, speak English, and now he saves my life. He explains that the plane is late, it's always late, even though it's there. He tells me you don't give them your bag, you let them weigh it, and you check it yourself on the first floor of the former Aeroflot monstrosity. I joke that I hope the pilot isn't drunk. He says seriously that he better be; it's worse when they have the DTs.

When we land he is waiting for me. I look like hell. I don't know why this guy is being so nice to me or why I put my complete faith in him. But I do. I have to go to another airport to get out of Moscow. He tells me he'll come with me in a taxi, they're all Mafia, they'll rip me off. I feel like Blanche DuBois with all the kindness from this stranger. He has an apartment in Moscow where we go to pick up his car. He will drop me at the airport on his way to his country house, next to Rostropovich and Gorbachev. He takes me to change money, to buy caviar. At the airport, he helps me find the first plane out—to anywhere—and I buy a ticket to Frankfurt. He steers me to the restaurant where he leaves me, shaking my hand. "How will I ever thank you?" I ask breathlessly, the helpless movie maiden. "There is no need," he says, Tom Hanks–like. "Maybe now you will have a better impression of Russia."

On the plane to Frankfurt, I talk nonstop to a very attractive admiral in the Indian navy who's been in Russia buying "things." I never talk to people on planes, and now I'm giving my address to an Indian admiral. I wonder what in the world is happening to me. And then I realize that after two days and 150 women, I'm starved for male conversation. I must be emanating some kind of pheromone to that effect. Men are suddenly following me everywhere. In Frankfurt, I talk to an adorable American banker working in Moscow. In London the taxi driver gives me butterscotch and the British tabloids and tells me my boyfriend is a lucky man. It's his birthday, and I kiss him goodbye. I've been traveling for about eighteen hours, but I honestly don't think I've ever been happier. On that last night, before I got off in Novosibirsk, I had asked Marie-Françoise if she missed anything, being on the train for so long. No, she said. For a feminist like herself, the train was "true orgasm." To each her own.

18

Extreme Makeover

(2003)

The first thing you see upon landing in Kabul is a sort of accidental airplane graveyard, with bits of jet carcasses—a nose here, a wing or tail there—strewn everywhere, alongside the occasional entire passenger plane on its back, wheels sticking straight up in the air like the feet of a gigantic dead chicken. Between the dust (there are frequent, blinding dust storms) and the exhaust (the city had virtually no traffic during the rule of the Taliban—now there are almost 200,000 registered vehicles) it is almost impossible to breathe. And as you drive—slowly, harrowingly, without any visible rhyme or reason—into the center of town, it becomes apparent that much of the city is essentially a pile of rubble. Many of the buildings still standing are riddled with bullet holes; the thousands of giant metal cargo containers that used to carry American supplies over two years ago now serve as makeshift homes or businesses—a DIS-ABLED CYCLE repair shop, vegetable stands overflowing with radishes and scallions and eggplants, stores selling L&M's and Fanta and bags of dried chickpeas—and may well be Kabul's soundest structures. Before I arrived I received an email from a contact in Kabul warning me that "in some parts of the city the destruction is so awful that my mind wanted to believe I was at the site of an archaeological dig and I was looking at the ruins of an ancient city."

The author of that message is Patricia O'Connor, a British-born

marketing and development consultant to the beauty industry charged
with the seemingly unlikely task of opening a beauty school in Kabul,
smack in the middle of the chaos and destruction she described. The
idea of putting up a school in such a place makes more sense than it
sounds. Before the Taliban gained power in 1996, beauty salons were
among the few small businesses owned and operated by women. During
the Taliban's regime, clandestine salons in private houses were often the
only means by which whole families were able to survive (though the
women literally risked their lives to operate them). Given this history—
and the fact that there was a pool of Afghan American beauticians who
would likely be willing to return and share their skills—a beauty school
seemed a natural.

It all started at a *Vogue* photo shoot, where Terri Grauel, a New York
hairstylist, met Mary MacMakin, an American activist, in the winter of
2001, when the Taliban was still in power. MacMakin had been thrown
out of her adopted country by the Taliban on the grounds that she was a
spy. She wasn't, of course, but she had founded PARSA (Physiotherapy
and Rehabilitation in Support of Afghanistan), which helped women
get off the streets and broke Taliban law—by putting them in business
making traditional Afghan handicrafts that MacMakin then sold to
fellow expats and aid workers. When MacMakin returned to Afghanistan after 9/11, Grauel called and offered to sell some of the work to
her clients. MacMakin had a more ambitious idea: Why not tap into
another Afghan tradition and open a beauty school?

Grauel first recruited O'Connor, whose own interest had been piqued
by a CNN documentary that included footage of Kabul's secret salons,
to spearhead the project. MacMakin talked the women's ministry into
leasing them the space, and Grauel rounded up Afghan-born teachers
from all across America and Canada. *Vogue* kicked in $25,000 to cover
the cost of building the school and enlisted the support of the beauty
industry at a lunch in Manhattan. MAC, a division of Estée Lauder,
shot a training video in Dari (the language spoken by the majority of
Afghanistan's varied population) and created the core curriculum for
makeup. "One of the huge problems is illiteracy, so it was important

to create visual materials for the women," MAC Cosmetics president John Demsey has said. They also contributed $25,000 and a shipment of foundation, lipstick, mascara, and eye shadow worth the same amount. Clairol cut a check for $60,000, and sent loads of hair color, but, most important, the company created the school's hair-coloring curriculum (and agreed to monitor the students' progress reports via weekly email to see where the course might need to be tweaked). Paul Mitchell, Matrix (which is owned by L'Oréal), and Frédéric Fekkai all donated styling and hair-care products. Revlon sent nail polish, John Frieda donated $17,000, and the John Barrett Salon gave the proceeds of an entire week devoted to the cause. Pennsylvania's Wilkes University developed a business curriculum and helped translate all the texts for the three-month-long course, which includes instruction in everything from color and cut to bookkeeping and customer service.

By the time I arrive, in August, the Kabul Beauty School has been officially up and running for a week and three days, and the first group of twenty students, aged sixteen to forty, are learning how to give a round-brush blow-dry. Bending over their practice "heads" (whom they have named Natasha, Christina, Zam Zam, and Apollo), they painstakingly wrap sections of hair around their new gold brushes and await comments in Dari from Vahida, an Afghan American from Falls Church, Virginia, and in English from Grauel. (One of the side benefits of the school is that the students get to work on their English.) A teething baby gurgles softly from his makeshift crib (a box top labeled MAC BLUSH DIS-PENSER, lined with a lavender blanket), and in a small kitchen off the classroom, two cooks clean the lunch dishes. In the makeup area by the door, a young bride-to-be comes in to have her eyebrows plucked by Grauel (Afghan women traditionally do not pluck their brows until they are married), and Razia, another Afghan American who has volunteered as a teacher, arrives for the standard three-week stint.

"I never thought that my profession would bring me here again," says Razia, who fled her native country, on foot, twenty-three years ago. Her husband was killed by the Soviets in 1980, when one daughter was two and a half and she was one month pregnant with the second. After

Razia got herself and the girls to New York, she worked as a cashier, finally wrangled a job in a salon, and managed to put both girls through college. For the last five years she has owned her own shop, in Queens. "I didn't allow myself to look back," she says. "I didn't pay attention until 9/11 and so much of what I saw on TV about Afghanistan, the lives of the children, of the mothers, affected me. I felt so guilty, I was uncomfortable thinking about anything else. So when this program came about, it was like God had heard my voice."

Razia fights tears as she watches her former compatriots work. "Look at them," she says. "See how desperate they are to learn."

The women in the classroom have, in fact, led desperate lives for decades. The twenty years of fighting after the Soviet invasion of 1979 left 2 million Afghans dead—and 20 percent of the female population widowed. Under the rule of the Taliban (from 1996 to 2001), women were not allowed to work, nor were they allowed to educate their daughters. Most were reduced to begging in the streets. Illiteracy rates soared, as did the rate of such diseases as tuberculosis.

It is no wonder, then, that it was of great interest to the numerous female passersby. (In the daytime, there are as many people about as there are cars and bicycles; after dark, the only pedestrians are men.) When word got out that the structure would house a beauty school, so many women applied that, in the end, a lottery had to be held in order to fairly distribute the first twenty slots, and now there are more than two hundred on the waiting list. The organizers narrowed the class by accepting only those with prior experience. The women wanted to improve their rudimentary skills—but the building was a draw as well. Though small (2,300 square feet), it is by far the best-looking in town—much nicer, for example, than the rather gloomy and run-down "palace" shared by Prime Minister Hamid Karzai and King Zahir Shah. A gleaming four-room oasis carved out of what was previously the guard station at the newly created Ministry of Women's Affairs, it is light and airy, with floors of pale marble (a plentiful resource in Afghanistan and, therefore, very cheap) and picture windows overlooking a well-tended garden—there's even access to the Internet.

The fact that such an efficient operation exists in the chaos that is Afghanistan is testament not only to the generosity of its benefactors but to the determination of the three women who made it happen. In another email that arrived before I did, O'Connor recounted the saga of ninety mannequin heads that had been lost in transit from Shanghai: "I went with Roshaan [an Afghan-born Australian who came over to help manage the project] to airport customs to see if they had them, but the customs officer spoke little English and had no idea what a mannequin was. There is no word for it in Dari, so Roshaan told him that they were heads but not real ones. The officer still had no clue what we were describing and looked at us as if we were mad. He kept bringing more and more people over until there must have been twenty Afghans trying to figure it out."

Other dispatches were less amusing: "The women on the waiting list would not leave me alone," O'Connor writes the week before classes started. "Some were crying: One woman was a widow with five children and no means to support them. Another was pregnant with two young kids at home and a husband recently paralyzed in a land-mine explosion. Writing this now makes me want to cry: I feel so overwhelmed and so helpless, but in front of them I had to hold it together, as otherwise it would have descended into chaos."

Neither of the two women mentioned in the email won places in the first class, but another did: a woman named Aadila, whose husband, a rare supportive one, had come to the school and implored the teachers to give his wife a spot. He said she was suffering from severe depression, and that going to the school every day, learning and expressing herself creatively, would be the best medicine for her. Vahida tells me that while Aadila waited for the winning names to be called, her face was "so scrunched up, it was tiny." Then, when she heard her own name, "it looked like the picture on TV that shows a flower blooming."

By the time I meet Aadila two weeks later, she seems anything but down. Unlike the rest of the women, who generally wear long, loose pants and tunics, with long hair to match, she sports men's trousers with white shirts and ties and a short brown coif streaked with blonde.

On the street, she covers her head, but a pair of Elvis aviator glasses are propped up on top of her white chiffon scarf. She is a great character and, in some ways, luckier than most. Both her parents were doctors, and throughout the rule of the Taliban, the family lived in Pakistan. Still, says Vahida, "her life just spiraled downward." Prior to the Taliban, a girl from a family with means, like Aadila, would have had many options. Not only did women operate their own beauty businesses, 70 percent of all the teachers in Afghanistan were women, and they made up 50 percent of all government workers and 40 percent of all doctors. Now Aadila is in her late twenties, with two children, and her best hope for employment—her only one, really—is salon work.

Depression in Kabul is hardly rare. The psychological impact of the Taliban's regime was as intense as the economic impact. In Kabul alone, 7,700 teachers were immediately put out of work; 8,000 women were forced to leave the university. Burqas, the body sleeves that had been voluntary since 1959, became mandatory. In addition to being hot (most are made of polyester), they are indescribably hard to maneuver in because the mesh eyeholes do not allow you to look down. "You have no eyes to see," one student says when I ask what she hated most about wearing a burqa. Others talk of constantly tripping, of breaking the heels off their shoes, of terrible headaches, of feeling as though they would suffocate. It was a mixed blessing, then, that women were rarely allowed out of the house. Although a woman could run crucial errands if escorted by a close male relative, if so much as a wrist was exposed, she risked a public beating. Worse, if a man spotted an unmarried woman and was attracted to her (how could he tell?), he could show up at her door and demand her for his wife. Anything that might have provided comfort or diversion was denied. There was no TV, no movies, no music. Photography studios, once big business in Kabul, were closed down; sports arenas were shut. "You can't believe," says Vahida, "the number of suicides."

Those who survived relied on the only things they had left, their self-respect and their ability to maintain what dignity they could by making themselves beautiful. Bashira, a redheaded mother of five, tells me that she learned to do hair from her "own passion" and by watching her cousin, who also operated a salon. Word spread of her talent, and friends would come to see her, pretending that they "were visiting family." Her husband had been a metalworker, but when the shop where he worked had been shut by the Taliban, she became the family's chief breadwinner. Her two oldest sons found work after school as maids; her daughters studied at home by reading textbooks disguised as the Koran. These days her husband makes meager wages at the university, working as a gardener and a cleaner, and Bashira hopes to expand her business at her no-longer-hidden home salon (called Shaam, which means "candle") after she completes the course. Best of all, says Vahida, who has been translating for me, "she can open the door without a burqa on and have no fear of being shot. And you know what? She can wear makeup, and that is so sweet."

Bashira's classmate and neighbor Farah had been a teacher of history and geography, but after the Taliban she was ousted from her position and her family had no income, so, she says, "I picked up the scissors." Like Bashira, she had no formal training, but her business spread by word of mouth, albeit whispered. She was so terrified that she would be found out that some days she wouldn't comb her hair and purposely made herself look "bad and dingy" in case the Taliban "would walk in the house and see." Mirrors were covered with curtains, products were smuggled in from Pakistan, and makeup was so precious it was buried.

It is two days after my arrival, and the women (whose names have been changed) are sharing their stories with me at a class picnic. (It's Friday, the official day of prayer in Afghanistan, and their day off from the school.) To see them now, sprawled out on carpets, eating kebabs and drinking tea while their grown children lounge and the small children play in the distance, I can hardly imagine the lives they describe. Though most of them still have water and electricity for only a few hours a day and many of their husbands are unemployed, they seem so happy just to be in the world again.

Still, their world is not an entirely safe place. Inside the school, blue, hand-painted lines in Dari are written above the door: WELCOME. THE DOOR TO A NEW WORLD IS OPEN. YOU CAN COME IN, YOU CAN STAY, YOU ARE AT LIBERTY. Outside, however, the guards sweep cars coming through the gates for bombs. The week of my visit is "one of the bloodiest since the toppling of the Taliban regime," according to *The Gulf Today*, the *USA Today* of the Arab world, which reported a death toll of "nearly 100"—including policemen just south of Kabul who had been ambushed by Taliban insurgents, and government troops in the Uruzgan province who had fought at least three hundred Taliban.

Every day brings a new incident. Two guards at a small hotel near my own were murdered and thousands of dollars were stolen from guests; $132,000 was taken from a German aid office. (Adding to the general danger of things, Kabul is a cash-only city.) In the northern province of Badakhshan, a gunman opened fire on a van belonging to the British charity Save the Children. No one was killed, which is a good thing because the children do need saving: A week after my return to the States, *The Washington Post* reported that a school—little more than a shed, really—in the Logar province had been doused with gasoline and burned to the ground. Leaflets scattered at the scene warned that girls shouldn't go to school, and now the lone teacher says she is too afraid to teach the fifty students who had been in her charge.

Even in Kabul, it is sometimes hard to remember that the year is 2003 (according to the Afghan calendar, it is actually 1382). While there I attended Roshaan's wedding. Even though he has lived most of his life outside of Afghanistan and will likely return to Australia, Roshaan's father and the father of the bride, old friends, have arranged the marriage. (The day after the ceremony, I learn that so far he has only held hands with his bride.) At the wedding, guests followed custom—the men danced with men, while the women danced with the children. Still, the event itself was joyous, complete with colored lights and a full wedding feast. Few of the women covered their heads, and toward the end, the bride changed out of her traditional wedding garb, an embroidered tunic and pants, and into a fluffy pink gown.

Weddings, arranged and otherwise, are big business in Kabul—on almost every commercial block there are wedding stores and formalwear stores, and cars bedecked with ribbons and pink net are common sights on the streets. It's as though people are ready to celebrate—something, anything. The students, in fact, dress up, every day, in spangled tunics or brightly colored suits. Makeup is applied with heavy-handed enthusiasm by those denied access to it for so long (Aadila, for example, though almost always in her shirt and tie, wears glitter on her cheekbones and eyelids and shiny purple on her lips). At the picnic, a camera crew had been shooting scenes for a BBC/Discovery Channel documentary, and one of the women shyly asked the director if she ever wore makeup. They are all mystified at our lack of jewelry and lipstick, at our wrinkled linen clothes and the flip-flops or espadrilles on our feet. Bashira and Farah have just presented me with one of their old perm "rods," a crude, hand-carved piece of wood with a rubber band attached that had been all they had to work with, and suddenly I am appalled at my own messy hair.

It doesn't matter. "They're just so happy to be seen by the outside," Grauel, who has been in Kabul for four weeks, tells me. "They're so happy that we're paying attention." Now that the school is up and running, she is returning to New York on the day after the picnic, and the students are tearful as they bid her farewell. "I'm going to miss all this love," she says. "I got twenty kisses every morning—actually, it was sixty because they kiss three times."

The majority of the students arrive at the school courtesy of the two drivers the school employs—public transportation in Kabul is notoriously bad, and they would never make it in time for eight o'clock classes. They are given breakfast and lunch and, obviously, instruction. Even those who have worked as hairdressers for years are working for the first time with scissors that don't look like pruning shears; they are mastering techniques they never knew existed ("Today we will learn the solid-form haircut"). They have their own textbooks and a chance to make a serious income. Farah, for example, has returned to teaching, but she'll make more money doing hair on the side. The hope is that as the quality of the city's beauty services improves, the Western aid workers who are streaming in will no longer wait until they get to India or Dubai to have their hair cut or their nails done, that they will spend their money in Kabul, along with the locals.

But a self-reliant future involves more than just lessons in color; it involves the new and luxurious chance for the women to socialize in the open, to speak freely about their plights and desires, having a place to seek help when it's needed. One student was miserable sharing the house of her controlling mother-in-law and worried about the toll it was taking on her marriage and her children. Vahida told her about a similar experience with her own mother-in-law and counseled her to move out with her family, which she did. "I told her that you have to stand up for yourself," Vahida says. "It's not just teaching hairdressing. It's sharing our lives, giving them a little encouragement. They are not used to love and affection."

Ultimately, the goal is to train at least one or two of the local women in the first three-month session to teach future students, but for the next year or so they will be instructed by their former compatriots. The experience of getting to know one another has been moving—the stories are different yet familiar in their hardship. When Razia is introduced to the class as Vahida's replacement, she tells of the walk with her children out of Afghanistan, eluding surveillance helicopters by hiding in caves, of being saved from starvation by the gift of a single piece of dough from someone they encountered, which they "fried" on a rock. After the Soviets killed her husband, she was never allowed to see his body, so for years she reflexively searched TV footage and newspaper photographs of Afghanistan for a glimpse of his face. As she talks, there is not a dry eye among the women, but the real tears come when she gets to the triumphant part, when she says that in America all she had was her pride and her strength and her dignity, but that she worked hard and built a business and that her achievement in life is her children, that she was able to educate them because of the skills she learned. "I want you to know that I am one of you. I left because of my circumstances, but I am back to share my skills with you. You are the strong women now. You stayed here, and you survived. Everybody is coming and going right now, but you must stay strong and stand for yourselves."

One class at a time they are learning to do that.

PART 5

Scenes from a Life

19

Dis Engaged

(1996)

I t would have been my sixth anniversary this month, an iron year, I believe, had I actually gotten married on June 23, 1990, like I was supposed to. I didn't—leaving almost one thousand people with nothing to do that weekend, the prospective groom a bit disconcerted, to say the least, and myself currently bereft of gifts of iron (what does that mean? Would I be getting steam irons, for example, or golf clubs? Or lots of those ubiquitous little iron picture frames from Pottery Barn?).

He is a wonderful man, my former fiancé, brilliant and funny and dear, and in this case extremely understanding, but I never should have said I would marry him, so in the end, rather at the last minute actually (a few weeks before the big day), I called it off.

Immediately people began to treat me like I had just had a nervous breakdown. They kept asking me in very hushed tones if I was all right. (When my mother told the man who had designed the lighting for the reception, he responded by baking her a loaf of bread.) People looked at me in the same way I imagine they look at someone just diagnosed with a brain tumor—they were sympathetic but wary. Or they told me how brave I had been. Not really. Once I'd finally faced the fact—albeit a bit tardily—that to get married was the wrong thing for both of us, there simply was no other choice to make.

This was not easy for people to accept. Why in the world would a woman almost thirty years old who had the chance to marry a good guy not take it? It had only been a few years, after all, since *Newsweek* had reported that a single woman at thirty-five had only a 5 percent chance of getting married, and at forty she had better odds of being killed by a terrorist: news that had sent women screaming into the streets.

My friends raced to the altar instead. By the time I announced my own engagement, one of them was already divorced with a child (and would get married again, have another child, and separate); one had just married a genuine psycho (whom she is thankfully now rid of) on the rebound from another boyfriend with whom she is now reunited; one had run off to Tennessee (where there is no blood test or waiting period for anyone over eighteen) with her ex-boyfriend (now her ex-husband) in the middle of a cocktail party. Everybody I knew was getting married, and since I had been with this man, off and on, for seven years, it seemed crazy not to, and even crazier to call it off.

At first I decided I was just being selfish and too scared to make a commitment. Maybe it was simply a matter of discipline. I made an appointment with a psychiatrist friend. "Should I straighten up and get married?" "Julia, you would kill him." Good enough. I called a friend of my father's, whom I love, to tell him he might not need to come to Mississippi after all (he was going to be an usher), and the only thing he said back was "Relief is a wonderful emotion, isn't it?" Yes indeed. So I told the groom, who was lovely and gallant, and called my father, whose feelings were a bit harder to fathom since for a full ten minutes he repeated the same two phrases over and over: "Oh, God" and "Your mother, your mother."

My mother had in fact spent a whole lot of time designing tents and tablecloths and generally working like a dog. Plus, she'd had to fight with horrible me every single day over things like whether we should have green or plain mayonnaise for the poached salmon, so I was sort of hoping that my father would tell her the news. Not only did he refuse, he told me that he planned on leaving the house while I told her and devised an elaborate phone code to signal me when he saw her car approach (she had driven two hours away to re-mat some prints because as part of the wedding preliminaries she had decided to redecorate the whole house) so that he could get out in time. At one point, when it dawned on him that he had not been behaving in a very fatherly manner, he pulled himself together and made his one and only pronouncement on the subject of my canceled nuptials: "Fifty percent of the people in this country who think they want to get married end up getting a divorce, so I guess you're doing the right thing."

They do and I was. In addition, the divorce rate is 50 percent higher for couples who live together before they get married, a statistic not nearly as surprising as it sounds. Getting married is easier, somehow, less immediately painful, than splitting up once you've gotten that far.

Moral commentators love to use statistics like these but what no one will say is that the numbers also have a lot to do with the basic stupidity of women's choices (coupled with the fact that once you make a bad choice, it is easier than ever to get out of it—even the Prince and Princess of Wales can get a divorce). What is truly stunning is how many otherwise intelligent women make the same stupendously starry-eyed and absurd choice as a nineteen-year-old virgin with an eating disorder. But that's just it—we all want to be the future queen of England, at least for a day.

Some of my friends married because they had been taught that a woman still needs the imprimatur of a man's proposal; some did because it was easier (they thought) to commit to a marriage than a career; some were afraid to wait to have a baby; and some, like me, did it because they could not bear the thought of hurting someone they love, and it was, you know, time. But none of us thought much past the fairy-tale wedding, past the party, the attention, and the finery. And when it's over, everybody is surprised by a real life full of ups and downs, a life of commitment even when your beloved is weak or petty and not always what you always wanted, a life that requires a staggering amount of attention. So they bail.

When I was in the eighth grade, my best friend and I would entertain ourselves in algebra class by planning our nuptial extravaganzas. We would draw dresses and list the bridesmaids and the flowers and the music and even the guests, but there was always a blank by the word *groom*—he was the least important part. I had barely met the man to whom I ultimately did get engaged when a good friend who was a designer sketched my dress one night on a napkin. In the end it was to be silk encrusted with beaded lilies of the valley, but I never saw it, not even in muslin form. He had made every frock for every other event surrounding the wedding and most of my mother's clothes, but not the Dress. When I asked him later what he would've done if I'd actually needed a gown to get married in, he said he didn't know, that he had to visualize people in his clothes in order to make them and he could just never quite see me at the end of the aisle.

I couldn't either, but I could certainly see everything else. Weddings in the Mississippi Delta are so legendary that Eudora Welty devoted her greatest novel to one. For my own outing, my good friend André Leon Talley had me make index cards with the details of each event so he would know what clothes to have made. (My father said the only reason he's sorry I didn't get married is that he really wanted to see André in the white piqué suit lined in fuchsia silk he would have worn to the wedding.) I flew home for summit meetings with flower designers and caterers. A team of electricians dug so many trenches in our yard that it looked like the site of a gopher invasion. ("At least," my mother said when it was all over, "I have a beautifully lit garden." But then an ice storm came, and all the trees and the lights are gone.) My mother and I spent whole days listening to tapes of orchestras and poring over hotel floor plans deciding where to put each guest, and one of the most entertaining dinner parties I've ever been to was held to see if the salmon flown in from Maine was good enough for a wedding supper. (The groom was not in attendance, which should have told me something.) The next morning, hung over, I posed for my engagement pictures, possibly the most unflattering photographs taken of anyone in the history of the world.

It was only when I ceased to wrangle over the execution of every detail that my mother said she knew something was terribly wrong. When I finally told her what it was, the invitations had been stamped and addressed, enough cases of French champagne to quench the thirst of 1,000 people had been delivered to our door, and I possessed 1,000 sheets of pale-gray-and-white stationery bearing what would have been my married initials of JRC. The champagne could not be returned (this was Mississippi, after all, and it had been special-ordered from out of state), so we became very festive around my house—if the dry cleaner delivered the clothes on time, my mother would ask him if he would like a drink. My uncle told us to use the stationery anyway and say the monogram stood for "Julia Reed canceled," which I didn't have the guts to do, but I did keep the china and silver my grandfather gave me because he died before I could give them back.

Everybody involved was so gracious that the only truly sticky moment, not surprisingly, was the planned wedding night itself. I was scared to call home, where there would have been an orchestra in full swing, and champagne being poured and cucumber sandwiches being passed and people dancing and laughing and hollering into the hot Delta night. But I called anyway, and I asked my mother what she had planned. And she said she was on her way out to the levee with a bottle of champagne, which she was going to drink, and a box of invitations, which she was going to make into paper airplanes and sail out over the Mississippi. I think she was kidding, but she was smart enough, thank God, to celebrate the belated good sense of her only daughter.

20

The Party Line

(1996)

So far this season I have bought: a chocolate-brown wool-jersey evening gown with a slit up the front and five-inch chocolate *peau de soie* Manolo Blahniks to match; an aubergine chiffon Empire-waist cocktail dress like Emma's and Josephine's, not quite but almost as brilliant as Galliano's interpretations; a navy silk Oscar de la Renta with a bow at the neckline and a crinoline beneath the skirt (very un-me, but so pretty and party-girl and *cheap*—I got it at the Super Sale in Washington to benefit breast cancer research); a black velvet Saint Laurent dress and a black YSL ottoman-silk suit; a long, skinny black wool coat with a Mongolian-lamb collar; two evening bags; another pair of Manolos; and a wad of Chanel pearls. This does not mean that I am very social or very rich (it means, in fact, that I am broke and devoid of anything to wear at any time prior to, say, eight o'clock at night). It means that I have a wardrobe for which I have no immediate plans. And I really wish someone I know would have a Christmas party.

Not an office Christmas party like in the movies, where everybody gets drunk and wears funny hats and somebody invariably gets caught with somebody else on top of the Xerox machine. Nor do I mean a real-life office party, one of these boring corporate affairs where people wear slightly dressier versions of what they wear to work every day, and it's always in a restaurant where they start setting tables for real customers at eight o'clock, so everybody has to clear out. And the ones that drag on are even worse, full of all that obligatory camaraderie—there's no romance, no glamour, not even the hint of surprise. What I want to go to is a real old-fashioned holiday party, one that's big and lavish and even a little magical, where all the guests look beautiful and the setting could be a stage—a party like the one in the opening scene of *The Nutcracker* (my favorite version is Baryshnikov's, because the wife gets a diamond necklace just before the guests arrive).

Nobody has these anymore, but they used to. One year my mother had three of them back-to-back, with at least one hundred people each, and I got to wear the blue velvet dress with the white lace collar I wore in my aunt's wedding and take the coats at the door. A very sexy Englishman I'd never seen before tipped me $2, which I kept for years as a souvenir, a link not only to this unspeakably handsome man but also to the soigné night in which I had played a tiny part. My mother had a different outfit for each party, and my favorite was the white silk crepe pantsuit, with narrow pants and a short-sleeved tunic that had hunky glass sapphires, emeralds, and rubies around its sort of Greek neckline. It was very chic and very Versace and I would wear it now myself, but for the fact that about two minutes before the guests arrived my little brother threw a cup of Welch's grape juice from his high chair, and it landed across my mother's snow-white front, and she had to change into the red-and-gold plaid hostess skirt and red satin blouse she'd worn the night before.

I will never forget the preparations that went into those parties, the garlands everywhere, and the huge tree with literally hundreds of strings of tiny white lights, and the dozens and dozens of votive candles that had to be lit with long matches at the very last minute. There were bartenders in white coats and hordes of people in the kitchen making homemade rolls and mayonnaise for the turkey, pouring sherry into the seafood Newburg and icing petits fours. And the guests made an effort, too—they looked different, better, far more glamorous than they did at any other time in the year. The ladies wore hairpieces or even tinsel in their hair, and dark eye makeup and big earrings (this was the sixties);

the men wore red vests and holly pants and ties with tiny Christmas trees. They laughed more and talked faster. Their cheeks were flushed and their senses heightened. Turned on by the brisk weather or the pine scent or the booze or the sheer built-in anticipation of the season, they all acted as if they knew something exciting and wonderful was going to happen before the evening ended—they just didn't know what it was yet.

New Year's parties are always awful because they are about pressure (to have fun, to get drunk, to be kissed); at their best, Christmas parties are about possibility. School's out and work's over and people's houses aren't their houses anymore—the furniture's all rearranged to make room for the Christmas tree; angels fly from the ceiling. They've become sets, and the thing about sets is that whatever happens inside them is fantasy.

Now I am overdue for a dose of fantasy, not to mention possibility. I have worked like a dog this year, and I want a reward before the next one starts. I want to do more than just get through my work and finish my shopping, have my packages frantically FedExed, all in time to race home to my family where everybody is exhausted, too, and we put on sweaters and sweatpants and lie around on the sofas to watch videos, and all the people who used to have festive parties are at their houses doing the same thing. I'm ready for some sugarplums to be dancing in my head; I want my pulse to quicken as I pick up my long skirt and mount some stairs to greet something wonderful that I don't know about waiting at the top. I want something surprising and grand and intimate all at the same time. I want to see people I love and people I'll want to. I want a buzz. I want to return home trailing my evening coat with an empty champagne glass in my hand and a dreamy look on my dramatically made-up face.

I just saw an Estée Lauder ad that said "Sparkle for the Holidays" with lip and cheek and nail color that "shimmers between silver and gold." I would like to shimmer, but I need a place to do it, along with a place to wear all the clothes I bought this year, not to mention the ones I've stockpiled virtually unworn from all the long years before: skinny red velvet pants, green chiffon pants with black-and-white velvet daisies, a black-and-silver beaded shift, black satin Manolos adorned with loose strands of crystals and pearls.

The first clothes I wore to Christmas parties were the ones I got for Christmas. We always had lots of people over on Christmas night, and my earliest ensembles at these events included a chamois Indian-chief costume with full headdress from F.A.O. Schwarz, a pink tulle tutu and matching leotard with satin slippers, and a gypsy dress with a multicolored striped satin skirt with a black velvet sequined bodice and matching headpiece with ribbon streamers. My friends all wore velvet dresses with big sashes and the boys wore matching jumpers or pants with white oxfords, and we would drink sparkling Catawba grape juice and pretend it was champagne and set off Roman candles on the front porch and eat dressing balls and bourbon balls and spy on the adults, which we could not wait to be.

All my parents' friends had parties, too. When I hit adolescence, I would get my tips on what to wear to those events from my twin style bibles, the holiday issues of *Mademoiselle* and *Glamour*. One year *Mademoiselle* recommended spray painting an old pair of shoes silver, so I sprayed my scuffed white clogs and pinned rhinestones to the pink pleated chiffon blouse my grandmother had given me. I wore this with some pink pants to the huge Christmas Eve party we went to every year, and it was the first year I didn't have to go upstairs and eat cookies and drink punch with the children. Downstairs, the drinks were served in silver julep cups and there were all kinds of things in chafing dishes to eat with toast points, and red velvet cake and caramel cakes, and women with long legs and long necks sitting on the stairs looking up with bright eyes and naughty smiles at the men they were talking to. One year at one of these parties I kissed a man I still secretly adore on the roof of the house (it was Victorian, and you could walk right out the upstairs dormer windows and find a level place to stand); another year a man got locked in the bathroom (adorned with greenery and red and white bunting and scented Christmas candles) and there was so much noise that nobody heard him, so he called his babysitter at home and told her to call back and tell whoever answered the phone to come and find him. It took the babysitter three tries to find anybody who cared enough to stop what they were doing long enough to get him out.

When I was about twelve or thirteen there was—in *Glamour* this time—a red satin dress that I really wanted. (Actually I wanted it for the rendezvous with Robert Redford and Paul Newman that my best friend, Jessica, and I had planned—we were going to send an invitation to each man for a surprise party in honor of the other and explain that the location was Greenville, Mississippi, so as to avoid the media.) The rendezvous, needless to say, did not work out, and I didn't get the dress, either, but my friend M.T. got one almost like it, red taffeta with a full, long skirt and a tight bodice with two rows of ruffles around the breathtakingly low scoop neck, to wear to the Christmas party her parents always had. Her grandmother took one look at that neckline and told her that people would talk and she said, "Oh, Nana, if they only would!" Exactly. That same year her mother wore silver moiré pants with a sash and a silver organza blouse and looked like an angel, and another year to the same party I wore a brown velvet suit with a gray satin blouse that I had to get a job at McDonald's just to pay for.

The great thing about the holidays is that people you've never seen before turn up—people's relatives, their college roommates, boys who went off to college years earlier and return as accomplished cellists or brilliant surgeons. One year at M.T.'s house I met somebody's long-lost brother just back from South Africa, all mysterious and exciting with curly dark hair and a mustache. Years later M.T.'s own brother returned from the Peace Corps in Mauritania and gave his father an African boubou, which he proudly wore to the party instead of his usual red pants with the holly stripes up the sides. At one of my own parents' parties an old beau of mine walked, uninvited, through the front door at midnight, sat down, and started playing the piano. The next thing I knew someone had woken up my neighbor to get a guitar, and somebody else found a tambourine, and we stuck holly in our hair and drank gin and danced and made up song lyrics about everybody we knew till dawn. I remember that I had on a burnt-out green velvet dress and earrings so long they grazed my shoulders, and that my fiancé at the time had gone to bed extremely early. It was raining so hard when it was finally time to go that everybody's cars got stuck in the front yard. So we ate breakfast and sang some more instead.

That was a long time ago and, unfortunately, the last great Christmas party I've been to. I asked a friend of mine how long it had been since she'd been to a great one and she said never. Another friend said it was about fifteen years ago, when she ended up with somebody in a closet. Closets are a recurring theme. My old boarding-school roommate ended up in one with her old boyfriend at a Christmas party, and they eloped that very night. Now, I don't have to have something that extreme happen to me this Christmas, but a little something unexpected would be nice, festive even, true to the season. Every year when I was little I had an Advent calendar, and each morning before I went to school, I got to open up another tiny cardboard door and a nut or a piece of candy or a little surprise was behind it. Well, I would like to put on one of my new dresses and my new coat and my five-inch heels and some false eyelashes and glittery lipstick and open a door and find a little surprise behind it. It shouldn't be too much to ask.

21

Whose Life Is It Anyway?

(2005)

About a year after my grandmother entered what is now widely known as a "persistent vegetative state," my parents attended a dinner party in Washington. The host, a newspaper columnist who was also a close friend, asked my mother how her mother was doing, so she told him. She sleeps; she wakes up; she responds to different voices—but there is absolutely no consistent level of awareness. The other guests, who included members of Congress and the odd cabinet secretary, murmured polite words of sympathy and then the overserved wife of a powerful senator stopped everyone cold. "Mama was like that," she said. "But after a while we just put a pillow over her face."

We did not put a pillow over my grandmother's face. Nor did we remove the clear plastic nasogastric tube that allowed liquid nourishment to pass through one of her nostrils, down her esophagus, and into her stomach during the eleven years that she lay silent inside an increasingly gnarled and twisted body. This was, after all, the late seventies, more than a decade before the Supreme Court would rule that the right to privacy extended to unwanted medical procedures, including a feeding tube, and more than two decades before the debate over whether or not to end Terri Schiavo's life cast a spotlight on that twilight zone called PVS. Short of the pillow, our choices were fairly limited and unpleasant at best (and my grandfather didn't want to talk about any of them), but like the families of the 30,000 other Americans in roughly the same shape, we grappled with them in private.

There was, of course, nothing private about Schiavo's last days. They were intensely, often excruciatingly public, involving a spokesperson (the antiabortion activist Randall Terry, late of Operation Rescue), who informed the press that after the final removal of Terri's feeding tube, "she looked like she just came from Auschwitz," and creating such bizarre bedfellows as Tom DeLay and Jesse Jackson—who arrived to comfort the family, twice, in a white stretch limousine. Her plight attracted the attention of major celebrities (Mel Gibson) and long-forgotten ones (Pat Boone). Most notably, it played into the political aspirations of Senate Majority Leader Bill Frist, MD (as he prefers to be called), who apparently forgot about the Constitution (the judge who overturned the "Palm Sunday Compromise," crafted to bypass ten court decisions and keep Schiavo alive, wrote that the congressional body Frist leads acted "in a manner demonstrably at odds with our Founding Fathers' blueprint for the governance of a free people"), not to mention his professional ethics (the good doctor diagnosed Schiavo from the Senate floor after viewing a three-year-old video in his office for "an hour or so"). Frist once lived close to my grandmother, in Nashville, but he never examined her, either up close or via videotape—in those days he limited his practice to the transplants of hearts and lungs, which would seem to be impressive enough.

The Schiavo case was an anomaly—an unusual confluence of meddling politicians and a torn family adept at using the Internet—but these days the law in most states is actually pretty clear. If you are incapacitated, you can assert your right to refuse life-sustaining medical treatment either through a "living will" or through a single, "surrogate decision-maker" who can present evidence that, stuck in a vegetative state, you would prefer to die. In thirty-three states the surrogate is a husband or wife (unless they are deemed unfit or someone else has already been designated). Even after a marriage of one week, spousal rights trump parental ones, and the reaction of Terri Schiavo's mother and father can be taken as an example of why: Parents are hardwired to fight for their children's lives.

Still, the first "right to die" case was brought, in 1975, by the parents of Karen Ann Quinlan, a twenty-one-year-old New Jersey woman who had overdosed on gin and barbiturates and whose breathing was assisted by a respirator. Her doctors told the Quinlans that Karen, who was emaciated and confined to a waterbed, would never recover, but after a year, when they asked privately that she be removed from the machine, the same doctors refused. The Quinlans sued, asking that their daughter be allowed to die with "grace and dignity." The New Jersey Supreme Court ruled in their favor, but she lived for another ten years because, tellingly, they had not requested that her feeding tube be removed as well. When asked why not, her father said simply, "That is her nourishment," and her mother explained that while the respirator caused her daughter obvious discomfort, she could not imagine denying her food or medication.

Even now, it is much easier to apply the label *artificial means* to the cold, gray, computer-driven machine that is an MA-1 respirator. The feeding tube, on the other hand, has been around in one form or another for centuries—after he was shot in 1881, President Garfield lived for another seventy-nine days on a mixture of milk, beef broth, and brandy. As late as the early 1980s, removal of sustenance via feeding tube was anathema to the majority of health professionals—indeed, lawyers have said that if the Quinlans had asked for that in their suit, their request would almost certainly have been denied.

By 1990 when the US Supreme Court reviewed Nancy Cruzan's parents' request to remove their daughter's feeding tube the thinking in both the medical and legal communities had changed. Cruzan, thirty-three, had been injured in a car accident and was being kept alive, like Terri Schiavo, by what was then a new type of feeding tube embedded directly in her stomach. But in his majority opinion, Chief Justice William Rehnquist asserted that Cruzan had the right to refuse life-sustaining measures, and attached no significance to the fact that the particular measure involved was artificial feeding. Concurring Justice

Sandra Day O'Connor explicitly rejected the idea of making a distinction between the feeding tube and other forms of life support. When the ruling came down, my grandmother had been dead two years.

She had her first stroke in January 1977, just after Christmas, when I was sixteen. She'd come to see us over the holidays in Mississippi, where I heard her tell my grandfather over and over again that her left arm was numb. He did not, typically, pay a whole lot of attention, but when she returned home she bought diamond engagement rings for her three grandsons (who were fourteen, ten, and eight at the time), and another ring for her longtime cook Ernestine, who drove her on these errands. I think she sensed she was going to die. Instead she became a woman with an almost entirely different personality who could not walk at all or talk very well or feed herself, though at least she was fed real food with a fork or spoon.

When the second stroke came several months later, it was massive, and a relief in a way. I was named after my grandmother; I loved her more than anybody on earth. When I was a child I flew to Nashville, by myself, on a Southern Airways jet, and we would shop and go to the movies and have chicken-salad sandwiches with fresh orangeade at Moon Drugs. When my brother was born, I was five, and she gave me a charm bracelet with an amethyst fly and a topaz heart and an emerald four-leaf clover. I happened to be glad he had come along, but she wanted to make sure I knew she still loved me. She was extraordinarily generous and a little shy, although she spoke her mind—a lot. To see her morph into someone I barely recognized, surrounded by caretakers neither of us knew, had been awful. But surely, in a fetal position and unable to speak or eat at all, she would finally be allowed to go in a matter of days at most.

But, again, she didn't. She was brought home, to the guest room, where the same caretakers fed her, this time through a tube in her nose. Her own doctor bemoaned the fact that my grandfather had the means to take such excellent care of her—had she been left in the hospital just a bit longer or moved to a nursing home, she would have been a victim (or, more to the point, the beneficiary) of "judicious neglect," the surreptitious way doctors and nurses used to let vegetative patients die before they could legally do so. She would have been allowed to contract pneumonia, for example, or some other infection, but having been installed on her husband's wishes back at home, where she lay on her own monogrammed sheets beneath a pair of Redoute prints, she never once developed so much as a bedsore.

My grandfather, who, like her, was born in 1907, had no intention of doing otherwise, and he was not a man my mother or my aunt had ever been able to argue with successfully. It was not until at least five years into it, when his own health had begun to decline and my grandmother had gotten to the point where she appeared to be almost unbearably uncomfortable, that the doctor, who was also their friend and neighbor, even broached the subject. Even then he didn't make a direct recommendation—he merely sat the family down and described as best he could what would happen to her if they agreed to remove the tube. He didn't pretend to know how she would feel, but he made the case that it could be a peaceful death—taking to one's bed and refusing to eat or drink was once a common way for the sick and the elderly to choose to go. My grandfather, who was riddled with anger and guilt and gin and confusion, called him a murderer and told him never to come back.

He did not. By then the life of the household had settled into a routine, a process that had taken some doing. Darlene, the head nurse who had been hired after my grandmother's first stroke, remained devoted to her until the end, but finding qualified and trustworthy night nurses proved to be a nightmare. One of them had heard gossip about her patient's impressive collection of jewels and enlisted an accomplice to come steal them from my grandfather's safe. When all he found were such valuable artifacts as my mother's first-grade report card, he emptied the house of silver instead.

Then there was the problem of the hangers-on, the folks who come out of the woodwork during what they like to call "your time of need." Though we weren't plagued by phone calls from Pat Boone or subpoenas from Tom DeLay, the new wife of my grandparents' next-door neighbor was almost as bad. This was a woman to whom I'm pretty sure my grandmother wouldn't have deigned to give a cup of sugar, but she kept turning up with a dog-eared, Post-it Note–marked Bible, which she read over my grandmother's bed when she wasn't laying hands on her, an action that would have gotten her slapped, or worse, had my grandmother been even partially aware. The Presbyterian minister, who was finally thrown out of his church for displaying unsettling charismatic tendencies, came by almost as frequently, praying ostentatiously for my grandmother's salvation while keeping one eye firmly on my grandfather's checkbook.

After those nuisances had been dealt with, there was the less-practical problem of getting used to the fact of my grandmother's condition. In the beginning, when I was in boarding school, my mother reminded me to pack a funeral suit whenever I went away on weekends in case I had to fly to Nashville from wherever I was, but we soon had to realize there was no real point in being prepared for something that no longer seemed remotely imminent. Nor was there any point in Darlene's continuing to paint my grandmother's nails with Revlon's Windsor—her fingers were so bent that what had begun as a loving act seemed almost cruel. George Spero, the man who had cut and set her hair in the same style as the queen's for thirty years, continued, initially, to do it at her bedside. But after a few months, Darlene took over the job and let it grow longer so she could brush it away from her increasingly flaccid face. Even my mother stopped reading and talking to her as much as she had in the first year or two. Whenever any of us did, her eyes were blank, or, far worse, fearful, but we all hoped that was our imagination acting on what we most dreaded.

My mother told me that every day she asked God to let my grandmother go, followed by "Please don't let Mama be inside there." It is doubtful she was—my mother told me that on the X-rays my grandmother's brain looked "beat up," and it is likely that spinal fluid had replaced dead neural tissue in the damaged cerebral cortex, which is the thinking part of the brain, just as it had in Terri Schiavo's.

Whether she was there or not, what was left of her had absolutely no privacy. (It is significant, I think, that the right to privacy is what the high court invoked when it ruled that people like my grandmother could get rid of the feeding tubes prolonging their lives.) After her first stroke, she required—and often demanded—our constant, rapt attention. It was so frustrating for her not to be able to express herself, not to be herself, and it was equally frustrating—and, admittedly, often tedious—to witness. But after the second stroke, the nurses were really the only ones who had to pay attention to her, even though we all constantly occupied her space. On evening visits, I gave her perfunctory kisses before settling down with some Scotch and a cigarette to visit with Darlene or Janice, the night nurse we were finally lucky enough to find. In the afternoons, Ernestine would make us fudge cake and we'd all watch *Another World* and *The Price Is Right* and shriek at the TV set while my grandmother lay snoring away in the background. At one point, Ernestine's father, Louis King, the houseman who had worked for my grandmother for almost fifty years, had his leg amputated. When I went to see him in the hospital, we played cards together on the bed—he had taught me to play stud poker when I was six, at my grandmother's kitchen table—and I realized I was sitting where his leg had been. Later it came to me that it was as though my grandmother had been amputated. We were all hanging out where she used to be—and yet she was right there in the room.

One of my favorite things to do growing up had been to watch my grandmother dress. To this day I have never seen anyone more meticulous. If there were a hair out of place or the faintest crease in her skirt, she would not come downstairs until it had been taken care of. Even her nightgowns were the most beautiful and well-cared-for things I'd ever seen. It was heartbreaking to see her in a hospital gown, with yellowed nails and hair lank across the pillow. I knew, of all the people in the world, she'd rather be dead than for anyone to see her like that, completely exposed and childlike.

Finally, after eleven years, she did in fact die, of a respiratory infection that, thankfully, no one could cure. My mother had left home quickly, and I had come direct from San Francisco, so that, after all our early planning, neither of us had the proper clothes. My grandmother had been the first person to buy me designer dresses (at far too early an age, according to my mother), so I went out and bought a black-and-green Ungaro chemise and persuaded my mother to buy a black Calvin Klein suit and I was so busy trying to find some shoes that I failed to notice at first how really, deeply sad my mother was. I had lost the grandmother I idolized, but I had lost that woman a long time ago. My mother had lost her mama, a different thing entirely, and she had not allowed herself to fully grieve until she was gone in body as well as mind.

I was sorry for my mother, and for Darlene, who had only known my grandmother as someone she was charged with taking care of, and for Louis, who had named his eldest daughter Julia, and for Ernestine, who by this time had uterine cancer and was dying herself. But the person I felt the most sorrow for was my grandfather, a man who had not always made it easy to sympathize with him. But in this case, he'd done what he thought was right, and it had proscribed his own life almost as much as it had the woman he'd been married to for the last sixty years, and now she was gone.

I think I knew my grandmother as well as or better than anyone (though, by the time she died, not very many people did—at her funeral the preacher included great-grandchildren she didn't have in his prayers, prompting one funeral goer to ask me which of us had the hidden illegitimate child). And I think I know that she absolutely would not have wanted to live in the state she was in. But as easy as it would be to judge my grandfather—and as easy as it was to judge Terri Schiavo's parents and the strange coalition of would-be saviors they had in their camp— I'm glad I didn't have to make the call myself. I honestly don't know what I would have done. It's a tough thing, in the end, to put that pillow over the face of someone you love. I do know that if I am ever in that state, I hope someone has the strength to do it to me.

22

The "I Don't" Honeymoon

(2011)

The honeymoon was to begin in Paris because that was, more or less, where we began. When I met my fiancé, I was in my early twenties and living in Washington, D.C. He was almost twice my age and living in London, so Paris is where we got together—where he romanced me over the course of seven years.

Sometimes our visits were fevered two-day jaunts; sometimes, when we had the use of his sister's sprawling apartment, they'd last for more than a week. On one trip we stayed at a tiny hotel called the Sévigné. On another, it was the ultra-discreet San Régis, said to be a favorite of Lauren Bacall.

Like a lot of Aussies I've known, the man in question was determined to prove that he was more cultured than the Brits he lived among, and I was happy to benefit from his efforts. We ate Gilbert Le Coze's dazzling pounded tuna at Le Bernardin before he and his sister, Maguy, moved the restaurant to Manhattan; we toured the de Menil collection at the Centre Pompidou before it went off to its permanent home in Houston. I learned to enjoy a pastis before dinner, thrilled to the Jacques-Louis Davids at the Louvre, and happily drank a hell of a lot of Château Giscours, his favorite Bordeaux.

The problem was, that had all taken place back when there was an "us"—an entity I'd rather abruptly shattered when I called off the wedding a few weeks before it was supposed to take place. Still, much to the disbelief of my mother and a great many other people who were similarly sane, we chose to take the trip that had been meant to celebrate our union.

I thought I was doing the civilized thing. I thought I'd be letting him down easy, that he could save face with friends and family (many of whom lived in Paris) if he could say it was the wedding and not the marriage I feared. There was also the fact that we already had first-class tickets (by this time we had racked up a gazillion miles), a suite at L'Hotel, and, on my end, a particularly swell trousseau.

We got over the first hump, the bottle of champagne left in the room to welcome the new "Mr. and Mrs.," by drinking it—quickly. My jilted groom spent his days catching up with fellow foreign correspondents; I had my own pals in the form of my then-colleague at *Vogue*, André Leon Talley, and George Malkemus, CEO of Manolo Blahnik USA, who was in town with him. André had a new wardrobe whipped up for my wedding, which included a double-breasted seersucker suit with matching shoes by Manolo. We dressed to the nines and lunched at Caviar Kaspia or on the Ritz terrace. We shopped at Madeleine Castaing and an ancient place George knew where I bought ropes of green cut-glass beads that looked like emeralds.

I wore the latter with a white silk dress to dinner à deux with my would-be fiancé at Restaurant Jamin, Joël Robuchon's first place of his own in Paris. Tucking into Robuchon's justifiably famous potato puree (accompanied by lots of the aforementioned Giscours), I remembered why I'd fallen in love in the first place.

But the next morning we were off to Lyon, a city not nearly so romantic nor containing a single soul we knew, and by the end of day two we'd almost killed each other. (I fear we actually might have killed the Michelin three-starred chef Alain Chapel—all the electricity went off in his restaurant the night we dined there, and he died of a stroke less than forty-eight hours later.) By that point, I'd decided to bail on the rest of the journey, a foray farther south to Cannes, and called André, who told me in typically colorful language to get myself on the first fast train back to Paris, where he would meet me in the bar at the Ritz.

Thus ensued one of the most entertaining nights of my life. For one thing, it was the occasion of my discovery of the Pimm's Royale, a Ritz specialty consisting of Pimm's No. 1 topped off with champagne and garnished with lots of sliced fruit and seriously potent brandied cherries. Somewhere around the third one, it seemed like a good idea to invite my almost-groom and his sister. By this time the room had filled up with people André knew, from Alain Mikli to Donna Karan, and we were all very jolly. Toward the end of the night, I found myself seated between a former Los Angeles Ram, who was one of Madonna's bodyguards, and actress Arlene Dahl, of all people, to whom I poured out my story.

The bill for the evening remains one of the largest of my life, but it was a small price to pay for finishing the "honeymoon" off in style, and even with a modicum of grace. I kept it as a reminder that even misguided intentions sometimes end up being not so crazy and that Paris can be a forgiving place—Bogart and Bergman are not the only ones who will always have it, after all. A Pimm's Royale remains one of my very favorite cocktails.

PART 6

Food and Feasting

23

Southern Sideshow

(2018)

In June 1980, the inaugural year of the Mississippi Picnic in Central Park, a group of us made the trek to Manhattan from Washington, D.C., where I was attending college at Georgetown. Our crew included: D. Gorton, the talented *New York Times* photographer who had grown up in my hometown of Greenville, Mississippi; two of my roommates; and Joe Hemingway, a flamboyant character and transplanted Mississippi Delta fixture who originally hailed from the boot heel of Missouri. Sadly no longer with us, Joe was one of those people who made you feel as though you'd been on intimate terms with him all your life (though you never knew how it was exactly that you knew him), and, like Zelig, he popped up everywhere. For whatever reason, he'd popped up in Washington for most of that summer, and it was his idea to repair to the picnic, an affair put on by a handful of New York–based expats "to preserve the culture and heritage of Mississippi."

Our own collective goal was rather more simple—to get out of town and have a little fun. So to that end (and under Joe's typically over-the-top direction), we brought along an Oriental rug as our blanket, a silver ice bucket and pitchers for the Bloody Marys, baskets loaded with pâtés and fruit and cheeses from the much-missed Neam's Market, and an ice chest filled with wine and champagne. There were about five hundred folks in attendance that first year, but we spread out in the shade and generally kept to ourselves. Mississippi, I've often said, is made up of more tribes than Bosnia, and we Deltans have been known to flaunt our perceived superiority (aided in this case by my grandmother's silver and a frayed entrance-hall carpet). Our former senator Trent Lott, who was born in the hills and raised on the coast (and who, in later years, attended the picnic), once described my fellow tribe members as people who read *The New Yorker*.

Now, I happen to be crazy about Trent and he knows it, and when he uttered that line, in a British accent no less, I got his point. Still, I have to say that in all my years growing up in the Delta I never, ever saw anyone engage in a watermelon-seed-spitting contest, one of the activities featured at the picnic. I was agog. Was this an actual pastime in the rest of the Magnolia State? I mean, I love watermelon as much as the next person (in fact, had we been thinking clearly, we would've injected one with rum and toted it along), but when I find the occasional seed in my mouth, I discreetly drop it in a napkin, I do not attempt to send it as far as possible into the distance. Yet here was Mayor Ed Koch being cheered on as he engaged in an enterprise that became an annual fixture at the event.

We did not participate in the contest, nor did we accept the glasses of sweet tea on offer (let the record forever show that I cannot abide the taste of sweet tea). Instead, we piled in the car with D. and headed downtown to the very cool Greenwich Village town house of some Columbia professors he knew who were throwing a party. Let me say first that they regarded our now fairly sodden appearance with the same wariness (and not just a little disdain) with which we had regarded the seed spitters. This was 1980, don't forget, so there was lots of warm white wine and some hash brownies, and in the middle of the living room a bathtub had been filled with melted chocolate in which a nude woman bathed. In retrospect, she might well have been my first experience with performance art. Whatever. It was a hell of a lot more interesting than watching people launch seeds from their mouths, a ludicrous undertaking that might be referred to as Peckerwood Performance Art, along the same lines as, say, the annual mullet toss at the justifiably revered Flora-Bama bar, or indeed the screaming contest that was added to the picnic roster as a tribute to the Mississippi-born Tennessee Williams (all the screamers were told to make like Marlon Brando and shout "Stella!").

Let me hasten to add that I'm not so much of a snob that I would object to a contest that allows people to let off a little aggression, and I am a big fan of the mullet toss. Its utter ridiculousness elevates it to high art, plus it's fun to get drunk and watch people try to throw slippery fish around in the name of the late great Kenny Stabler. But I had to wince when one of the founders of the picnic told the Jackson, Mississippi, *Clarion-Ledger* that "from the beginning . . . our goal was to change perceptions New Yorkers had from the '60s." This is the kind of stuff that brings out the worst in me, so I'll apologize up front, but my first thought was "Nope, we don't lynch people anymore, we're too busy hollering and spitting out watermelon seeds."

Further, the perception of folks in New York (where I lived for almost twenty years) was probably not aided by the passage of the so-called "Religious Freedom" bill, a piece of legislation that promises that citizens who refuse to provide services to people because of religious opposition to transgender people, extramarital sex, or same-sex marriage will not be punished. The law, recently upheld by the Fifth US Circuit Court of Appeals, effectively killed the Mississippi Picnic, which the founders canceled in 2016, the year the bill passed. They have since announced that the event, which had grown to include more than three thousand picnickers, will not be resurrected, and now I'm sort of sorry I never returned after that first summer. Perhaps it was because I've really never been very good at the talents, peckerwood or most others, that we Southerners are supposed to possess.

I do not whittle, for example, nor have I ever been able to whistle—"Dixie" or otherwise. I used to smoke, but I draw the line at chewing (or spitting) tobacco and cannot for the life of me play the spoons. I would probably make biscuits, except that the good people at Marshall's and Callie's and Mary B's make it easy not to. (Similarly, my former Greenville next-door neighbor once won the Mississippi Picnic pie contest by submitting a pecan pie baked by the esteemed Upper West Side bakery Sarabeth's.)

The one extremely useful and extraordinarily delicious Southern skill
I have mastered is the making of cheese straws—and by that I do not
mean the kind sold at Sarabeth's and countless other Manhattan empo-
riums that persist in selling twists of puff pastry glazed with cheese and
calling them straws. A true cheese straw is an ineffable combination of
butter and cheese and flour that melts in your mouth and is a de rigueur
addition to every Southern cocktail hour. The only thing better might
be a hot cheese olive, made with the same dough. They are the perfect
briny, cheesy bites (otherwise known as a salt-and-fat delivery system),
as well as my tiny but successful attempt to redeem the reputation of
my home state. The New Yorkers I served them to never failed to chase
the trays around.

Julia Reed's Hot Cheese Olives

Yield: 50 hors d'oeuvres

INGREDIENTS

8 tablespoons (1 stick) butter, at room temperature
8 ounces extra-sharp cheddar cheese, grated (about 1⅔
    cups)
2 ounces Parmesan cheese, grated (about ⅔ cup)
1½ cups all-purpose flour
¼ teaspoon cayenne, or more to taste
¼ teaspoon salt
1 large egg
50 small pimento-stuffed olives, drained

PREPARATION

In the bowl of a stand mixer, beat the butter until light
and creamy. Add the cheeses and blend well. Add flour,
cayenne, and salt, and mix until smooth.

In a separate bowl, beat the egg with 2 tablespoons
cold water. Add to the dough and mix until just incorpo-
rated.

Preheat oven to 350°F. Take a piece of dough about the size of a walnut and flatten. Place an olive in the center and shape the dough around the olive, rolling it in your hand until smooth and pinching to repair any breaks. Place on ungreased cookie sheet. Repeat with remaining dough and olives.

Bake for about 15 minutes. Let rest for a couple of minutes and remove to a serving tray to pass at once.

24

Food Memories from the South (of France)

(2018)

I spent the second week of July in a lovely stone farmhouse in an equally lovely village in Provence called Vernègues. My dear, dear friends Ellen Stimson and John Rushing had rented the place and assembled an intimate but jolly house party made up of people like me who love to cook and eat and drink pastis and lie around reading books in the sun. On my first night, John, who knows more about music than pretty much anyone I know, got us tickets to a jazz festival in a nearby town where we sat beneath enormous plane trees, drinking large glasses of French beer and listening to Pat Metheny make such magical music on his guitar that we all cried, including Metheny himself. We also watched soccer and shared the whole country's increasingly frenzied excitement as France got ever closer to winning the World Cup; we had a languorous lunch in Cassis (where I ate the most divine gratinéed mussels probably ever cooked and where we toured the majestic limestone calanques from a boat skippered by an impossibly adorable brown sea otter of a boy named Louis). Mostly, though, we shopped at nearby farmers' markets and butchers and roadside stands and made lunches and dinners in the enormous kitchen carved out of a stone embankment and featuring a commodious oven and a fridge that held a constantly replenished supply of rosé.

As is invariably the case (with me and like-minded folks, at least), food—choosing it, handling it, cooking it, and, almost always, talking about it while eating it—triggers food memories. Just about every significant meal I've ever sat down to is marked in some way by recollections of or nostalgia for another. Because, as Proust so emphatically made the case with his madeleines, food is about much more than mere physical sustenance. Each taste or smell opens a doorway to one's past, long buried or recent, and the memories bound up in each bite.

On my first trip to Provence, I stayed in a house rented by my late first cousin Frances, who was born a month before me and whom I loved more than I could any sister. I was living in Madrid that summer and had discovered *pisto*, a Spanish stew of zucchini and tomatoes more delicate than the French ratatouille and the specialty at the venerable Casa Paco. When it was my turn to cook, I made it for dinner with a tender leg of lamb and cherry clafouti for dessert. There was an enormous cherry tree in the backyard (along with two horses we rode bareback), and when we pitted the cherries before adding them to the batter, deep red juice flowed down all our arms. Images of that glorious evening almost twenty years earlier came flooding back as I stood this summer on a roadside near Mallemort, feeling the tomatoes and piling zucchini in my basket. There were insanely plump cherries too, and I had thought to pack a pitter in my suitcase.

Once again, I was in charge of the meal, so when we stopped at the boucherie on the way home, I bought skinny lamb chops and Spanish-style chorizo sausage, and then we all got to work in the kitchen. I chopped the vegetables for the pisto I'd decided to make after so long a time and marinated the chops in rosemary and garlic and lemon, an act that prompted yet another memory—of a lunch off the Adriatic coast of Italy. I was with a man who was beautiful to look at but also insecure and cruel, and we were making our way to Rome from a fancy resort where the food had been both forgettable and pretentious. The antidote appeared like a mirage as we came around an especially treacherous curve: a rustic restaurant filled with noisy families still dressed for church whose good humor and just plain goodness seemed palpable (though it was no doubt heightened in comparison with the disposition of my companion). Everyone around us was enjoying platters of crispy lamb chops, so we ordered them too, a pile of perfect bites fresh off the wood-fired grill, scented with rosemary and flavored with sizzling fat. To this day, the memory of them transcends that supremely ill-advised entanglement, and I attempted to re-create them for our own happy group in Vernègues. We never made the clafouti—the cherries were so good we ate them before we unpacked the rest of the groceries, standing in front of the deep copper sink.

Ellen had armed each of us on the trip with a copy of *Provence, 1970*, a wonderful book by Luke Barr that uses a moment in time when six iconic American culinary figures—including Richard Olney, Julia Child, and M. F. K. Fisher—found themselves together in the South of France, to chronicle the subsequent food revolution in America. Fisher is not just my favorite food writer, but my favorite memoirist, period, so I also brought along her lovely *Long Ago in France*, which I've probably read a half dozen times. In it, she recalls the year 1929, when she was a young wife having just moved to Dijon, where a favorite meal was a casserole of cauliflower, served with a salad and "cheap but good" red wine. She remembers the cauliflower, "small and very succulent, grown in that ancient soil," which she boiled for a few minutes and covered in heavy cream and "a thick sprinkling of freshly grated Gruyère, the nice rubbery kind that didn't come from Switzerland at all, but from the Jura. . . . It was grated while you watched, in a soft cloudy pile, onto your piece of paper." In the end, she and her guests "cleared [their] plates with bits of crisp bread crust and drank the wine," and made big plans, but when she moved back to California, she found that she could never replicate the dish. The cauliflower was watery, the cream not thick enough or unpasteurized, the cheese dry and oily. But the ingredients weren't the problem, not really: "Where was the crisp bread, where the honest wine? And where were our uncomplicated hungers, too?"

That's the thing: Food is about not just where you are when you make it, but who you are. Some meals are tinged with joy or regret, some, like Fisher's, with an innocence that can never be reclaimed. My own most memorable "innocent" feast was consumed yet again with Frances. We were in our early twenties, on holiday in Guadeloupe, nursing broken hearts. But we were young with what we thought was all the time in the world—the future was so spread out right in front of us that we couldn't stay too sad, and anyway the setting was beautiful and the food delicious. One morning, we drove to the opposite side of the island to visit a rain forest, where I purposely ripped the seam running up the middle of my linen Calvin Klein skirt so I could hike to the top of an unexpected waterfall. Afterward, exhausted and famished, we drove along the cliff road and stopped at a tiny store for what we hoped would be a cold beer and maybe a bag of chips. Instead, the proprietor ushered us onto a hidden terrace overlooking the sea and sent a small boy scrambling down to spear a fish. The man stuffed the barely dead snapper with stalks of fresh thyme and threw it on a grill while he sautéed a pan of diced breadfruit with wild mushrooms. Frances, who hated fish, made do, tragically, with a heated can of Spaghetti-Os while I gulped cold white wine and dug into a bowl of homemade mango sorbet for dessert. When people ask me to name the best meal I've ever eaten, I almost always return to that one, while my friend Mary Thomas says hers is a plate of corn bread and sun-warmed sliced tomatoes with her maternal grandmother's artichoke relish eaten in her childhood kitchen. Both could not be simpler or more vivid, touchstones suffused with memory to turn over again and again.

When I ask other folks about their favorite times at a table, most Yankees always tell me the name of a famous restaurant, not what they put in their mouths. I've had life-changing restaurant meals too, most notably at Le Bernardin when it was still in Paris. It was in 1984, and I was madly in love with a man whom I later, at the last minute, would decide not to marry, and I can still describe in painstaking detail the pounded raw tuna with chives placed before me and the salmon paillard in a garlic cream sauce that I wish more than anything I was eating right this minute. When the restaurant made the move to Manhattan two years later, it would change the way Americans thought about and prepared fish. On my first outing in its new home, I was given a plate of plump, lightly cooked oysters still in their shells and napped with truffled cream, a perfect marriage of earth and sea that moved me to tears. A very sweet French waiter, now retired, once told my dining companion,

"We love it when she comes in here—she gets so emotional." Well, yes. Food is emotion. When I talk about a food chain, I don't mean Webster's "arrangement of the organisms of an ecological community according to the order of predation in which each uses the next usually lower member as a food source." I mean the chain of memories composed of single bites and whole meals and who we were and what was and might have been.

Herewith, I offer the very tangible and easily re-created pisto, with which I plan to make many more memories:

Casa Paco's Pisto

Yield: 6 to 8 servings

INGREDIENTS

3 tablespoons olive oil

4 cloves minced garlic

2 chopped yellow onions

2 pounds zucchini, cut into half-inch cubes

2½ pounds ripe tomatoes, peeled, seeded, and chopped
   (or use 1½ large cans of whole peeled tomatoes,
   chopped)

½ teaspoon sugar (or more, depending on the sweetness
   of the tomatoes)

1 teaspoon salt

½ teaspoon freshly ground pepper

2 large eggs, lightly beaten

PREPARATION

Heat the olive oil in a large skillet over medium heat. Add the garlic and onions and cook until soft, about 7 minutes, stirring frequently to make sure the garlic doesn't burn. Stir in the zucchini, tomatoes, sugar, salt, and pepper. After about 5 minutes, add ¼ cup water and simmer, stirring often, mashing down on the vegetables as they soften.

(A potato masher is useful.) Add more water if it cooks out before the vegetables are soft.

When the vegetables are done and the mixture resembles a chunky puree, taste and adjust the seasoning if necessary. Add the eggs, stirring quickly to incorporate, and remove from heat. Check for seasoning and serve hot or at room temperature.

25

Crazy for Catfish

(2019)

Years ago, sometime around the mid-1980s, the Catfish Farmers of America asked me if I'd be willing to represent them in the Mobile Mardi Gras parade, where I would ride on a float and reign as Catfish Queen. I was living in Washington, D.C., and writing for *U.S. News & World Report*, and that sounded (correctly) like something happening on another planet, so I politely declined. Looking back, I find it unimaginable that I did not jump at the chance. My father couldn't believe it at the time—but then he's always found the whole concept of what he calls "titled women" wildly entertaining. You know: Miss Pink Tomato, Queen of the Turtle Derby, Poultry Princess, and so on. We have a lot of them down here. Miss Pink Tomato (along with Teen Miss Pink Tomato and Little Miss Pink Tomato) has been crowned every year in Warren, Arkansas, since 1957. So why not a Catfish Queen?

Let me hasten to add that I have never exactly been the titled woman type—unless of course there was an actual title and an especially lovely English country house involved. Sadly, I am certain I was asked to be queen not because I was even remotely pageant material (you've got to compete for the "real" crown, after all), but based on my support of farm-raised catfish, an industry now worth about $450 million a year but which was fairly new at the time. The 1980s were not the kindest to cotton and soybean farmers in the Mississippi Delta, which prompted many of them to try their hands at the fledgling catfish business by converting their fields to ponds. Since 60 percent of US farm-raised catfish are grown within a sixty-five-mile radius of Belzoni, Mississippi, just down the road from my hometown, Greenville, I wanted to do my part. I wrote my first piece showcasing the industry during my brief tenure as a business reporter for the *Orlando Sentinel*, and then, when I landed at *U.S. News* a short time later, I wrote another. Hence the CFA's gratitude—when I declined to accept the title, they sent me a plaque instead.

Anyway, the marketers and lobbyists were clearly busy during this period. Ronald Reagan declared June 25, 1987, National Catfish Day. And now of course there is an official Catfish Queen—actually, she's called Miss Catfish—who is properly chosen in the annual pageant in Belzoni during the World Catfish Festival in April. The contestants all have shiny hair and brightly glossed lips and curvy dresses that are usually red to match the roses they carry. Had I been in charge of the crown, it would have been made of two rhinestone catfish kissing in the middle with whiskers that move when you walk, but I missed my chance when I declined the float ride.

The fact is that I didn't need the possibility of a crown or Reagan's proclamation or, especially, a slew of titled women to solidify my love of catfish. For one thing, the cat is a mighty entertaining creature. It can be wily, hanging out on the bottom of lakes and rivers, hiding in the reeds or inside logs, where some of my crazier friends try to grab them, an entirely slimy (catfish don't have scales) and very muddy enterprise that I enjoy watching but will never, ever participate in. Also, there are those fetching whiskers. After my ex-husband thoroughly botched a big birthday, he tried to make amends by giving me a giant gilded papier-mâché catfish with superdramatic whiskers I'd spotted, incongruously, in a fancy antique store in Charlottesville, Virginia. It had once done duty on a New Orleans Mardi Gras float, so ownership of it kind of brought everything full circle. For years it hung out atop a grand piano in my former house; now it serves as the mascot of (shameless plug) Reed Smythe & Company, a business my dear friend and fellow Mississippi Deltan Keith Smythe Meacham and I started in the spring.

Also, if the first solid food I remember eating was a hot tamale, the second had to have been a fried morsel of crispy, salty, cornmeal-crusted catfish, followed closely by a hush puppy and a forkful of slaw. Many decades later, I still can't get enough of the stuff—when I'm home I hit the drive-through at Gino's or get the Friday plate lunch at Jim's Café, where the slaw is homemade and pretty damn perfect. I also accept all invitations to catfish fries, especially when the master fryer is a man named Dan Hammett, who makes the best fried catfish and hush puppies I've ever tasted. Every year at the Delta Hot Tamale Festival, so many of my astonishingly generous chef pals bring their time and talents (and yummy, yummy food) to Greenville. The only way I can think of to thank them is with a catfish fry with Dan manning the fryer. His hush puppies are ethereal, his fish crisp and expertly seasoned. I've seen him add lemon pepper and red pepper to his cornmeal, but even he can't tell me exactly what the trick is. I think it must be like biscuits or pie dough—everything depends on the hand of the cook, and Dan's timing with all that gurgling grease is clearly spot-on.

One of the chefs who regularly attends is James Beard Award winner Stephen Stryjewski, who is Donald Link's partner in the Link Restaurant Group in New Orleans and just about the funniest, sweetest man who ever walked. Stephen has a mighty fine hand at catfish himself— six months after he opened Cochon in 2006, he developed a superlative version of catfish court bouillon that thankfully remains on the menu. Cochon is nominally a Cajun restaurant (albeit a very sophisticated one), and Cajun court bouillons are always roux based. But, Stephen says, "it was hot and steamy out, and I wanted the dish to be lighter and more about the fish and tomatoes and peppers and less about the typical roux-based version, which I love but tends to be more of a stick-to-your-ribs-type thing." He also didn't want the catfish to cook forever as in a stew, so he fries it first and then adds it to the sauce, finishing it with some bright herbs and grilled scallions. "The fresh parsley and mint add a counterpoint to the heat of the chiles, and the scallions boost the roasted vegetable flavor." Stephen says he loves the taste and texture of catfish, but he is partial to the "muddy edge" of the "wild stuff." I am too, but I would be remiss in my role as CFA cheerleader not to add that the farm-raised variety would do just fine in this dish.

Either way, it is a masterpiece. What follows is Stephen's recipe the way he wrote it, but if you can't get your hands on lard, bacon grease or even safflower oil would work fine. Hoppin' John's excellent stone-ground corn flour (which is also great on fried oysters) is available at hinsononline.com, and if I can't find good tomatoes to roast, I use about four or five canned whole peeled ones. Stephen might wince, but I am also not above using some boxed fish stock in a pinch. No matter what, it's a perfect summer/fall offering and a delicious homage to the noble cat.

Cochon's Catfish Court Bouillon
Yield: 6 servings

INGREDIENTS

1 large onion, diced

6 ounces lard

¼ cup chopped raw garlic

2 red bell peppers, roasted, seeded, and peeled

2 green peppers, roasted, seeded, and peeled

2 poblano peppers, roasted, seeded, and peeled

1 jalapeño pepper, roasted, seeded, and peeled

3 medium-size ripe tomatoes, roasted and peeled

1 head garlic, roasted and separated into peeled cloves

2 cups fish stock

½ cup red wine vinegar

Hot sauce, to taste

Salt and pepper, to taste

2 pounds small catfish fillets

2 cups Hoppin' John's Stone-Ground Corn Flour

¼ cup whole mint leaves

¼ cup whole Italian parsley leaves

4 scallions, grilled and sliced

1 lemon, halved

PREPARATION

In a large deep skillet or a sauté pan, sweat the onions in 2 ounces of the lard. When the onions are soft and just beginning to pick up color, stir in the chopped garlic. Cook, stirring, for a minute or so and set aside.

Place the peppers, tomatoes, and roasted garlic in the bowl of a food processor and pulse until a nice chunky consistency is achieved. Add to the onion and garlic mixture in the skillet. Stir in fish stock and vinegar and bring to a simmer. Let simmer for 30 minutes and season to taste with hot sauce and salt and pepper. It should be the consistency of a thick stew and have a nice balance of heat and vinegar.

Season the catfish with salt and pepper and dust liberally with corn flour. Shallow fry the catfish in the remaining lard. Add to the sauce along with mint, parsley, and scallions.

Taste to see if more hot sauce, salt, and/or pepper is needed. Sprinkle with lemon juice and serve with white rice.

26

Secrets of a Southern Hostess

(2019)

Once, in my very early party-giving days, I was agonizing—on the phone with my mother—over what to serve at a dinner party for a famous book critic, a stories op-ed columnist, and some of my colleagues at *Newsweek*'s Washington Bureau, where I worked part-time. All the guests were older than I was and, clearly, more accomplished; I was still in college, lived in a three-room walk-up, and had exactly one byline to my name. But I could cook, and for weeks I'd been clipping recipes from the food pages of *The New York Times*, mostly overthought and fairly soulless stuff under the heading "Nouvelle Cuisine," which had just been invented.

Anyway, long distance cost a lot of money back then, and I was driving my mother crazy with a long list of choices that must have sounded pretty terrible because finally she interrupted me and said, "Why don't you just serve something that tastes good?" I have told this story many times, but it bears repeating because I took it to heart, and almost twenty years later—after I'd served a whole menu of things that tasted good at a party in my Manhattan apartment to a crowd that included an editor from *The New York Times Magazine*—I ended up writing about food for the very paper from which I once cut out all those pompous recipes. The editor who hired me apparently had never seen a pimento cheese sandwich or a deviled egg or a fat piece of rare beef tenderloin on a hot

yeast roll until that night, and it impressed him. It impresses most people, which is why my mother's long-ago advice remains my first rule of
throwing a good party: The food does not need to be formal or "fancy"
or even necessarily expensive to have an impact. In fact, the opposite is
usually the case.

For example: Journalist and famed D.C. hostess Sally Quinn tells a
story about a night when the caterers screwed up the date of a formal
dinner and she had the bright idea to send the babysitter to Popeyes.
Chicken and biscuits and red beans and rice were piled into pretty silver,
the guests took seconds and thirds and demanded to know the name of
the cook, and even the most august cabinet members took off their ties
and rolled up their sleeves so as to better get at the good stuff in front of
them. Quinn says that her male guests kiss her when she serves mashed
potatoes; I get the same response to squash casserole and cheese spoon
bread. But this kind of "simple" food takes a certain amount of fearless-
ness. During my first-ever summer in the Hamptons, I was told by the
formidable wife of an editor friend that under no circumstances could I
serve the pot of seafood gumbo and platters of fried chicken and potato
salad I'd planned on having at my debut gathering. "That's not what we
do here," she said, instructing me instead to have a seated supper of plain
grilled swordfish that was as ubiquitous that summer as shoe leather, and
just as tasteless. I was slightly terrified, but I ignored her and I've never
seen people so happy. By offering up an exotic (to them) antidote to the
asceticism to which they'd unwittingly been subjected weekend after
weekend, I set a tone I hadn't even realized I was setting. They drank
more and laughed louder, ate the chicken with their fingers, and stayed
very, very late (except for the aforementioned arbiter who ostentatiously
refused to eat a morsel and left her grateful husband behind when she
drove home in a snit).

It was then that I realized that every party should be an antidote—to
boring everydayness, to toil and strife, to clean living or the opposite lure
of TiVo and takeout Chinese. A good party should enable you to step
outside your humdrum existence and into a virtual theater of someone
else's creation, a stage set that encourages you to be your best, most

hopeful self. And that does not happen when bossy, humorless hosts or hostesses put you on accidental diets or orchestrate the conversation. The two words I feared most during the years I lived in New York City were "table talk." At one point during the meal, a glass would be clinked, and the dread words would be uttered. Each guest was then obliged to offer up his or her opinion on the latest Supreme Court nominee or some equally contentious subject, a forced march that completely shut down all the things that make being around a dinner table worthwhile: witty repartee, serious flirtation, an actually impassioned argument that ends in good-natured bread pelting rather than oration about the state of the latest immigration bill.

Those table-talk evenings always led me to the nearest post-party saloon where I could have a real conversation and enough booze to get over the previous hours' trauma. Which leads us to the next and most important rule. It is not possible to overbuy the whiskey and wine, and both should be easily accessible from moment one of the event. To that end, there is not a thing wrong with offering people a pre-drink drink, a flute of champagne, say, or a special cocktail mixed up for the occasion and served on a tray (preferably by an actual person) just outside or inside the door. This eliminates any initial stress on the part of your guest and enables festive and well-lubricated passage along the way to the actual bar. If you've got a packed house, make sure you have circulating waiters taking more orders once at the table; no one should ever have to ask for more wine. By far the most useful gifts my mother ever gave me were a pair of Irish crystal wine decanters that hold almost four bottles apiece. People reach over and refill—a lot—but the wine's still there. It's like the miracle of loaves and fishes but no one sees the magic. Which is the point. Most people don't want to be reminded that they're pounding down a bottle or two of wine all by themselves. They sort of don't want to be reminded that they are drinking at all, rather that they are simply morphing into their most lively and charming and brilliant selves, sort of like Romy and Michele in the high school reunion dream sequence where they look really hot and explain how they invented Post-it Notes, complete with the formula for the glue.

But back to the stage set. Outdoor lanterns are always festive; inside, candles are a must. Flowers too, but just as the food should not be too fussy, do not have someone come in and do your house up as if a bride is about to emerge from upstairs on the arm of her father, or worse, someone has died. If you have a yard, use it. My mother has done amazing things in her time with not much more than Johnson grass, and my own favorite trick is to smash grocery store lilies or roses or whatever looks pretty into a collection of julep cups or wine rinsers on the table.

Music is also a must. I once hired a Cajun band whose washboard player did backflips across the stage. That definitely got things going, but you could also press into duty your piano-playing best friend to re-invigorate the after-dinner crowd with a rousing version of "Twist and Shout" or "What'd I Say." There is scarcely a woman alive who does not secretly fancy herself a Raelette, and a generous host or hostess will give her the opportunity.

Finally, if the occasion demands it, have a toast ready, but for God's sake make it funny—and short. At the rehearsal dinner the night before my good friend Anne McGee's first wedding (an occasion she now refers to as "My Big Party"), all the super-serious friends and relations of her Yankee groom went on so long that the bride's brother-in-law passed out at the head table during a recitation of Rudyard Kipling and her uncle finally yelled "Bullshit!" during an especially fawning tribute that made the groom out to be something other than the man-child we knew him to be. The rest of us gave Anne just the right amount of grief in the form of brief musical tributes and suitably hilarious stories that entertained our own selves and (almost) everyone else in attendance.

On the day of the wedding, my parents threw a wedding lunch at which the backyard crowd looked a tiny bit like the Red Sea, featuring the (by now forewarned) Yankees on one side and the rest of us on the other. Not surprisingly, one side stayed later than the other, so that I was late arriving at the bride's house for the ceremony itself. As I slipped inside, I noticed the McGees' good-looking neighbor in front of me wearing a sexy chiffon cocktail dress accentuated by a pair of evening sandals, the straps of which she had tied together and slung over her shoulder. She'd been to a great many of Anne's mother's big parties and well knew the fun she was going to have. Why slow things down later when you can have your dancing feet at the ready? This is hopeful, this is what you aim for, this is the sign of a very good party to come.

27

Cooking Through COVID

(2020)

On Monday, March 16, I launched into a full-on cooking frenzy. I had left New Orleans, where I live part of the time, for the Mississippi Delta to avoid the end of Mardi Gras. As the world now knows, I avoided a lot more than that. On the same day, the New Orleans mayor more or less locked the place down; on Friday one of my oldest and closest friends came down with COVID-19. She is now fine, but within two weeks cases had exploded across the city. Feeling helpless and isolated (well, not completely—I had the ever-trusty Henry the beagle and a veritable bird sanctuary for company), I ordered a ton of food online. If I am honest, I was driven at least as much by the desire to never ever set foot inside Kroger or Walmart again, or at least not for a very long time. And then, you know, the food arrives in all these coolers and boxes and you feel compelled to cook it.

Included in the stash were whole briskets with which I made my own corned beef (not nearly as good as that found at Stein's in New Orleans—first lesson learned) and a supremely time-consuming recipe from my beloved Suzanne Goin that involved marinating and braising the meat, which was then accompanied by a horseradish crema and a potato puree that required two types of potato. I made Lidia Bastianich's Bolognese sauce, ramp pesto, and at least three of Nigella Lawson's ridiculously easy and tasty clementine cakes. In the weeks leading up to

Easter, I researched English hot cross buns, ordered a slew of dried fruit to go in them, and ended up opting for an English muffin with marmalade on the morning of. I learned to spatchcock a chicken (why have I not been doing this all my life?) and made tons of stock with the bones. One day I went especially bananas and ordered two dozen cans of sardines and mackerel in olive oil—each. I had visions of making a French potato salad with tarragon and chives and the mackerel with a lemony aioli on the side. Sounds lovely, doesn't it? Next month perhaps, when I can face peeling another potato. As I type, there is another brisket and an entire side of bacon in the freezer.

What I realized is that while cooking for oneself is supposed to be a healthy expression of self-love, self-care, whatever, it is cooking for other people that really brings me joy. In those very early days, the only beneficiary was Henry, who will now barely eat his own food, knowing as he does that if he is patient enough and makes enough noise (an unsettling new development), he will be the happy recipient of sourdough croutons, morsels of chicken, a chunk of Parmesan or Vermont cheddar, or a slice of prosciutto that is better suited to wrapping round the incredible cantaloupe my friend Rabbit brings me every Thursday when the melon man sets up a stand on the highway. I was, until not too long ago, a creature of restaurants and the night. Henry knew he had best eat his own food if he wanted to eat at all.

By the end of the first week, I was sharing with two-legged folk, leaving packages on the hoods of my friends' cars and receiving the same. Rabbit brought me the melon, fresh eggs, homemade wine vinegar, divine runny cheese, and the best vichyssoise I've ever tasted. In return, I took him olive oil cake, the aforementioned pesto, tarragon from the herb garden I planted, the pâtés I continually overorder. My mother sent me bits of almost everything she made (including tomato aspic, blackberry cobbler, and a congealed cranberry salad I have loved since childhood), and I returned the favor. On Mother's Day we sat at opposite ends of my outdoor table and shared a rack of lamb with an inspired mint sauce (chicken stock, fish sauce, honey, a ton of mint, and the lamb jus).

It was magic. We had missed each other. We had cocktails and looked at the trees I'd just planted and drank a bottle of delicious Pomerol with dinner. Then came the gnats. It is not enough that we are living through a full-fledged plague. If you live where I do, you also have plenty of pestilence. This year, during one of the most beautiful springs of my lifetime, millions of buffalo gnats (so named because they are fat, brown, and furry) were encouraged by the high water to cross the river from Arkansas, effectively ruining our lives. Nothing kills them, though they are (very) mildly deterred by a spray called Buggins, which is not ideal perfume for dining, or (rumor has it) a scent from Victoria's Secret that I imagine to be worse. They stick around until it's too hot to go outside, which means I'm going to have to start sleeping on plastic sheets—my brand-new embroidered cotton numbers (food is not remotely the only thing I've been ordering online) look like Zorro has been after me. The welts (which don't respond to even the highest prescription of cortisone) make mosquito bites look like pinpricks.

I realize that in the hideous and highly unfair world we are living in, it seems pretty petty to bitch about gnats. And perhaps even pettier to damn the whole of Arkansas as their benighted source. I have a lot of fine friends from the Arkansas Delta, but I personally have witnessed some seriously bad stuff going on in the rest of the state. When I was twenty-two and working for the summer in *Newsweek*'s Atlanta bureau, a lot of white-supremacist groups were rearing their ugly heads, and the editors in New York sent me to check out the Covenant, the Sword, and the Arm of the Lord, a particularly nasty bunch who referred to the US government as ZOG (Zionist Occupied Government) and were preparing for the end-time in a camp somewhere in the Ozarks, not far from where the Netflix show starring Jason Bateman and Laura Linney is set. In retrospect, I should have been a tad more nervous about charging up in there in the company of a mouthy photographer, but when I called the leader, I realized he craved attention and, anyway, I knew these guys. Like almost every redneck with whom I grew up, they didn't want to pay taxes, didn't want to send their kids to school with African Americans (though that is certainly not the term they used), didn't want to hear from their "women" (whom they housed in a separate dorm with the kids, who received little education and went mostly barefoot), did not, when it came down to it, want to have their dubious manhood messed with in any way. They sat around and told dirty jokes and read porn and scratched their hairy stomachs. But they also wore MAC-10 submachine guns crossed over those big bellies and had a fleet of tanks on the premises, along with an anti-tank rocket launcher and piles of sawed-off shotguns. For fun every night, they practiced shooting moving plywood cutouts of people inside "homes" in a "community" they dubbed Silhouette City. After three days, I badly wanted to get out of there and urged the magazine not to give them the cover story they so desperately craved. The FBI finally took them down, but not until after they'd trained many like-minded folks to go out and wreak their own havoc and one of the members shot a gun store owner and an African American police officer. I drove away over a gorge on a bridge the Klan was said to have wired with explosives in case they needed a no-access safe harbor, and what I know now is that I should never have been so cavalier in my assessment of these bozos, examples of another kind of pestilence that has infected American life from the get-go. These guys were like the damn gnats: You don't always see them coming and you don't know the harm they've done until you're practically bleeding to death.

So what to do? While we are faced with larger reckonings, the smaller act of cooking suddenly doesn't seem so crazy. We are, most of us, in the midst of a national wake, grieving for an ever-growing number of lives lost and dreams—still—deferred. Where I come from, a wake demands food, a lot of it. My mother is a master of the art of the funeral lunch. Black churches usually call them repasts. By any name, I see piles of fried chicken, squash casserole, pound cakes, corn bread, green beans cooked forever with ham hocks, potato salad, macaroni with a ton of cheese. When my aunt died, I arrived at her house after a long drive, expecting to see at least one or two of those things on the dining room table. Instead there was bad takeout Chinese. Where the hell was the love in that?

Everyone I know has a signature dish for such occasions. My dear friend Helen Bransford, who knows a lot about a lot of things, always brings tomato sandwiches, an inspired idea if you think about it, perfect for nervous pickup eating and exactly what anybody with any sense wants to eat. I will be making a whole lot of those in the coming days, peeling the tomatoes, as my mother always does, and spreading the crustless white bread with her sublime homemade mayonnaise. I want the lobster roll I perfected last summer on Martha's Vineyard, Gulf shrimp boiled for a nanosecond and eaten, still steaming, from the colander in the sink. I'll make "fried" corn off the cob, okra and tomatoes, thick Roman steaks with garlic and rosemary like the ones at Nino in Rome, a place I will most likely not visit anytime soon. This is less ambitious than my original crazed efforts but far more soul filling. Meanwhile, if the end-time does come, I have a whole lot of mackerel and sardines to get me through.

PART 7

The South

28

The Southern Name Change

(2018)

I come from a long line of people on both sides of my family who named their children after folks they were actually related to. For this I am profoundly grateful. Had my mother made like, say, Gwyneth Paltrow and named me after a fruit, I might have ended up as Fig, her favorite. (Though come to think of it, she likes peaches an awful lot too, and in that case, where I live at least, I wouldn't have been the only one burdened—or blessed—with that moniker.) Or she could have gotten the jump on the Kardashians and given me and my two brothers names that begin with the letter R. The Kardashians irritate me in ways that you do not want to get me started on, but I am not necessarily against siblings with names possessed of the same initial consonants. I have very fond feelings, for instance, toward a man named Rudy Smith, the owner of a now-defunct towing operation, who once fished my car out of a canal in Harahan, Louisiana. While I sat in Rudy's office waiting happily for him to declare my car a total loss (it was an ancient Plymouth Acclaim and pretty much of a loss even before I accidentally drove it into a really deep ditch), I leafed through his brochure, the cover of which featured him posing in a suit in front of the St. Louis Cathedral flanked by his brothers, Ricky, Ronnie, and Randy. I liked that. But then, unlike those of the Kardashians, those are names that actually exist in nature.

Also, when Southerners make up new names, it's usually a more meaningful exercise than simply slapping a K where it does not belong, like when people name their girls after their daddies. This results in the likes of Raylene, Bobette, Earline, Georgette (one of George Jones's daughters), Georgine, and my personal favorite, Floy (feminine for Floyd). As it happens, I almost got a masculine name (unfeminized) myself. I was named after my maternal grandmother, Julia Evans Clements Brooks, and my mother was dead set on calling me Evans until my father put his foot down on the grounds that that was the kind of stuff that Yankees did. Maybe, but we do plenty of the last name/family name business for girls down here, too. Off the top of my head I can think of three Southern women I love a lot: Keith, Cameron, Egan. Still, it's a practice not without risks: My former daughter-in-law's daughter is named Winslow, and she is a very smart, pretty little girl, but it took monumental control for me to resist the urge to call her Homer.

In the end, we did it in my family too. My two nieces are named Evans and Brooks. Which is where it gets confusing. I've got a male first cousin named Brooks and a male second cousin named Evans, which was also the name of his father and grandfather. All the recent generations of men not named Brooks or Evans are named Runcie, and all the women are either Julia or Frances. My cousin Brooks even married a woman named Frances, the name of his sister and mother and great-grandmother and probably plenty of girls further back than that. I am not qualified to venture into the Freudian implications of his choice (and this particular Frances is a fine human being), but it does make dividing the passed-down monogrammed linens super easy.

My niece Brooks named her daughter Serena, my maternal great-grandfather's mother's name. I am so proud of her in a way that I decidedly would not have been had she lifted it from Blake Lively's character on *Gossip Girl* (in my generation it would have been Samantha's cousin on *Bewitched*). I love that she reached way back. If I'd had a daughter, I always knew I'd have named her Eliza Bouldin, the name of my father's maternal grandmother. There are some epic names on that side of the family: Sterling Price Reynolds, Gideon Crews, William Thomas Bouldin Crews. My youngest brother was saddled with the name Reynolds

Crews to assuage my father's irritation over my other brother being a junior (he'd wanted to honor his ancestors and not himself). Our pediatrician joked (sort of) that we should just call him R.C., but when you get down to it, that's like naming someone MoonPie.

It didn't end up mattering much because both boys were almost always referred to as Brother or Bubba, and to this day no one in my immediate family or its orbit has ever called me anything but Sister. Which leads us to another Southern phenomenon. There's Tennessee Williams's Sister Woman, of course, and a character in a Lee Smith short story is named Uncle Baby Brother. Sometimes it's hard to tell whether these sorts of sobriquets are simply early nicknames that stuck or actual appellations. For example, I have an especially lovely friend in New Orleans named Sweet. Hers is a family name and the middle name she goes by, and it's a good thing she really and truly is a very sweet person because no one wants to be a walking, talking irony. But I have known other people all my life—Baby Doll Walker, Bebe Shackelford, Buddha McGough—and I have no idea if the names they go by are on their birth certificates or if they're what their mamas or nurses or whoever started calling them when they were young. I know my friend Bo Weevil Law is actually named Sid, that Honk Morson's real name was Andrew and that his nickname was short for "honky-tonk," that Ug McGee's name was Humphreys but he was so pretty they dubbed him Ugly and abbreviated it to Ug. (In Honk's case, when his stickball teammates asked him if he knew what a honky-tonk was, he replied that it was a donkey. After howls of laughter, they dubbed him Honk. Naturally.)

Some folks give you clues up front that their nicknames are just that. There were two famous state legislators from the Mississippi Delta whose names I never saw in print any other way but H. L. "Sonny" Merideth and C. B. "Buddy" Newman. The latter even has C. B. "Buddy" on the marker alongside his memorial highway. The former, who is buried in a field not far from that stretch of road, was also a lawyer and had a client married to a man named Marty "Bullets" Albinder. When Marty's wife caught him messing around with another woman, she lay in wait and pumped the contents of two guns into his chest. There are three miracles here: Marty survived the shooting, Sonny managed not to have his client charged with the "alleged" crime, and Marty gave his own self his nickname and was so proud of the new handle he had it printed on the nameplate he wore at the riverboat casino where he found employment after his recovery.

Southerners also have a famous proclivity for the double name. My favorite show as a child was *Petticoat Junction*, largely because of the three sisters, Betty Jo, Bobbie Jo, and Billie Jo (the blond and gorgeous Meredith MacRae, the one I most wanted to be), even though I'm sure that show was set somewhere in Upstate New York (Hooterville was the same town, after all, to which Eddie Albert and Eva Gabor decamped from Park Avenue on *Green Acres*). But since the characters were supposed to be bona fide country bumpkins, the surest way for Hollywood scriptwriters in the 1960s to get that across was to give the girls Southern names, as in Elly May Clampett (the daughter on *The Beverly Hillbillies*, who was in fact born in Tennessee). Once when I was bitching about Siri's persistence in misunderstanding most everything I say, my pal the artist David Bates suggested that some enterprising Southerner should invent an app called Siri Ann. I laughed hard at that, though I have to say I prefer Siri Sue. But double names can be a tad dangerous. My best friend's middle name, LeAnn, is a mash-up of the names of her paternal uncle and aunt. When they divorced, she kept the name—and the friendship with both—but then she's an angel and most people are not.

My niece is currently pregnant with her second child, and she is digging deep into my father's family tree rather than turning to the countless baby-name websites that have become so insanely popular. On babynames.com you can even find out what names are trending daily. As I type, the second most popular boy's name is Caleb, but I'd be willing to bet that a whole lot of the mothers and fathers out there randomly choosing that particular forename have no idea where it even came from (son of Jephunneh, representative of the Tribe of Judah during the Israelites' journey to the Promised Land, Numbers 14:30). If she lands on the name Gideon, which goes back to at least my great-great-great-great-great-grandfather, she'll have to remind people of that fact lest they think she is like so many of her hipster contemporaries, picking stuff like Atticus, Noah (number two on mom365.com), or Liam (number one on the same site). They are time-honored names, to be sure, but to me, grabbing them out of thin air is not unlike buying a Shinola watch. Still, my niece and everybody else for that matter could do worse than Gideon. He's a biblical figure too, a military leader, judge, and prophet whose battles were won through strategic thinking and faith rather than arms alone.

To be fair, I do get the impulse to turn away from family for a name. There might well be too much baggage there. Also, sometimes people just come out looking like what their name should be, like my dog Henry, whom I realize is not an actual person but close enough. Some sweet baby might simply look like a Jack or a Sam or a Mary or a Jane. (Still, while I'm beating this horse, I bet no one comes straight out of the womb looking like Madison, one of the most popular names of 2017, nor does anyone look like a Khloé or a Kourtney—at least not without a boatload of filler and silicone and God knows what else.) But here again is another slippery slope. We should keep in mind that one of Honk's teammates on the stickball team was Moonface Abernathy. Sometimes looks can't help but name the man.

29

Cat Tails

(2019)

This past September, while the temperature hovered in the high nineties and the humidity was its usual unbearable self, 7,556 homes in New Orleans lost power after a cat wandered into a substation at 8:30 in the morning and caused a flash by touching the equipment. Entergy New Orleans claimed to have installed "protective devices" to keep cats out, but apparently it does not know the wily ways of the feline race. Since I was not among the thousands without power, naturally I felt most sorry for the cat. In a tweet, Entergy said, "When this happens, the animals unfortunately do not survive the high-voltage contact." And there you have it: one more reason to despise power companies.

While it pains me to say anything even remotely in this particular company's defense, cats have been known to wreak a little havoc. When I was in college in Washington, D.C., I adopted a kitty from my beloved *Newsweek* colleague and Georgetown neighbor Jane Whitmore. Jane and her two daughters had taken in a stray they named Bob and then Bob surprised everyone by turning out to be Bobbie Jo and pretty much immediately giving birth to a litter of kittens. The one I chose, Sam, was the bruiser of the bunch—one of his siblings had died in infancy because Sam hogged all his mother's milk. I picked him up without a crate—we had maybe a two-minute drive and I figured I could hold him in my lap.

Wrong. By the time we made it home, my favorite silk blouse looked like one of those multi-tailed kites blowing in the wind.

As a kitten, Sam woke me up each morning by jumping on my chest of drawers and knocking over, one by one, every antique cut-glass bottle that I'd painstakingly collected from London's Portobello Road until I got up and fed him. Closing the door was not an option. He simply got a running start and hurled his entire bulk against the door, creating a sonic boom more powerful than any alarm clock. And his bulk was not insignificant. He weighed thirty-five pounds and had an enormous handsome head and long black hair, which made him seem even more massive than he was. Such was his appearance that when Sam and I lived in Orlando, Florida—in a house with a jalousie glass front door— the Orkin man mistook him for a bear. He was a new guy, so when he called me at work to say he couldn't go in the house, I figured he didn't know where the key was hidden. "No ma'am," he said, "it's not that. There's a bear cub loose in your living room."

I was proud that Sam was such a notable—and noble—beast. I had my friend the great painter John Alexander capture his lordly beauty in a portrait just before he died, after twenty years of loyal and entertaining companionship. I loved Sam and I am crazy about cats in general. So I was happy for my mother when she called to tell me she had acquired one of her own. (She had already nixed another dog, saying she could not repeat the trauma of the demise of our last yellow Lab, Bo, ever, ever again.) But that was before I met the cat, to whom, rather irritatingly, she gave the late, great Sam's name.

The luckiest day of Sam II's life was the day he decided (wisely—cats have scary good intuition) to wander up our long gravel drive and into the loving arms of my super compassionate mother. (She once almost killed us all braking for a butterfly. "They have such short lives already," she said after we wound up in the ditch.) He weighed almost nothing, he'd been chewed on by some critter or other, and he was skittish as all hell. The plan had been to clean him up and give him the run of the air-conditioned utility room outside. But that was before the discovery that he was afflicted with feline immunodeficiency virus, otherwise known as feline AIDS. The cat immediately became ruler of the house. In the summer, so that her prized pet could still enjoy some semblance of the outdoors, my mother opened every single screened window, which meant the thermostat was set to something like thirty-two degrees. Further, every morning, to this day, he gets newly washed and ironed six-hundred-thread-count pillowcases on all the numerous spots where he likes to lounge. Now, I have known and loved my mother all my life, so not a bit of this stuff surprised me. The cat, she said, had lifted her from her depression (which none of us knew she had); the cat could do whatever he wanted. The only thing she could not allow him to do was be in the presence of my sainted dog, Henry.

This was sort of a deal breaker. I go home a lot; Henry likes to go with me. My mother, dead serious, informed me that the mere sight of the dog would give the cat a fatal heart attack. She actually tried putting those words in the vet's mouth, but again, I've known my mother all my life, and I know the vet well enough to know that he would not in fact make such a pronouncement. Still, when Mama has a theory, it is iron-clad even if it's a tiny bit insane. Finally, after two years, I decided it was way past time to test it. As soon as I let Henry in the kitchen door, the cat not only did not have a heart attack, he pounced on my poor, peace-loving pup and beat him over the head with his paws. When Henry finally escaped and ran yelping for safe harbor beneath the living room sofa, the cat followed and commenced beating him some more. Since Sam II is clearly going to live forever (he has far better health care than the great majority of this country's human citizenry), there was nothing to do but build what is essentially the most expensive doghouse in the Mississippi Delta, now almost at completion. Henry and I both need a safe place to sleep.

Much as Sam II might irritate me, I have to admit that cats, even those not allowed outside, do possess several useful traits in addition to being mood lifting and extremely entertaining (as evidenced—interminably—by umpteen zillion cat videos). When I moved into the apartment that would be Sam's and my first home together, it was inhabited by so many mice that I had repeated nightmares of rats crawling all over me, as in a scene from *Willard*, a movie that scared the hell out of me when I was a kid and haunts me to this day (although not as much as the demented *Frogs*, starring Ray Milland, but I digress). As soon as Sam turned up, the mice vanished and so did my bad dreams. My childhood cat West Virginia, a regal gray American shorthair, was fond of leaving bird carcasses at the back door each morning. I love birds as much as the next person, but Virginia's prowess—and her own pride in it—never failed to amuse and impress me. Really, now that I think of it, it's a shame cats don't go after bigger birds as a sort of public service. They can wreak far more regular havoc than the power station's tragic kitty.

To take a famous case in point, there was the "Miracle on the Hudson" in which a US Airways jet struck a flock of geese after takeoff from New York's LaGuardia Airport. The cool handling of the situation made the pilot Chesley Sullenberger a hero, but this stuff happens all the time. For example, a few months ago, after a seriously splendid few days in Tangier, I was standing in line to board a plane (on Ryanair, which I would wholeheartedly *not* recommend) when the gate agent inexplicably locked the door to the tarmac through which all the plane's passengers were about to walk. The Moroccans are not big on information (or on much-needed airport bars, which are forbidden), and not a single announcement was ever made. Flummoxed, I called on a lifetime of reporting skills. After many, many interviews with everyone in anything that remotely resembled a uniform, I managed to ascertain that a bird had flown into one of our plane's engines, where it had not met a happy end. ("Big bird! Barbacoa!") The engine had already been repaired, but a Ryanair engineer had to be flown in from, I swear, Bergamo, Italy, to sign off on things. Ten hours later we peered into the night and watched a tiny woman disembark from a plane, shine a flashlight into our aircraft's engine, and scribble her name on some paperwork.

We were then released, but all day long, and well into the night, I had been priding myself on my Zen-like attitude. Somebody I follow on Instagram had that very day posted a line from Galatians that read, "But the fruit of the Spirit is love, joy, peace, patience, kindness, goodness, faithfulness, gentleness, self-control." As Richard Gere once said to me, apropos of his hero the Dalai Lama, "Keeping your heart open is a tough gig, man." Yep. So is the long list contained in the aforementioned Bible passage, but I endeavored mightily. Things did not fall apart until we boarded the plane and I ordered a double Dewar's on the rocks, which I had assumed—incorrectly—would be on the house (let me add here that Ryanair is such a supposed bargain because you must also pay—dearly—for coffee, water, tea, you name it). When I very politely mentioned our long wait to the flight attendant, she shot back, "Well, we had to wait too, you know." Patience, kindness, gentleness, and self-control thus met the fate of the unfortunate bird.

Birds are not the only airport problem. Last year planes in Utqiagvik, Alaska, were delayed for hours by an extremely large seal that stretched itself out smack in the middle of the runway and refused to budge. Animal control was summoned (presumably not from Bergamo) and it was at last removed, but that's the kind of stuff that's too amusing to be irritating. Likewise the hares that are fond of darting around the runways of Milan, a situation the shambolic Italians have chosen to remedy by enlisting volunteers to blow whistles and wave.

As it happens, all these airports would be far better served by a single call to my very own father. More than sixty years ago, he bought a patent from some Belgians and formed a company, Reed-Joseph International, that sells Scare-Aways to farmers and airports and any other entity that wants to keep various varmints from interfering with its business. Among Reed-Joseph's wares are radio-controlled cannons, Bird Bangers, Screamer Sirens, and many more items all designed for the "harmless, effective dispersal of birds and wildlife." About twenty years ago, an off-duty fireman was repairing one of those items and managed to blow up Daddy's entire office, unleashing a series of booms and sirens so loud that half the town thought we'd been the victim of a terrorist attack (the Atlanta Olympic bombing had taken place the day before, so, of course, Greenville, population 32,704, would be next). Anyway, when operated correctly, these things are as safe as the day is long and are extraordinary deterrents. Yes, this is indeed a shameless plug, but also a plea of sorts. Think of the cats these things could save. I also am going to strongly encourage Daddy's far younger partner, Barthell Joseph III, to get himself to Tangier forthwith. I never want to spend ten hours in an alcohol-free airport again. It is a seriously tough gig.

30

A Delta Housewarming

(2019)

Since I was twenty-five, by which time I'd been away from home for almost ten years, I've fantasized about building a house, a retreat of sorts, in or near my hometown in the Mississippi Delta. I hadn't realized how long I'd actually had this particular dream until a few weeks ago when I found a love letter from the man I almost married that brought me to my knees. In it, he envisioned the place that even then he knew I'd always wanted, and that he had wanted for both of us. "Could you hang orchids from the veranda like you do in Malaysia, and grow mangoes in the garden?" he wrote. We would have a Vietnamese cook who would do miraculous things to catfish; we'd gaze out at the Mississippi in reclining wicker chairs "having some sort of long drink" or maybe "a fine old Armagnac."

An obvious first question might be why in the world I called off my wedding to this lovely, poetic man. The answer to his own question is no, you cannot hang orchids from the veranda except maybe in the dead of summer, and we'd need a greenhouse for the mangoes. When he sent the letter, he had not yet made the trek to my home state, which is not quite as tropical as he clearly thought—he had been born in Australia, at the time lived in London, and was a foreign correspondent who had spent a lot of time in the Far East. Still, his was a deeply romantic image and one I carried around in one guise or another for three more decades.

And then, at the beginning of last year, I started building the house. Two things had happened. One, I got divorced. I became, you know, myself again and remembered how much long-dormant thoughts, hopes, plans, visions had meant to me. About the same time, my mother, in a healthy fit of unsentimentality, decided to put our family house up for sale, which conveniently had a skinny strip of land behind it on the other side of a tall fence, one on which she had grown tomatoes and roses, across the private dirt road from the pasture where I'd kept my horse Hi Joe. (Okay, so there's no view of the river, but the pasture is green and gorgeous and populated with picturesque paint horses.) "Please, please, *please*, whatever you do," I begged, "do *not* sell that land." She did not, which turned out to be a good thing since for the past couple of years I'd been secretly, actively thinking about a house there, scribbling plans on legal pads, starting a folder titled simply "F" for Folly. I kept a folder on my phone too, of Instagram images that inspired me—posts of wide unstained floorboards just like the ones now on my floor, of an English sofa with a French chintz slipcover, almost exactly like the version that sits in front of my new mantel, painted in the same Farrow & Ball Card Room Green I'd been obsessed with for years.

I'd renovated one grand house in New Orleans' Garden District and gotten a book out of it, but believe me when I say that is not an experience I would ever repeat. Also, this house would be mine and only mine, imagined from the ground up and full of things I truly, madly love, like my books (the great majority of which had been languishing in storage since the sale of the house) and Henry the beagle (who for the first time in his life would be able to go outside without a leash, in a small hedged-in garden built just for him). I wanted an enormous meadow of daffodils (bulbs rot in the wet ground of my adopted city) and a mini-orchard of the pear trees and crab apple trees I'd climbed as a child. I decidedly did not want or need a ton of square feet (been there, done that), but I did want floods of light and the feeling of space and tall, tall windows I could throw open wide.

For that last bit, I needed an actual professional, so I immediately turned to my great friend the Birmingham architect James Carter. We scribbled on yet another legal pad in his office, talked details over dinner at Frank Stitt's glorious Highlands Bar & Grill, and the house was not just born but pretty much perfect. Overnight, James produced a colored sketch featuring a green house with simple white columns and the orange trumpet vine I told him I'd always imagined on the front (the next best thing to orchids). We toned it down a bit—for a hot minute it looked a little like Monticello—but James knew instantly what to do and gave me one great soaring space with the necessary bits added on (bedroom, mudroom, kitchen, dressing room, and bath). We consulted, a lot, with our mutual dear friends, the talented team of Courtney Coleman and Bill Brockschmidt, designers based in New York and New Orleans who share my sensibility almost to a T and who have worked on lots of projects for people I know and love.

On the ground, my sainted friend Hank Burdine, who can do pretty much anything, sweetly agreed to guide the project. Hank once built roads for a living; now he is an über-ambassador for where we were both born and raised, spearheading festivals (most recently the Delta Blues and Greens Festival in Clarksdale), serving on the all-important Levee Board, grilling the world's best duck poppers, and chronicling what's important in his brand-new memoir, *Dust in the Road: Recollections of a Delta Boy*. Hank had already introduced my mother to her new favorite carpenter, Tommy Carnell (and she's had a lot), so he left her new house and started work on mine, puzzling over some of James's seemingly more arcane instructions, but getting it done with his crack—and very entertaining—team, who also managed to crack me up almost daily along the way.

And then, miraculously, it was all but done less than a year after we broke ground—without any of the horror stories that had filled up whole book chapters, without me throwing myself on the ground weeping or threatening to beat anyone's head in with his own hammer, with a few, ahem, overruns, naturally, but still, it was there just in time for Thanksgiving in all its green glory. So I did what I always do and decided to have a party.

In my experience, the best way to pull a house together is to have a lavish party that seems insanely premature or even impossible. Otherwise it will never, ever be finished. For example: In the midst of a fairly extensive redo of my Manhattan apartment, Jon Meacham's wife, Keith, and I decided to throw him a huge birthday bash with a guest list that included such fancy (and disparate) folks as Katharine Graham and Manolo Blahnik. On the days leading up to the party, I had been sleeping under painters' tarps. The morning of the event, the carpet layers arrived with new sisal for the entire place, and my mother was hanging pictures down the upstairs hall. Minutes before the guests arrived, my father was dispatched to Citarella for five more pounds of crabmeat *just in case*, and Keith ran to Gracious Home for a bedspread. And it was great. Mrs. Graham, who had just had both hips replaced, arrived early, so we ensconced her in one of the few comfortable chairs. Manolo hung out in my bedroom, where he noticed my empty shoe closet (it had just been painted), which resulted in the generous gift of multiple boxes of new shoes with which to fill it. People walked through the French windows to smoke on the fire escape; at one point it was so crowded people were holding glasses over their heads à la *Breakfast at Tiffany's*.

With that triumph in mind, I figured Thanksgiving in the new abode would be a cinch. After all, I'd put on a seated lunch for twenty-four in New Orleans on the first Thanksgiving after Katrina when no more than a bare bulb hung from the dining room ceiling. A call went out to festive friends near and far. Ellen Stimson, her husband, John, her three kids, and her friend David, who is by now also a friend of mine, made plans to drive from Vermont, where they live, all the way to Montreal just to fly down to Memphis, where they would then have to get in the car again. My pal Courtney, a close friend since boarding-school days who has a PhD in theology and an iPhone home screen featuring a shot of her with her buddy the archbishop of Canterbury, offered to bless the house. My Georgetown roommate Anne Flaherty turned up early, thank God, since on the Tuesday night when she arrived, the place could still be best described as a box museum and there was no mattress on the daybed, which supplies much of the main room's seating. Still, we managed to get rid of the boxes, dry brine the turkey, and procure a mattress (and a mixer and countless other things) on multiple trips to Walmart, while my mother, once again, hung the pictures.

By Wednesday, things were looking good until I realized that while I had a shiny new Wolf range, there was no gas hooked up to it. Many, many increasingly frantic (hysterical, really) calls to the operators at the gas company's headquarters somewhere near Waco, Texas, ensued. (Polite, Zen-like operator: "Ma'am, I promise he is going to get to you today—there are a lot of emergencies in the area." Me, unhinged: "This is a freaking emergency! I have six people coming all the way from Canada to eat a turkey I cannot cook!") Then four of the six did not actually make the plane from Canada (the four who stopped for doughnuts), so by the time the stragglers pulled into town, they had been traveling for twenty-four hours and son Eli had toted two pies (an amazing pecan made with duck fat and a deep-dish cherry that Ellen knows is my favorite) in his mother's pie basket through four major airports so we could have them with our lunch. These are intrepid folks.

We all are: my ninety-year-old father and my mother, who, more than anyone, helped me will this house into being; so many of my closest friends who gathered around the long farmhouse table to break bread and christen a dream I'd held on to forever. We ate—a lot—and drank and were very merry, and the next night Courtney produced a script that included a blessing for almost every square inch of the house and an intermission featuring a group sing-along of the Karla Bonoff song "Home" led by the great blues pianist and singer Eden Brent, whom I've known and loved since she was four. Keith blessed the entrance, and Hank blessed the bar, and Anne blessed the living room, and John, who is a brilliant English teacher, blessed the library. While at least four people crowded into my fine new Kohler tub, Eli blessed the dressing room and bath, reading, in part, "Let [Julia] be adorned in splendid raiment, and may her feet always walk, shod only in Manolos, in your heavenly ways."

With that, of course, we had come full circle, as some of the same Manolos given to me by the master himself after that long-ago New York shindig now grace my new shoe closet. By the time this appears in print, more old friends will have come to celebrate Christmas and I'll have greeted the first morning of 2019 with Henry and the horses across the way. I'll also have played some of the tunes (my shelves are happily filled with all my old vinyl) that my former fiancé imagined us listening to in his letter: Jimmy Yancey at the piano on "At the Window" and Sonny Rollins and Dizzy Gillespie doing "After Hours." They are among my favorite songs, but in this case especially, better suited for a reflective solo sip or two. At the party, Eden closed us down with something far more fitting and joyful: a rousing and completely infectious version of Ray Charles's "What'd I Say." Everyone clapped and stomped and sang at the top of their lungs. By the end of the night, a few inaugural dents had been put in the heart-pine planks, and the house was blessed indeed.

31

All Praise Willie Nelson

(2019)

In January, on a very cold, rainy night not in Georgia (RIP, Tony Joe White) but in Nashville, I took my mother to the Bridgestone Arena to see a star-studded tribute to Willie Nelson, which was heralded as a commemoration of his eighty-sixth year and titled "Willie: Life & Songs of an American Outlaw." By now the show may well have been broadcast on the A&E channel (as I write the date has not yet been set), and if so, I hope y'all saw it because it was pretty damn amazing. Mama and I are inveterate concertgoers. We've seen everybody from Petula Clark and the Carpenters to Edgar Winter's White Trash (not entirely her idea) to the Rolling Stones. I knew she loved Willie and at least a half dozen of the umpteen folks featured in the show, but the real reason I invited her to go was to see Kris Kristofferson, whom she worships like no other. One summer night years ago, we sat on our Seaside, Florida, front porch with a couple of friends and a boom box and listened to *Songs of Kristofferson* about 150 times, in tears, naturally. Admittedly, we were fueled by more than one pitcher of frozen peach margaritas (well, actually, they were more like margarita daiquiris because I thought it might be interesting to add a bottle of rum). But you don't have to be drunk to be equally moved—five of the twelve songs on the compilation are quite simply among the best ever written. In the world. I once asked Chris Gantry (who wrote "Dreams of the Everyday Housewife," a seriously fine composition its ownself) to name the most perfect, most quintessential country song and braced myself for "He Stopped Loving Her Today" (almost invariably the number one answer), but he didn't miss a beat: "Help Me Make It Through the Night." As the kids would say, true dat.

But back to the concert. Chris Stapleton opened with a rousing "Whiskey River." Next up were Willie's sons Micah and Lukas, who are perfectly beautiful and super talented (Lukas cowrote eight of the songs in *A Star Is Born*) and sound exactly like a fifty-years-younger Willie. Nathaniel Rateliff, on the keyboards, did a soul-stirring version of Leon Russell's "A Song for You," and Jack Johnson sang a sweet and hilarious tune written for the occasion called "Willie Got Me Stoned." Gentleman Lyle Lovett (as I've decided to call him because he's clearly so kind and courtly and I have such a crush) did a terrific cover of "My Heroes Have Always Been Cowboys," and Vince Gill, another of the world's nicest men, killed "Blue Eyes Crying in the Rain." And then there were the breakout performances of the night: Alison Krauss singing "Angel Flying Too Close to the Ground" and Jamey Johnson doing "Georgia on My Mind." Now, I have heard both those songs a whole lot of times by a whole lot of people, but Krauss took my breath plain away (along with everybody else's), and Johnson brought me to my feet (along with the rest of the packed house).

There were a whole bunch of other people, including Jimmy Buffett and George Strait, who had never before sung with Willie—an astonishing fact given that the birthday boy had done duets with everybody from Julio Iglesias to Snoop Dogg, not to mention every other country star in America, and one that Strait lampooned with "I Never Got to Sing One with Willie." Toward the fourth hour, Willie and Kris did their own duet of "Me and Bobby McGee," and though Kris's voice was maybe not what I would term its tip-top best, Mama wouldn't hear a bad word about him and declared that he looked fabulous to boot. Also, there was the house band, which was worth the not-exactly-cheap price of admission alone. Pulled together by the brilliant producer Don Was, who played bass, it featured the great Matt Rollings on keyboard (he produced Willie's *Summertime* album and has played on every single one of Lyle Lovett's recordings, among countless more), Amanda Shires on fiddle (in a crazy-hot drum majorette outfit, she also did a ravishing duet with her husband, Jason Isbell), and Mickey Raphael on harmonica.

Mickey, who has been playing with Willie for forty-five years, is the hardest-working man in show business. Impeccably dressed, as always, in a slim black suit, he played on all but maybe two songs in the four-and-a-half-hour show. Mama was worried to death about him. Plus, he'd rehearsed for two days, unlike his boss, who does not do much in the way of rehearsing. (I mean, what the hell—he's eighty-five and he's long since paid back the IRS; and, you know, he's Willie.) Which meant that it was a good thing that on the dozen or so songs he sang himself, he had some stellar help, including Emmylou on the great Townes Van Zandt epic "Pancho and Lefty." By the time he and Stapleton came out with "Always on My Mind" (which, as my mother correctly pointed out, is the lamest love song ever), his pipes had opened up and he and the full ensemble closed things out with rollicking renditions of "On the Road Again" (of course), "Roll Me Up and Smoke Me When I Die," and "I'll Fly Away."

I first met Mickey on the same day I met Willie and Kris, sometime in the early nineties, on a bus in the bowels of the Superdome during that summer's Farm Aid. It was a memorable afternoon. We smoked a lot of dope and Kris quoted a lot of William Blake, and Mickey, who now rides the "straight bus" exclusively (yes, there are two buses these days), mentioned that one of his relatives had once owned a watch store in New Orleans, so we went on a stroll down Canal Street to try to find it. I was a guest on the bus, the first of many times, courtesy of my friend Susan Nadler, who really should have her gorgeous mug next to the definition of sui generis in Webster's. She grew up in Pittsburgh, a self-described Jewish American Princess, and spent time in Israel on a kibbutz and then in a Mexican jail (an experience you can read all about in her book *The Butterfly Convention*). In Key West, she was a muse of sorts to everyone from the artist Russell Chatham to the poet James Merrill and was married to the aforementioned Chris Gantry. When I first met her, she was starting over again in Nashville doing country music PR, and within a few short years, she and her partner Evelyn Shriver were moguls of sorts, owning George Jones's record company and producing *Soundstage*, among their long list of accomplishments.

It was in Susan's company that I found myself in Tammy Wynette's kitchen one morning while her husband, George Richey, made us his "prizewinning" biscuits with sausage cream gravy, and in the same kitchen a few years later, Susan and I stood beside Tammy and Leeza Gibbons, as Tammy's beloved "Meemaw"—in a hospital bed in front of the sliding glass doors overlooking the fan-club weenie roast going on in the backyard—literally breathed her last. We were together on Tammy's bus when her bus driver claimed a Vietnam flashback, jumped out into a ditch, and took off running. (He later surfaced via a tell-all about Tammy in the *National Enquirer*, but she, typically, forgave him.) And we were on Willie's bus once again when a seriously wired Tanya Tucker popped in to say hello to a seriously stoned Willie, Waylon, and Kris, prompting Willie's deadpan "Man, that girl has a lot of energy."

I have to confess that I have a bit of a country music connection myself—my maternal great-grandfather was one of the founders of the insurance company, National Life and Accident, that in turn brought the world the Grand Ole Opry (the radio station that to this day broadcasts the Opry every Saturday night is called WSM, which stands for the late company's motto, WE SHIELD MILLIONS). In those days, unlike now, "society" Nashville did not much mix with country Nashville, though my grandfather, who later headed up NLT, as it became, did play golf with Roy Acuff. I think I was the first member of my extended family to attend the Opry live—my mother was much more of an Elvis girl, though as a child she did have a chocolate-brown cocker spaniel named Goo Goo, after the nutty clusters whose company used to sponsor the show ("Go get a Goo Goo, it's good").

But it was with Susan that I learned the real stuff. As in the show must go on—and on. The night Tammy's mother died, Gibbons offered to go out and greet Tammy's fans in her stead, but a horrified Tammy wouldn't dream of it. Not only did she wipe the mascara from beneath her eyes and walk out among the adoring guests, she got on a bus bound for Canada that very same night. As Susan explained, there is still a lurking fear among members of Tammy's generation especially that they may be one failed record away from landing back in the cotton fields or the beauty parlor or wherever. On her living-room coffee table at First Lady Acres, Tammy kept a bowl of cotton to remind her whence she came. They don't know how to stop. A year or so before Merle Haggard died, I watched from backstage in Dallas when he opened for Marty Stuart. Such was the state of his lungs that his wife, Theresa Ann, who was also his backup singer, had to continuously leave her post to give him his inhaler. Likewise, in the past eight years, the ever-productive and marvelously eclectic Willie has recorded no fewer than eleven albums (bringing his studio album total to sixty-eight), including tributes to George Gershwin, Ray Price, and Frank Sinatra, as well as the aptly titled *Last Man Standing*.

Such was the breadth and depth of my experiences with Suse over the years that I tried and tried to come up with a way to translate them into a story for *Vogue*, where I was then employed. I never did, but that did not stop me from using my massive expense account (this was in the long-gone golden era of magazines) to try to figure it out, an exercise that involved multiple trips to Nashville and beyond. At Marty Stuart's suggestion, I flew to Dallas to interview Hank Williams's sister Irene just before she died and flew again to Montgomery, Alabama, to attend her funeral with Marty and his wife, Connie Smith. I took the brilliant fashion photographer Arthur Elgort with me to shoot the CMA Awards one year, and then to Fan Fair (where he was forced to protect his cameras in a rainstorm by lying on the dry ground beneath Clay Walker's bus).

I had wanted to get at the humor and deep-seated humanity of the people I had been lucky enough to spend time with, at their never-give-up gumption, at their all-too-rare lack of bullshit. (When Lorrie Morgan announced her engagement to Clint Black's bus driver, Susan tried to give the short-lived future husband a tad more gravitas by referring to him in a press release as a "transportation director," a bit of wordplay Morgan nixed: "Susan, he's a bus driver. Call him a goddamn bus driver.") And in some small way I may have wanted to pay tribute to my own roots. Though I didn't write the piece, at one point during my years-long "reporting," I was asked to write the liner notes for the Little Jimmy Dickens single "How Much Is That Picture of Jesus." Dickens, who was the oldest living member of the Opry when he died in 2015, was around in my great-grandfather's day. I like to think that "Dee Dee," as my mother called him, would have been proud that at least one family member found her way back home, as it were. And I'm sure he would have been gratified to see us cheering on Willie and the gang, even if his own music of choice was opera.

32

The Politics of a Summer Escape
(2019)

For an entire, glorious month this summer, I have rented a house on Martha's Vineyard, an act that makes me the first person in my family to make a sane summer vacation decision. I grew up in the Mississippi Delta, a place where the average high temperature in July is ninety-three degrees and where the low rarely dips below seventy-three. Worse, the humidity level hovers at 94 percent. On a website called climatemps.com, the summers of my birthplace are described as "hot and muggy with thunderstorms." Despite these facts—or, now that I think about it, in defiance of them—we steadfastly refused to head north (to lovely, chilly Maine, say, or perhaps Rhode Island), choosing instead the almost identical climate of Destin, Florida, except that the lows there drop no further than seventy-seven.

Don't get me wrong—we loved it. We loved the one-story Frangista motel, where the banging screen doors were just a few running steps from the water. We loved hanging out on the beach all day and crabbing by night. We loved the carefree, uncrowded nature of the place before it got so built up with near skyscrapers it started looking like the Gulf Coast version of Atlantic City. I still really love Seaside, about twenty miles southeast, but I am older and wiser and in charge of my own destiny these days, which means that the great majority of my visits occur in the fall, winter, and spring.

There was one all-too-brief period when we made it maybe halfway to Maine, during the two summers my grandparents took a house in Linville, North Carolina. It was made of logs and had a woodstove and a wide front porch, and my cousin Frances and I rode horses and built houses for the imaginary fairies out of twigs and moss and bark and mushrooms in exchange for the silver dollars the owner of the woods would leave us in return. In the Fourth of July parade, we wore the traditional embroidered frocks my grandmother had brought back from Switzerland, and for the country club costume party our mothers safety-pinned our matching Florence Eiseman frocks together at the hip and sent us off as conjoined twins. Much as we both hated our identical dresses and cardigans and red kid Mary Janes, even then I knew it was an inspired idea. The stuck-up blond chick in a pink tutu won first prize, and I sort of went off Linville after that.

So back again we went to Destin, but after Richard Nixon's ascendancy to the presidency in 1969, Washington, D.C., an even hotter destination, was added to the summer itinerary. To call D.C. a swamp is to not even use a Trumpian metaphor—the National Mall and parts of Foggy Bottom were once marshes or parts of the Potomac that were filled in, and large swaths of the city are barely at sea level. In July and August, the air is so heavy and wet with humidity it is possible to actually see it. Still, my father was heavily involved in politics, and D.C. increasingly called. "Out saving the free world, baby" was his unvarying response whenever my young self would ask him where he'd been. That sounded about right to me, and by the time I was twelve, I was allowed to accompany him on these missions alone (which is to say without my mother, who happily stayed home with my little brothers).

A little background: Such had been the economic and political isolation of our long-benighted state (as well as much of the rest of the Deep South) that until Nixon's election, the last sitting president to have bothered to visit had been Teddy Roosevelt in 1902, and he only came to hunt bear. My father and the Mississippi delegation had given "the Prez" (as Daddy called him, though not, of course, to his face) their support at the 1968 convention (as opposed to Ronald Reagan or Nelson

Rockefeller), and Nixon was a grateful man. I was grateful too—not only did he make more than one trek to Mississippi, my own summers suddenly got a whole lot more interesting. On one of my first D.C. visits, Agnew was still vice president, having not yet pleaded nolo contendere to charges that he'd failed to pay taxes on income that happened to come from bribes. During the election, I had been all in, sporting a "Spiro is my Hero" watch; now the veep presented me with a slightly more so-phisticated "gold" bracelet boasting a charm in the form of the vice pres-idential seal. There's a photo, currently holding a tongue-in-cheek place of honor in my powder room, and we're both grinning away, me in a chic cotton shirt printed in tiny green and orange elephants chosen especially for the occasion. Afterward, Daddy took me to lunch at the Sans Souci, the famed French power joint a block from the White House, and I had coq au vin for the first time along with a tiny glass of wine.

We stayed, as we almost always did, at the Hay-Adams, which over-looks Lafayette Square. This was decades before security breaches forced Pennsylvania Avenue to be closed to through traffic—via hideous con-crete barriers—and you could walk through the park and be at the White House gate in five minutes. I loved it there—it was the first park I'd ever been to without a swing set. Also, despite the early rumblings of Water-gate, it felt like an innocent time. During the day, when I wasn't feeding the squirrels or watching old men play chess, I ducked back inside the hotel, where I helped the Filipino barman fill up bowls with peanuts. At night, I tagged along with Daddy and formed opinions of his cocktail partners: thumbs-down for Howie Phillips, acting director of the Office of Economic Opportunity (who later opposed Sandra Day O'Connor's nomination to the Supreme Court); a resounding thumbs-up for the dashing Russell Train, chief of the Environmental Protection Agency, which Nixon had created. At the hotel restaurant, the waiters tossed Caesar salad tableside and shaved impossibly thin slices off whole sides of smoked salmon. We had steak Diane at the Jockey Club and clams casino at the Market Inn, where the jolly waitresses slipped me frozen banana daiquiris and I got an early education in jazz from the late, great piano/bass duo Tex and Lenny.

Nixon's 1972 reelection slogan, NOW MORE THAN EVER, had particular resonance with me—I did not want my education in the ways of the world to come to an end. Yet there we were in the summer of 1973 in Destin once again. My best friend, Jessica Brent, and I didn't spend much time on the beach in those weeks, glued instead to the snowy Frangista television set, watching John Dean and James McCord testify in front of Sam Ervin's committee. The following summer was marked by Nixon's resignation, but all was not lost. Gerald Ford ascended, and by June of 1975, I was back in D.C., this time with Jessica in tow.

It was a brief but halcyon time. Ford was a highly decent, blameless figure. The Ford kids were cute and seemingly wholesome—everyone had a crush on Jack. Betty Ford took the stigma out of both breast cancer and drug addiction. On the fledgling *Saturday Night Live*, the worst presidential trait the cast could find to lampoon was Ford's exaggerated clumsiness. Instead of having to smear on orange makeup and rant and rave, the only thing Chevy Chase had to do was fall down. Even Dick Cheney, Ford's young chief of staff, seemed normal.

Further, refugees were not only popular, official committees were formed to welcome them. Upon becoming president, Ford pushed through a bill to fund the resettlement of almost 120,000 displaced South Vietnamese and set up a task force to which my father was appointed. We sort of owed these folks one, after all, but even then, Ford was met with lots of resistance from the right (that many Vietnamese would never be able to assimilate, they said) and the left (even Jerry Brown didn't want them in California). "To ignore the refugees in their hour of need would be to repudiate the values we cherish as a nation of immigrants, and I was not about to let Congress do that," Ford said after the bill was passed.

The night before the refugee committee was due to be officially seated in a ceremony at the White House, Jessica and I had drunk so much champagne at a cocktail party given by a journalist friend of my father's, we thought it would be especially hilarious to teeter in our wedge heels on our narrow Hay-Adams balcony, no more than a ledge really, while loudly addressing the pigeons at Lafayette Square and pouring the contents of our ice bucket onto the awning below. So much for our much-longed-for sophistication. The next morning, feeling a tiny bit worse for the wear, we were waved in at the gates and ushered to the East Room for the swearing in. What Daddy had not known (or had forgotten to tell our mothers) was that the committee would then board Air Force One for Arkansas's Fort Chaffee, where the first wave of refugees was arriving and where he would be spending the night.

To say that Jess and I were elated to be on our own would be a dramatic understatement. We promised to behave and were then introduced to Cheney, who seemed like a nice fellow, devoid of the snarl of later years and so eager to be helpful he supplied us with the number of the White House security office. (It was, thrillingly, 456–7007.) Cheney implored us to use it if we ran into even the smallest hint of trouble, and believe me when I say that we tried mightily. In the end, alas, all was peaceful. We shopped at Garfinckel's, spent hours at the National Gallery on Daddy's orders, and ate a delicious room-service dinner. When we arrived back home a few days later, our mothers were none the wiser.

I have always loved that memory. Not only is it indicative of that less-hysterical era, one blessedly free of helicopter parenting and concrete barricades, it also captures a kinder, gentler America, not to mention a kinder, gentler Cheney. So it was that after years had passed, after I had graduated from both boarding school and college in the Washington area and spent some years covering politics for a living, I found myself at a dinner at the British embassy where Cheney, now vice president, was also a guest. I was sitting at a table nearby and could tell he was not in a happy mood. As he had just had one of his many heart episodes, the embassy's social secretary had thoughtfully asked the kitchen staff to send out a plate of fruit as his dessert—a gesture that so incensed him that he sent it back in favor of the rich chocolate mousse the rest of us were enjoying. Still, once the plates were cleared, I decided to forge ahead. I thought he would get a kick out of the memory of his kindness to two young teenagers, of his pressing that Bondian number (now changed—I've checked) into our hands. I was wrong. Instead, I chattered away as people do when the person they are talking to resolutely refuses to respond, and when I realized it was no use, I turned and walked away.

No matter what was up with Cheney, he could never ruin the story for me. It might have been hot in our nation's capital, but I was a lucky girl indeed to have had so many early seats at so many tables, and I am forever and deeply grateful to my father even though he never took us to Maine. Anyway, I've finally arranged my very own vacation with beloved friends in a cool clime, and even though this summer promises to be another marked by televised hearings, I will not be watching. I will be keeping my sanity well intact by cooking and swimming and reading and taking long beach walks with the dog while breathing in air that I will not be able to see.

33

Out to Pasture

(2020)

When I was a child in the declining days of the solidly segregationist South, when Jim Eastland was still a Mississippi senator and Herman Talmadge was his Georgia counterpart and George Wallace was governor of Alabama (the list of similar, ahem, "statesmen" goes on and on—and on), there was an extremely popular license plate containing the message "Keep your heart [with an image of a splashy red heart subbing for the word] in Dixie, or get your ass [garish illustration of donkey's behind] out!"

Now, I hated that thing even before I was old enough to grasp the offensiveness of its meaning, primarily on aesthetic grounds. It was super tacky, and I knew the noble donkey (otherwise known as *Equus asinus* and already among my very favorite animals) did not deserve to be used in such a way. But the long-suffering ass, which was first domesticated around 3000 BC and has been used as a working animal ever since, is a beast of burden that has borne far more than its share. I recall an image of Talmadge, the staunch segregationist governor and senator whose Georgia reign lasted from 1948 to 1981, rather stiffly wearing a suit and tie astride a donkey. He was finally banished from political life after his second wife, Betty, testified against him during a Senate investigation into a financial scandal in which he was found to have accepted substantial reimbursements for official expenses not actually incurred. Betty, whom he had married when she was eighteen, was not Herman's hugest fan. When they divorced, she accused him of "cruel treatment" and "habitual intoxication," but in apparently happier times, as First Lady of Georgia, she and Herman hosted lavish parties at their plantation in Lovejoy, where Betty was an enthusiastic slaughterer of pigs. Upon arrival, guests were greeted by soldiers in Confederate gray, Dixieland banjo players, and a pet donkey named Assley Wilkes. Take your pick about which is the most odious, but I'm going with Assley. I felt the same way about his namesake the simpering Mr. Wilkes as my man Rhett Butler did. No self-respecting animal deserves that moniker, especially not in that hideously cutesy version.

Donkeys have also been consistently derided as stupid and stubborn. Not so. They are, rather, intelligent and cautious, possessed of a healthy sense of self-preservation—their big, thoroughly adorable ears afford them excellent hearing so they are aware of danger way ahead of most creatures. Their so-called stubbornness, then, turns out to be an asset, a fact Andrew Jackson was smart enough to capitalize on. During the 1828 presidential campaign, supporters of John Quincy Adams called him a "jackass." Jackson ran with the comparison, putting donkeys on campaign posters and highlighting his "stubborn" nature as a weapon in his battle against corruption and elitism. By the 1880s, with the help of the political cartoonist Thomas Nast, the donkey had become the unofficial symbol of the Democratic party.

The Scots, who know a thing or two about a lot of things (including my favorite whiskey in all the world), are smart enough to use donkeys in Scottish heraldry as symbols of humility and patience. Exactly. And let's not forget Christ his own self riding into Jerusalem on Palm Sunday in "lowly pomp" astride the humble beast. How could anyone gaze into those liquid brown eyes and not immediately recognize the donkey's finer qualities? When I was on my first African safari, our group decided to choose what today would be dubbed our "spirit animal." I chose the antelope because I felt such empathy, as though the creatures could look inside me and read my very soul. On home ground, it's a donkey, hands down. For the last ten years or so, I've passed a seed barn in Chatham,

Mississippi, where two donkeys and a black-and-white paint horse are kept. Recently, I've been making the trek on purpose, armed with bags of carrots and apples just to commune.

I'll keep visiting my pals, but now I realize I could avoid the twenty-five-minute drive and install some of my own four-legged friends in the pasture across the gravel road from my new house in the Delta. I will have to rent or buy the space, but it will be worth it to wake up to the sight of my beloved donkeys, the odd horse, and a handful of mules (the offspring of the first two). I may even indulge in a long-held fantasy about freeing the sweet but miserable mules that pull carriages of overweight tourists around New Orleans' French Quarter in the hot sun. They suffer such indignities as wearing plastic "straw" hats festooned with flowers while listening to the driver/"guides" get pretty much every piece of New Orleans history wrong. Once, while residing on the lower end of Bourbon Street, I went out to get my mail only to find a self-liberated mule on the run, cheered on by the gathering crowds on the sidewalk. He was hauling ass (an extremely useful description, and here, only a half-bad pun), his harness sending up sparks as it scraped the pavement. It was a hell of a sight, and while I prayed he'd make it to safety in a field somewhere on the other side of the levee, I feel sure he was caught and pressed back into his dismal duty.

So, the pasture it is then. I will free some mules, buy a horse, collect some gorgeous long-lashed donkeys. I'll make like the St. Francis of the Mississippi Delta, though since I can't quite pull off the saint part, perhaps I'll go with Lady Julia of Asinus. Anyway, I've a history with this particular piece of land that goes way back. Our neighbor Mr. Smith, who owned what were then hundreds of acres of pastures and fields surrounding the house I grew up in (behind which my current house stands), kept some cows and a big old bull back there. Since Mr. Smith was not so good at maintaining his fences, the bull escaped into our backyard, walked out onto the flat swimming pool cover, and promptly fell through it. It was three days before he allowed himself to be led up the steps at the shallow end, which, it must be said, demonstrates no small amount of stubbornness. But you know, he was traumatized.

Several years later in the same pasture, I kept a horse named Hi Joe, who, when I was not riding him, did duty as a literal shoulder to cry on. In the winter I'd bundle up and lie down on top of him in the barn, weeping into his mane over various heartaches and reading novels that underscored my maudlin drama. Joe, a docile creature, did not seem to mind, and until I went off to boarding school and we put him out to pasture for good, he was my closest companion.

Unlike my late first cousin Frances, who was an accomplished rider, competing at Wellington well into her forties, I was not a serious horse-woman. When we were little, my grandmother bought Frances a fine chestnut pony named Key Biscayne, while I rode my riding teacher's fat white pony, Mary Poppins. The pony and I won a few ribbons in our country horse shows, and I adored my teacher, Sue Chick, who later graduated me to a dappled gray horse named London Fog. But perhaps my greatest triumph was my first-place win as Lady Godiva in the costume class astride Mary Poppins. My mother outfitted me in a flesh-colored leotard, and I sported a waist-length ponytail made from at least a dozen blond Dynel falls purchased at Morgan & Lindsey, the local dime store.

As usual, I digress. Let us return to my dear friends the donkeys. They are even useful when they don't carry packs in third-world countries. While they may not deserve it, their name has provided some of the greatest and most varied epithets of our time, especially when paired with such words as *hat* and, well . . . there are a lot. The insane Venezu-elan president Hugo Chavez once said to George W. Bush, "You are a donkey, Mr. Danger," but horses are not spared either. As Secretary of State Dean Acheson once said of Lyndon Johnson, "A real centaur: part man, part horse's ass!" One of the countless funny lines uttered by my friend the inimitable Howard Brent involves a horse, but the behind in question is his own. "That horse threw me up so high, birds were building a nest in my ass before I even hit the ground." And then there are the mules, also erroneously tagged as stubborn—among their many exceptional qualities are hardiness and longevity. There's a passage in Andrew Lytle's short story "Jericho, Jericho, Jericho" in which one of the characters insults the protagonist's fiancée, who comes from the "new" industrial city of Birmingham rather than the fine old agrarian South. "Birmingham," says Miss Kate, "I've got a mule older'n Birmingham."

But back to my pastoral—or pastural—pursuits. I might actually ride my new horse, in a wholesome, healthy way, fully clothed in jodhpurs or breeches and posting properly up and down or galloping along the levee. I have photos of my last riding expedition about twenty years ago and most involve my friends atop their mounts, putting on lipstick and drinking beer. There's one of me passing my lit Marlboro to a fellow rider so she could light her own. The actual riding part is a tad hazy. But the donkeys' mere presence will change all that. I'll gaze at them and get all centered and Zen and ride the horse and feel good about the rescued mules. In this particular case, my asinine plan feels like the opposite of what that adjective usually implies. I can't wait.

34

JT in My Mind

(2020)

James Taylor is a hardworking man. In droll Instagram videos, he splits seemingly endless piles of logs into kindling for the woodstove in his studio in the Berkshires of Western Massachusetts. Already this year, he has celebrated the fiftieth anniversary of his second album, *Sweet Baby James* (which means it's been almost that long since I first fell hopelessly in love with that face, that voice surging forth from my beat-up eight-track and breaking my young heart), and by the time this column appears, he'll have brought out a new one, *American Standard*, his twenty-ninth. In January, Amazon released the Audible book *Break Shot*, which describes the first twenty-one years of his existence, including his oft-harrowing family life and struggles with addiction, in moving and extraordinarily articulate detail. (Says the project's producer, Bill Flanagan: "He's one of the only rock stars you'll ever meet who speaks in full paragraphs.") In it, he describes how his mother, Trudy, never got over the trauma of being uprooted from the New England seaside where she grew up and plopped down in civil rights–era North Carolina. She was deathly afraid her five children would grow up to be "hillbillies" and took solace in the fact that they did not speak with obvious Southern accents. And yet.

Taylor himself all but credits his career to his idyllic early childhood in the South (the family wouldn't reach its breaking point until a few years later), shooting BB guns and building forts with his four siblings on their isolated creek-side spread near Chapel Hill, where his father, Ike, was the dean of the University of North Carolina medical school. "If I had not had all those free days to let my imagination roam, I'm not sure I'd be a songwriter."

A songwriter he is, of course, one of our very best, but he is also a fine singer and superlative stylist, up there with or surpassing (don't shoot me) Frank Sinatra and Ella Fitzgerald. His ability to infuse songs that are part of the lexicon with something else, something ineffable, is what makes *American Standard* so damn good. But decades before he tackled "Ol' Man River" and "The Nearness of You," he was doing the same with beloved Southern classics like "Oh! Susanna" and "Mockingbird." More than that, though, he preserves a particular way Southerners express themselves that I fear we are fast losing. I don't mean the cornpone flim-flam Bill Clinton whipped out whenever he got in trouble or strived to seem "authentic": cartoonish expressions about hogs and dogs and wood ticks and turtles on fence posts. I mean the poetic, subtle, but unmistakably Southern rhythm and dialect that so often creep into a James Taylor phrase or sometimes an entire song.

There's the occasional "y'all" ("One Man Parade") as well as the odd expression or sobriquet ("natural born fool," "Mama Roo" and "Lou Mama Lou," "up and gone," "pretty as homemade sin"). One of my favorite tunes is the infectious "Sweet Potato Pie," which, not surprisingly, he recorded as a duet with Ray Charles, whom some have erroneously identified as its writer. I can't tell you how much I love the fact that Anna Davis, my mother's brilliant African American nurse from Nashville, opened every letter she wrote to Mama with "Dearest Sweet Potato Pie" until the day she died, well into her nineties. Taylor has written whole songs about pigs ("Mona") and dogs ("Sunny Skies"). His late older brother, Alex, introduced him to stock car races, moonshine, and, most important, soul: Ray, Wilson Pickett, Percy Sledge, Sam Cooke. His close friend and collaborator Danny Kortchmar introduced him to the blues that he says "transported" him: the music of Mississippi John Hurt, Muddy Waters, Howlin' Wolf. You can tell. Though he met the

New York–born Kortchmar on Martha's Vineyard (his mother hauled the kids up in the station wagon the minute school was out every summer), had he grown up exclusively in Massachusetts, I'm not sure we'd have songs like "Steamroller Blues," "Chili Dog," "Fool for You," and "Woh, Don't You Know." He may be devoid of the dread drawl, but he managed to pick up plenty.

Trudy Taylor became a civil rights activist and was an artist herself—she'd studied voice at the New England Conservatory, helped design the family house that her son calls "a work of art," raised sheep, and spun wool on a loom. Like a lot of privileged white Southerners of the era, the Taylor kids were exposed to a lot of culture—museums and Broadway musicals on trips to Manhattan, their parents' sophisticated American record collection that included the soundtrack to *Oklahoma!* and Aaron Copland's "Appalachian Spring," which Taylor says he absorbed in his bones. There is no question Taylor was at least partially "raised up" Southern (he has a song called "Raised Up Family" about that very thing), and the roots of his father's rather gothic North Carolina family reach back generations. But in the end, he is quintessentially American, singing the songs of our collective soul in his clear, precise, vibrato-less voice. On *Covers*, he does a number by another great American songwriter, Jimmy Webb. I defy anyone who has heard him hold the notes toward the end of "Wichita Lineman" not to drop to his or her knees. Songs, phrases, even notes, can be little miracles, and miracles are everywhere in Taylor's music. He supplies constant reminders of the beauty and grace that exist all around us, even when he's singing about the most gut-wrenching stuff. Always too, there is the generosity. In *Break Shot* he says, "The initial motivation for writing a song may be some personal experience but if it doesn't speak to other people, if it doesn't offer solace or entertainment or identification or make you want to . . . hum along, it's going to fail as a song. The success of an artist is not measured by how much he makes himself feel. His success is how much he makes other people feel." He may have written "You Can Close Your Eyes" with Joni Mitchell more than four decades ago, but when we buried my brother Crews last summer, two of my closest friends sang it and it was perfect. (It also almost killed us, until another friend carried us off with his trombone.)

Taylor's "Carolina in My Mind" has become an anthem of sorts for generations of Southerners, and I smile every time I hear the line "peace and quiet and dogs that bite" (he occasionally subs "peace and quiet" for "geese in flight"). Sometimes, live, he pronounces "quiet" as "quite," a rhyming tactic that reminds me of the country folks with whom I grew up. As a transitional tactic of my own (!), I will also single out the lines "The signs that might be omens say I'm going, going . . ." I've been thinking a lot about both signs and omens of late. (Taylor does too, apparently—see "Home by Another Way.") My own nurse and chief childhood protector, Coatee Jones, was never without a rabbit's foot in her purse. She had a .22 in there as well—she learned early on to hedge her bets—and while she never let me touch the gun, I rubbed the hell out of that lucky foot. Not long ago, a dear friend, knowing I was in need of a talisman and not just a little good karma, gave me a rabbit's foot key chain just like the one I'd been so fascinated by. I carried it with me everywhere until one day I stepped on something sharp and realized that my trusty beagle, Henry, motivated by the unstoppable forces of DNA, had eaten the whole thing, leaving only the tiny metal cap and ball bearing chain. My New Orleans neighbor, upon hearing this news, told me about a Sufi mystic who set up camp on the sidewalk in front of the house where he once lived in Khartoum. The holy man's chief job was to pray constantly for the minister of finance so as to increase his barakas, or blessings, but as a sideline he wrote bits of Koranic verse on slips of paper. The passersby he sold them to dipped them into glasses of water, dissolving the ink, so they could literally drink the holy scripture. This delightful anecdote only confirmed what I already knew: Henry was indeed my good-luck charm.

Since Henry is also my constant companion, I had no need to acquire another rabbit's foot, but I collect feathers and nests, hold in my hand a heavy silver heart given to me by a dear friend and then-suitor in London decades ago, and keep a carved wooden rabbit given to me by my lifelong best friend by my bed alongside a silver one of my mother's.

I still have the Kennedy half-dollars that Coatee gave me for my childhood birthdays; I stick the four-leaf clovers for which I am forever on
the lookout inside the pages of my Book of Common Prayer as well as
my copy of the book *Good Dog*, which is sort of the same thing. Most fe-
licitously, on New Year's Day this year, my most spiritual friend, Courtney Cowart, also a collector of feathers (they find her, she insists), gave
me a bright yellow-and-black specimen she'd discovered in the backyard
of the house I recently completed in the Mississippi Delta. (Like James
Taylor, I went often in my mind to the Delta, where I spent my own
free-roaming childhood, until last year when I finally came home, at
least part-time, for real.)

We'd never seen a feather like it, but it was so exotic we knew it must
be important. I immediately called Giles Kelly, son of the same friend
who gave me the wooden bunny. He'd just graduated with honors from
the wildlife and forestry program at Mississippi State; now he does the
Lord's work for Wildlife Mississippi, a conservation nonprofit my father
and Giles's grandfather helped found. He got right back to me: The
feather belonged to a yellow-shafted flicker, a woodpecker that sticks
around the eastern United States. A beautiful bird with a fawn-colored
head marked by a red stripe, it has a speckled body, but the undersides
of its wings are the glorious yellow that caught Courtney's eye. It is also
the state bird of Alabama, where it is known as a "yellowhammer," a
term given the state's Confederate soldiers due to the yellow cloth at
their sleeves and coattails. We chose to ignore that ignominious piece of
bird baggage and concentrate instead on the far more exciting news that
the feathers of these particular flickers are believed to bring good luck
and healing. Further, unlike that of pileated woodpeckers, the flickers'
pleasing call is a sustained laugh—*kikiki*—and they are proficient and
steady drummers, playing their tunes on dead limbs and wooden houses.
I swear I thought someone was knocking on my door before dawn the
other day, and then I realized it was probably my new friend the bird.

Of course, it could have been the coons or the coyotes or the enormous possum who resides in the hood. This was once a primeval forest,
after all, and the critters still think they own the place, which is actually

fine with me, as long as they are furry or feathered. I've even readjusted my thinking about rats, now that I've found out I am one. This year, 2020, is the Year of the Rat according to the Chinese lunar calendar, and it is my sign. The rat also is the first sign of the Chinese zodiac, due to its quick thinking in winning the competition held by the Jade Emperor to decide the order of the animals—the wily creature hitched a ride on the back of an ox and jumped off just before the ox crossed the finish line, beating him to it. In addition to an obviously tricky nature, people born under the sign of the rat are said to be inventive, charming, and shrewd. George Washington and T. S. Eliot were both rats, so I'll take it.

Best of all, the rat played the flute while on the ox's back. Given that I've got a veritable posse of drummers currently in my yard, we have the beginnings of a band. I really think my man James should come visit. He could bring Jimmy Johnson on bass and Lou Marini on sax to round things out. I'll be the one dancing with the yellow feathers in my hair.

35

Sheltering...at Home

(2020)

The first thing I did at the dawn of our new era of social distancing, sheltering in place, hunkering down, holing up—pick your preferred term for the new normal—was to order a ham. I know, I know. Dorothy Parker said, "Eternity is a ham and two people," and a week into it, a lot of folks were already feeling as though an eternity had passed. But this is a beautiful, manageable ham, made of superior Berkshire pork, bone-in, uncured and smoked, from D'Artagnan, the New Jersey–based purveyor of deliciousness that has long been one of my lifelines. (I live in two places where the butcher, if such a person in fact exists, looks at you as though you have lost your mind when you request such exotica as a simple lamb shoulder or a breast of Muscovy duck.) Also, since the second "person" with whom I am isolating is my beloved beagle, Henry, the ham would not last close to an eternity, but about two and a half minutes tops, should I let him anywhere near it (though I do share part of my lunchtime sandwich).

Henry and I are extraordinarily lucky. At this point, I swear I've ordered enough food to feed us and the friends and family for whom I carefully drop off packages until well into the next decade. Our particular shelter is a light-filled, book-lined house with green pastures out the windows and a yard in which the bulbs, trees, and vines change almost daily and the increasingly plump birds flock to my six constantly refilled feeders. I have always been something of a scaredy-cat—even as an adult I was terrified to stay in my parents' house alone—but I feel safe here, nourished. I cook like a demon, read the poems of Mary Oliver and Jim Harrison, and rejoice in nature and my solitude. So far.

I've also been thinking a lot about the other, earlier places where I've been happiest and most secure, which means I've been revisiting my maternal grandparents' house in Nashville. On the face of it, that particular dwelling is an unlikely choice. Countless cases of Beefeaters were consumed on the premises along with daily packs (or two or three) of Pall Malls (and later, Vantage), and there was a great deal of hollering back and forth (out of anger, oh yes indeed, but also out of necessity, as my grandfather was deaf as a post). The phone rang often in the early morning hours because in those days my aunt, who lived nearby, was not what we might call in the very best shape. Still, such was my love for the place and the depth of my memories there that the long-out-of-use phone number is still my most frequent password. (The ancient black phone resided on a game table in the back hall along with a bronze bear on a marble base that is now in my possession.)

I adored my grandmother beyond all reason, but to the outside world she was anything but warm and fuzzy. Always immaculately put together, even when she wasn't planning on leaving the house, she rarely descended the stairs in anything less than full makeup and perfect hair (styled almost exactly the same as Queen Elizabeth's), and never once did I see her bare fingernails, which were forever sheathed in two coats of Revlon's Windsor. People called her "the Duchess," but I always knew that stuff was armor protecting a kind and very shy soul, and to me her only title was Ga. Until I got too big to fit, I slept with her in one of the two single beds in the bedroom she and my grandfather shared. The image is enough to startle Child Protective Services, not to mention my mother, who will quake at the description: Ga and my grandfather, each flat on their backs beneath their respective sheets, wearing black satin eye masks and snoring away while I watched my grandmother's last cigarette burn to the end in the dark.

In the daytime I explored the house, which in those hours was hushed and cool, protected from the outside world by heavy silk damask curtains and wildly unlike our sprawling, light-filled, board-and-batten one-story house in the Mississippi Delta, where I actually lived. It had a basement that smelled like laundry and country ham, an elevator (!) that I wore out, and a kitchen where Ernestine Turner, both my and my grandmother's most constant companion, made black-eyed peas with fried hot-water corn bread pretty much every day for lunch (though Ga opted instead for jellied madrilene or chicken salad on toast).

In the basement laundry room, I'd curl up in the big old wooden bed and listen to the endlessly entertaining chatter of Josephine, Ernestine's sister, and Louis King, their father, while the soul channel played on the radio. They taught me how to do the Funky Chicken in that room, the only dance I've ever mastered. But my favorite place, my hidden, *private* place, was the luggage room off the bar. It smelled thrillingly of leather and old canvas, and the suitcases themselves, covered in labels from my grandparents' travels, served as the perfect head- and backrests for reading. I'd spend hours lost in the exploits of the Bobbsey Twins or the Melendy family, breaking only to cadge olives and cocktail onions from the tiny bar fridge next door.

Now, of course, I'm acutely aware that the safety I felt was made possible by the help that made our days so easy, the sheets crisp and tight as a drum, the surfaces dust free and gleaming. When I slept in the tiny room between the basement door and the kitchen, my wake-up call was Louis crushing ice in the hand-cranked crusher (also in my possession) and the sizzle of frying sausage. Without them there would not have been nearly as much love and laughter and camaraderie or just plain fun. Louis and Josephine took me fishing at Centennial Park, where we'd sit on overturned buckets, thread our hooks with worms, and wait patiently while eating tomato sandwiches. Fishing with my grandmother was an entirely different affair. One of my favorite photos from that era is of my cousin Frances and me in matching shorts and shirts on the edge of a stocked trout pond while my grandmother stood some distance away smoking, in a crisp shirtdress and Delman pumps, sunglasses firmly on her face, alligator pocketbook hanging from her arm.

During the summer of 1969, my days were also spent around my aunt's pool, site of a constant house party that included endless pitchers of Bloody Marys and not just a little drama. Tupper Saussy, musician and songwriter ("Morning Girl," "Heighdy-Ho Princess"), watercolorist, and jack-of-many-other-trades, stood in the pool for hours on end reciting lines from *Cactus Flower* (he had a starring role in a local production), prompted by his wife, Lola. When the astronauts landed on the moon, we all gathered around the Sony Trinitron while Tupper took to the piano and scored the event.

I continued my prolonged annual visits to Nashville but eventually, as they always do, things changed. My aunt went off and got herself together, shut down the shindigs, and divorced my uncle (I stayed close to both until the end). My grandmother had a stroke. By then summers were more and more spent in the Delta, where the main goal was to get out of the house. First to our backyard pool, where our neighbors' kids and all their older friends were allowed over to swim after dinner. We played Splash and Marco Polo until my 10:30 curfew—just in time to pile in my bed with towel-dried hair and watch my number one boyfriend, Johnny Carson, who offered up a lesson in sheer brilliance every night.

Later, of course, summers revolved around cars outfitted with eighttrack tape players and loaded with twelve-packs of the Miller ponies we bought illegally at the Spur station on the corner of Broadway and Alexander. My friend McGee's mother overheard us making whispered plans to score some once and went bananas: "Don't think I don't know that pony is slang for heroin!" We doubled over at that and smoked pot and Marlboro Reds instead and put so many miles on my '66 Mustang convertible we could've driven to Canada and back twice.

So now here we are, not desperate to hit the road but discovering the joys of our own versions of the luggage room. At night I make a gin martini with both olives and onions and toast to the memory of my grandparents. There are stacks of books to read and reread (I may even take up the Melendys again), so many letters to write, and five tote bags to empty out, after which I will be filled with virtue. And maybe most important, there is my beloved collection of vinyl that finally has a home and a brand-new turntable on which to play the hits of summers past as well as a few that have newfound resonance.

36

My Home Is My (Animal) Kingdom

(2020)

First, a disclaimer: I know that we are in the midst of the most terrifying plague any of us have seen in our lifetimes (unless you are a hundred plus and good for you). I try hard not to stay perpetually mad as hell about our devastating lack of political leadership and the staggering stupidity of a great deal of my countrymen, both of which have cost this nation a whole lot of lives. I am in awe of those on the front lines, whether they be doctors and nurses or grocery store workers, people who fill essential jobs by putting themselves and their families at risk on public transportation, or scientists trying hard to make us see the light and bring us a vaccine. I am not struggling to put food on the table or wondering if I will still have a job. I know I am a lucky so-and-so, that I am in a position of pretty enormous privilege as I shelter in a swell new house in a place I love.

Mine, as they used to say, are first-world problems, white-people problems. Yes, indeed. However. Even in this cone of comparative luxury, some stuff still manages to penetrate, especially if it comes in waves of successive pestilence. I guess I shouldn't have been surprised—we're already living through the apocalypse. The white horse behind me in the pasture—the one I ply with apples and carrots and affection—could well be the Antichrist, bringer of said pestilence and infectious disease. I'm keeping careful watch. If the pale horse gets here, I'm gone.

It started out a bit slowly. I have mentioned previously on these pages that spring brought an infestation of large, furry brown gnats that caused such enormous and infected welts I was practically bleeding to death on my sheets every night. So it was that I did not notice until far too late that my bed—and my bedroom rug and shades and more upholstered surfaces than I cared to count—was infested with bedbugs. Since the pandemic began, I had been forced to stay in exactly one hotel room for a mere two nights, during which I was so worried about COVID-19 that I double masked and gloved and continuously cleansed every possible surface with Clorox wipes. Instead of bringing home the deadly virus, I provided transportation for hundreds of bedbugs, those insidious reddish-brown parasites that bite the exposed skin of sleeping humans and feed on their blood. (Note to self: Quit bringing your own pillows, and pack in plastic bags.) Now, I have read about bedbugs, about how horrible they are and hard to get rid of, but let me tell you that nothing prepares you for them. The first night I noticed the little bastards, they were about the size of a quarter of a penny (i.e., full-grown) and the same color, marching across my pillow in a line. I'd had the doors open for much of the night—I blithely thought they were some kind of beetle I'd never seen, flicked them away, and went to sleep. The next night I woke up to find them on my nightgown. *Hmmm,* I thought, and started googling away—in the next room. Within a half hour, I knew what I was up against, and it wasn't pretty.

I blame it on the gnats. If I hadn't already been bleeding like crazy from their bites, I would have realized that most of the blood was coming from an even more evil source. The bedbugs start out tiny. I'd brush what seemed like thousands of minuscule brown specks off the bed and all that was left of them would be pinpoints of blood—mine. What to do? I called our local Orkin man. He is a very nice fellow but has little experience with this stuff. He came over in a white plastic suit, sprayed a bunch of chemicals everywhere, sold me a nylon mattress cover that turned out to be useless, told me to get out of the house for a few hours and leave the bedroom doors shut for three days. Okeydoke. Problem solved. I slept on the living room daybed, which I quickly discovered is good for the occasional guest too drunk to drive home but extremely bad for relatively sober people trying to get some actual sleep. At the end of the three days, I was delighted to climb between some newly laundered sheets and get what I hoped would be a restful night of slumber. The next morning it looked like a slasher had visited. Clearly, it was time to leave town, a move that required me to take a steaming hot shower, cover my feet in garbage bags, and walk out of the house completely naked, whereupon I put on a waiting set of brand-new clothes and shoes, got in the car, and left for New Orleans. It was, a website assured me, the only way not to take the bugs with me.

While I was gone, an expert came in from Jackson, a steam cleaner cleaned all the furniture and rugs, every single piece of clothing from my closet and drawers was removed and laundered, far too many tote bags full of "important papers" I'd yet to go through were boxed up and taken away, and the expert came back to make sure the bugs had not returned. This was not an inexpensive enterprise, I assure you, but I swear I would have paid pretty much anything to get those critters out of there. I came home. It was lovely. My house was my haven again. And then, the bats came.

Let me hasten to say, I've always liked bats. My friend Helen Brans-ford loves them so much, I once gave her an eighteenth-century print of one for Christmas. They eat mosquitoes, and they mostly keep to themselves. As a child, I loved watching them swoop over our backyard pool when the light was on. But you know, the pool was far away from the house and my affection for bats might really have been sort of a theory. Still, I was not *all that* traumatized on the first night, when I noticed something strange and brown under one of the dining table chairs. A friend was with me, and we shooed it out the door. I live in the country, in the Mississippi Delta, a place that really never should have been inhabited—all the areas outside my doors are sprinkled with some kind of snake-away powder, a version of the goofer dust of old. We figured the poor thing had flown in somehow, lost its way out, and that would be that. Two days later, I got up to brush my teeth and one was in the sink. I am not at my tip-top best early in the morning in the first place, but this pretty much did me in. First, I grabbed the nearest thing to hand, toilet paper, with the intention of grabbing him. Who was I kidding? I immediately flooded the sink with water, put a cookie sheet with a stack of books on top—but not before I saw a little hand reach up. I have to confess that got me. It also turns out that it's illegal to kill a bat in Mississippi. One friend was so concerned about my bat karma she insisted I build a bat house. I actually considered this until the next bat turned up in the bathtub and another, grotesquely dried up and dead, in an empty cachepot.

The Chinese believe bats have such highly developed sensory parts that they can sniff out "auspicious chi" and that their presence heralds good fortune. But there's also Dracula. So again, I fled the house (but just to my mother's, down the road), and again, called in the experts. The same outfit with the bedbug department also has its own bat man. I'm not kidding. He informed me that bats need no more than a half-inch opening to slip into your house. Naturally, the mesh atop my chimney was a half inch rather than the specified quarter inch. The man spent a great deal of time with my carpenter identifying a dozen more possible entry points. We went to Lowe's, got some stuff to fill them up, and another pest, I hoped, had been dispatched.

At this point, my friend Ellen asked me if I'd killed a bunch of little babies earlier in life. You might well wonder. Because next came the fleas. Henry, being the perfect beagle dog, has had fleas only once in his fourteen years, and that doesn't count because we were in Florida. But there they were, hopping around like madmen in my bed, a.k.a. the Battleground. I checked Henry—not a flea on his precious belly. I checked my own arms and legs—red bites everywhere. I thought of giving up, of torching the freaking house (or at least burning the bed, à la Farrah Fawcett), of riding away on the white horse, exacting revenge on . . . whomever. Instead I poured a stiff drink and left a message for the Orkin man.

After the fact, nothing is ever as awful as you think it is, but I could have used a little help, a breather, a place to blow off some steam and take the immediate edge off. Which brings me back to the lunacy of our great leaders and the legions of folks who were drawn to the words of a woman who warns against "demon sperm" and believes Big Tech is suppressing a cure and masks are unnecessary (though it's sort of irresistible not to warm to her theory that reptiles are running the government). This is the kind of crap that is keeping the rest of us out of our beloved restaurants and bars, the places that have always provided solace, even joy, during times of trouble, or, yes, pestilence.

Had I been able to make the short drive downtown to the Grille, and had Don the Most Excellent Bartender set down before me a perfect martini with an olive and the faintest shards of ice floating in the stemmed glass, all would have been far better in my world—the daybed less uncomfortable, the bedbugs, etc., less pesky. You share a few tales of woe with your fellow men, and your own seem to fade. Cold gin, camaraderie—hope!—win the day.

So let us strive to fill these beacons of light and life soon and do anything we can to help keep them alive in the meantime. Until then, I'll be keeping a watchful eye on the pasture.

Index